To Laura

Eve

27ᵗ Set ₄.

4

Frank

From Pillar to Post

The Indo-Caribbean Diaspora

Frank Birbalsingh

TSAR
Toronto
1997

© Frank Birbalsingh 1997

Except for purposes of review, no part of this book may be reproduced in any form without prior permission of the publisher.

We acknowledge the support of the Canada Council for the Arts for our publishing program. We also acknowledge support from the Ontario Arts Council.

Cover art: photograph courtesy of Simon Archer

Canadian Cataloguing in Publication Data

Birbalsingh, Frank
  From pillar to post: the Indo-Caribbean diaspora

Includes bibliographical references and index.
ISBN 0-920661-66-1

1. Caribbean East Indians - Foreign countries.
I. Title.

F2191.E27B57 1997   909'.0491411   C97-931548-4

Printed in Canada by Coach House Printing.

TSAR Publications
P. O. Box 6996, Station A
Toronto, Ontario M5W 1X7
Canada

in loving memory of
Mariam S Birbalsingh (1912–1944)

Their [Indentured Indians'] status was rather similar to that of freed Negroes under Apprenticeship. They were expected to work for the master who fed and housed them. They could not leave his service without consent. Failure to work for him, without good cause, was a criminal offense. So was running away.

ELSA GOVEIA, *An Introduction to the Federation Day Exhibition on Aspects of the History of the West Indies*

A peasant-minded, money-minded community, spiritually static because cut off from its roots, its religion reduced to rites without philosophy, set in a materialistic colonial society: a combination of historical accidents and national temperament has turned the Trinidad Indian into the complete colonial, even more philistine than the white.

V S NAIPAUL, *The Middle Passage*

At the graveside [of Indian strikers killed by police at Enmore, Guyana, in June 1948] the emotional outbursts of the widows and relations of the deceased were intensely distressing, and I could not restrain my tears. There was to be no turning back. There and then I made a silent pledge—I would dedicate my entire life to the cause of the struggle of the Guianese people against bondage and exploitation.

CHEDDI JAGAN, *The West on Trial*

"Trinidad," I said. "In the West Indies. And You?"
He ignored my question. "But you look Indian."
"I am."
"Red Indian?" He suppressed a nervous little giggle.
"East Indian. From the West Indies."

V S NAIPAUL, *The Overcrowded Barracoon*

He could hope for death here but his grandchildren, maybe even his children, would continue the emigration which his grandfather had started in India, and during which the island [Trinidad] had proved, in the end, to be nothing more than a stopover.

NEIL BISSOONDATH, "Insecurity," *Digging Up the Mountains*

Contents

Preface

Although the Indian diaspora of around eleven million people is smaller than its Jewish, African, Chinese and other counterparts, it is unique in several respects. It is more widespread than others, and also both more varied in its religious and social composition and more uneven in its cultural achievements. It also has the distinction of having suffered greater harassment than most others, having been expelled from Aden, Burma and Uganda, partially repatriated from Sri Lanka, and subjected to discrimination and harassment in Kenya, Guyana, Surinam and Fiji.

For reasons having to do with their painful circumstances of migration, lack of historical curiosity, and the failure to throw up eminent writers, the Indian diaspora is the least well-researched. This is as true of the post-second world war immigrants to the West Indies as of their older counterparts in South Africa, Fiji and the West Indies. This is a great pity because it neglects an important pool of human experiences and the insights it offers into the mechanisms of colonial rule, sources of inter-ethnic conflicts, and the remarkably ingenious ways in which immigrants cope with their predicament. Frank Birbalsingh's excellent new book therefore deserves a warm welcome, not only for its contribution to the study of the Indian diaspora but also for highlighting the distinct cultural identity of the Indo-Caribbeans.

There is also another, far more important, reason to welcome the book. Much of the literature on the Indo-Caribbeans is either historical or social-scientific in its approach and orientation. While historical facts and empirical generalizations are important, they miss out the human dimensions, the struggles, the frustrations, the failures, the resourcefulness, and the achievements of the diasporic community. We need to find ways of integrating different disciplinary perspectives in order to capture the full range and complexity of the diasporic experience. Frank Birbalsingh shows one way in which this can be done. He narrates the basic historical facts about Indo-Caribbeans with learning and sensitivity, and makes them come alive by means of both skillfully executed interviews with carefully selected figures of the Indo-Caribbean community, and insightful analysis of literary writings. The book represents a novel methodological experiment which should set a precedent for similar future studies.

I learned much from this fascinating book and have no doubt that others will do too.

— Bhikhu Parekh,
Professor of Political Theory, University of Hull, UK.

Introduction

There are many reasons why Indo-Caribbean culture is not widely accepted either as a valid concept or as a legitimate subject of study. This is mainly because the Caribbean is viewed as African. The predominence of existing studies of Afro-Caribbean history and culture will readily confirm this. These studies also confirm an Afro-centric outlook towards a region whose main population consists of descendants of African slaves who provided the labour on European-owned sugar plantations for centuries, until slavery was abolished in British Caribbean territories in 1834. During a visit he made to the Caribbean soon after World War Two, a British traveller observed that the inhabitants there consisted of

> the ghostly Ciboneys, the dead Arawaks and the dying Caribs:
> the Spaniards, the English, the French, the Dutch, The Danes and
> the Americans; the Corsicans; the Jews, the Hindus, the Moslems,
> the Azorians, the Syrians and the Chinese, and the all-obliterat-
> ing Negro population deriving from scores of kingdoms on the
> seaboard and hinterland of West Africa.[1]

Although this confirms African predominance, it also acknowledges the presence of smaller ethnic groups, for example, Portuguese from the Azores (and Madeira), Hindus and Muslims from India, and Chinese, all of whom came as indentured labourers to replace freed Africans on the sugar plantations after 1834.

The devastation (the word "genocide" comes to mind) wrought upon the indigenous Caribbean inhabitants, for example Arawaks, Caribs, and Ciboneys, upon the arrival of Europeans at the end of the fifteenth century, made it possible for Africans to claim the most decisive cultural impact on the region through their greater numbers, their longer period of residence, and the totality of their participation in the region's dominant plantation mores. In turn, this produced an African-centred view of things, which is accepted in most Caribbean territories.

Indians, however, form a clear majority in Guyana and almost a majority in Trinidad and Tobago, and to apply Afro-centricity to these two territories contradicts the principle of majority rule and reduces the importance of Indian labour in the region since 1838. The entrenchment of African governments in Guyana and Trinidad and Tobago, for most of the time since the 1960s, when the larger English-speaking territories gained Independence and ceased to be British colonies, suggests that Afro-centricity is deeply rooted in the Caribbean as a whole.

Despite charges of mischief and corruption, the Afro-Guyanese leader, Forbes Burnham and his party, the People's National Congress (PNC) held unbroken sway in Guyana for nearly three decades (1964-92), without serious objection from either his fellow Guyanese or neighbouring Caribbean heads of state. Similarly, Eric Williams's People's National Movement (PNM) regime survived in Trinidad and Tobago for an equally long period (1956-80). As Afro-Caribbeans, Burnham and Williams successfully relied on African electoral solidarity that ensured that neither of them was likely to be replaced by opposition parties from other ethnic or minority groups. In the end, only death removed these two leaders from office. Even if external factors, for example American hegemonic considerations during the Cold War, did help Burnham to survive politically, it is unlikely that either Williams or Burnham would have yielded to electoral defeat by an Indian party, or that Guyanese and Trinidadians would have accepted two similar Indian-controlled regimes for such a long time.

In 1964, the Indo-Guyanese Dr Cheddi Jagan's (mainly Indian) People's Progressive Party (PPP) lost power because of strikes, riots, murder, and mayhem in Guyana. Dr Jagan's socialism or communism was blamed. But Burnham was also socialist, yet his party ruled continuously for twenty-eight years. No doubt there are external geopolitical factors having to do with the Cold War and American hegemony in the Western hemisphere that helped to maintain Burnham rather than Jagan in power. But Burnham's ethnic identity cannot be completely separated from his relative appeal to both his American sponsors and the Guyanese electorate. It is possible that because of his ethnic—African—descent, a government led by Burnham could be more readily seen to atone for centuries of African enslavement than an administration led by Dr Jagan, an Indian outsider, marginally connected to the mainstream of Afro-Caribbean history.

Indians were not the only ethnic group to be marginalized in the post-Independent Caribbean. Other non-African groups, for example the Europeans, Chinese and Portuguese, suffered in similar fashion; but none of these had invested as much labour on the land, nor did they have large enough numbers to form a government in Guyana or Trinidad and Tobago. The Indians' failed political possibilities and "body and soul" investment of labour greatly intensified their frustration and fomented more uncertainty, division and fractiousness among themselves than among any other Caribbean group. Their very name became a source of controversy. Indentured immigrants from India were described as "East Indians" to distinguish them from indigenous inhabitants of the Caribbean and the Americas who had been misnamed "Indians" by Columbus. At the same time, all Caribbean people were called "West Indians" to distinguish them firstly from the misnamed "Indians" and later from the East Indians. Since West Indians were mostly of African descent, the term "West Indian" became synonymous with "African" or at least with "Afro-Caribbean." People of Indian descent then properly became "East Indian West Indians"—an absurd term. This is why many Indo-Caribbean people still prefer the term "East Indian," which was used, for example, in the three Indo-Caribbean conferences held at the University of the West Indies in Trinidad in 1975, 1979 and 1984. "Indo-Caribbean" seems the most suitable term for describing people descended from Indian indentured workers in the Caribbean, for their experience has been substantially indigenized over one hundred and fifty years to create a new, mixed creolized culture, one that is less an entity in itself than part of a larger regional culture.

During the immediate post-Independence decades, Afro-centric social and political attitudes helped to create a sense of insecurity in minority ethnic groups and promote a second migration chiefly to Europe and North America. However, since Afro-Caribbeans themselves migrated in large numbers during the same period, Afro-centricity alone cannot be held responsible for this second migration. Other factors were involved, for example, an historic postcolonial dependency of the entire Caribbean region on the developed world of Europe and North America.

Although the need for higher education, professional skills and better economic opportunity traditionally suctioned off migrants out of the Caribbean, their number up to about 1960 was insignificant compared to the tidal wave that followed during the post-Independence period. Exact numbers of these migrants are hard to come by. So far as Canada is concerned, since official statistics list immigrants by their last county of permanent residence, we can find out how many Guyanese settled in Canada between 1962 and 1992, but not how many Indo-Guyanese. But if we estimate Indians as 80% of the Guyanese total and 60% of the Trinidad total, we arrive at a figure of about 100,000 Indo-Caribbean immigrants in Canada. Since Indo-Caribbean immigrants in Britain and the US are likely to be more numerous, an estimate of the total Indo-Caribbean diaspora should not be far below half a million, more than 90% of whom would be Indo-Guyanese and Indo-Trinidadians. Although this figure includes children of the immigrants who were born abroad, it gives some idea of the impact of the Indo-Caribbean diaspora on Guyana and Trinidad and Tobago, whose combined population is not much above two million.

The seven reviews and essays in Part One offer a condensed, impressionistic version of Caribbean history and its legacy of imperialism, oppression, exploitation, brutality, resistance, racial mixing, rivalry, nationalism, and disorder. These themes are central to a region whose history, as C L R James said, "is governed by two factors, the sugar plantation and Negro slavery,"; Caribbean social organization based on hierarchies of race and colour, has evolved a unique creole identity that has become a defining element in the region's culture. Ethnic groups which arrived in the Caribbean after 1834 prove their Caribbeanness mainly by the degree to which they adopt creole manners.

The problem is that the "creole" model itself is constantly evolving, and the word "creole" has gone through more semantic changes than almost any other word in the history of the colonies. Originally denoting Europeans and Africans who were born in the Caribbean, "creole" later referred specifically to French or Spanish people born in the new World of the Americas and the Caribbean, and later still to any Caribbean person of African descent, partial or whole. All this leads to a contemporary definition of "creole" simply as Caribbean with a major African component. This is why, for many people, "creole" is equated with African. But even if the African element is dominant in creole culture, it is not total. To equate "creole" with African distorts history and devalues the labour of Indo-Guyanese and Indo-Trinidadians who all but sustained the economies of their respective countries since 1838.

Part Two of this volume focuses on Indian indenture, which lasted from 1838 to 1917 in the Caribbean. It consists of eleven book reviews. Part Three, "Indo-Caribbeans," consists of fifteen interviews with Indo-Caribbean people from a variety of backgrounds; altogether the interviews contribute a multiplicity of attitudes, opinions, points of view and situations which convey a general impression of Indo-Caribbean experience. A majority of those interviewed are male and are either from Guyana or Trinidad; almost half are Christian, while the remainder are Hindu or Muslim; and almost all are professional—civil servants, doctors, school teachers, academics or authors. Although interviews were not conducted with labourers or manual workers, their experiences are adequately captured by the review of autobiographical accounts of labourers in *The Still Cry*, and by reviews of novels of plantation life, for example, Monar's *Estate People* and Shinebourne's *Timepiece* in Part Two. In addition, one third of those interviewed (Ramcharan, Jagan, Shinebourne, Kallicharan and Seecharan) grew upon plantations. Since labour is the hallmark of Indo-Caribbean culture, its effect cannot be neglected or underestimated.

The interviews make up the bulk of the text of this volume and contain the core of its argument: that the peculiar dislocation and fragmentation spawned by Indian indenture in the Caribbean reflect a more universal condition of homelessness as articulated most eloquently by V S Naipaul in his fiction, for example, in his story "One Out of Many," in which the hero Santosh comes to this sobering conclusion:

> "the knowledge that I have a face and have a body, that I must
> feed this body and clothe this body for a certain number of years.
> Then it will all be over."

None of the fifteen individuals interviewed in *Indo-Caribbean Diaspora* say this explicitly, but implicitly, their collective account is just as comfortless and unconsoling.

Since the basic form of the interview is biographical, and its medium oral, it is essentially a type of oral biography. It possesses the narrative capacity of short fiction by reporting events or reproducing dialogue as effectively as any short story narrated in the first person. The interview is equally versatile in providing commentary of an essayistic, nonfiction type. Most of all, the interview possesses the human and dramatic interest of a question-and-answer format, something which no academic commentary, however perceptive, can match. It is hard to imagine a scholarly essay capturing the dramatic tension, elemental power and spontaneous appeal of one individual's personal account in narrowly escaping death during the political riots in Guyana in 1962, or the limitations of innocence and naiveté in another individual's account of political awakening, as remembered through the mind and eye of a growing Guyanese village girl. Its ability to shift from first person narration to reported speech or dialogue illustrates the flexibility of the interview, which combines the functions of fiction and autobiography with more scholarly purposes of writing or commentary. In their presentation of Indo-Caribbean experience, therefore, the interviews collected here are both evocative and analytical.

Part Four opens with an essay entitled "Indian Migration," which is followed by three book reviews and two essays. "The Second Migration" reflects on the historical background of migration, firstly from India to the Caribbean, secondly from the Caribbean to Europe or North America, and then possibly, to destinations further ahead. The first review—of David Dabydeen's novel, *The Intended*—examines Asian and black experience in England in the 1970s. The hero is born in Guyana, and grows up in London, which he discovers to be an urban jungle with psychic and multicultural dangers of its own. The second review is of *The East Indian Diaspora*, a collection of essays by various commentators who consider all aspects of Indo-Caribbean diasporic experience in the US from social, cultural, and economic issues to psychological problems and mental health. The third review is of a volume of stories, *Jogging in Havana*, by Cyril Dabydeen, the most productive of Indo-Caribbean writers in Canada. The stories are set both in and out of Canada and illustrate a version of psychic alienation in which the author feels that his imagination is divided between "here"—his experience in Canada, where he has lived for more than twenty years, and "there"—memories of Guyana where he grew up.

The essay "Indo-Caribbean Canadians" attempts to survey the experience of one Indo-Caribbean diasporic community—the one in Canada. Using mostly literary sources, the essay argues that although most Indo-Caribbean immigrants have achieved a satisfactory level of material prosperity in Canada, they are ambivalent towards their new environment. Their feelings are best expressed in Bissoondath's story "Security" in which the main character—Ramgoolam—enjoys the creature comforts of Toronto, but misses the inner contentment that he enjoyed within his own Hindu community in Trinidad. The story also exposes an alarming gap between Indo-Caribbean Canadian immigrants who hanker after a Caribbean lifestyle, with its own satisfactions and pieties, and the more fast-paced life of their children in Toronto, with its secular freedoms and absence of taboos. This portrait of "insecure security" admirably encapsulates the diasporic dilemma of Indo-Caribbeans whether they live in London, New York, Toronto or Saskatoon—one of outward affluence and physical security combined with inward disquiet and a hidden sense of foreboding.

The final item in this volume, the essay "Immigration in the Fiction of V S Naipaul" acts as a summary to the entire volume, by arguing that the basic features of Indo-Caribbean experience, for example the dislocation from India, the heavy burden of labour in the Caribbean, ethnic victimization after Independence, and subsequent flight to England, Canada or the US, are simply one group's particular experience of a global phenomenon of placelessness and homelessness that affects all human communities. This theme forms the basis of V S Naipaul's impressive literary reputation as the finest writer of English prose to come out of the Caribbean. For all that, Naipaul's essential perceptions into Caribbean and global homelessness are neither as remarkable as claimed by his admirers—mostly Western critics, nor as treacherous as professed by his detractors—chiefly Third World and Caribbean critics. For Naipaul's perceptions derive from the subtly differentiated point of view of a unique cultural group (Indo-Trinidadians) who are doubly marginalized, firstly through their dependent creole-Caribbean condition on the fringes of the Euro-American metropolis, and secondly through their outsider status as Indians within this already dependent and devalued creole culture that relies for its very survival on its client status to Europe and North America. The tenuous precariousness of this double marginalization is what enables Naipaul to depict homelessness with such clarity and feeling in his fiction.

But Naipaul's literary distinction is not an unmixed blessing: whereas his perceptions are luminous within the enclosed, specific Indo-Trinidadian world of a novel like *A House for Mr Biswas*, they shine less brightly when applied to Caribbean society as a whole. This is why Naipaul has been so fiercely pilloried, mostly by his countrymen of African descent, whose worst nightmare is to be linked to the feudalistic, shifting and amoral plantation values from which they believe they had distanced themselves since the Emancipation era of the

1830s. It was galling enough for Afro-Caribbeans to be labelled with these values which applied far more to Indians with their fresh experience of the plantation; it was even more galling that the label indicated the truth: that Afro-Caribbeans had not completely succeeded in distancing themselves from their plantation past. They had not succeeded because of their continuing colonial dependency on Britain and North America. But they had not failed completely either. For example, they had come to regard the Caribbean as home, thereby shedding some of the transience and homelessness that still afflicted their Indian countrymen who arrived in the Caribbean much later than they did. Therefore when the acclaim of Western critics and commentators made Naipaul the foremost Caribbean spokesman in the 1960s and 70s, it aroused such blinding Afro-Caribbean animosity against him that it still rankles thirty years later, although the most wounded feelings have since been mollified by increased pride in the subsequent international recognition of Afro-Caribbean poets like Derek Walcott and Edward Brathwaite.

Nothing illustrates the tangled ambivalence of Indo-Caribbean diasporic experience better than this turbulent controversy over Naipaul's literary reputation, which has haunted the world of Caribbean letters for nearly four decades. Naipaul came, after all, from rather an insulated orthodox Hindu family, which limited his degree of creolization. On the other hand, Samuel Selvon, his Indo-Trinidadian contemporary, came from a Presbyterian family that was more creolized. Because it is more tolerant of creole disabilities, Selvon's writing has not aroused the animosity that has all but marginalized Naipaul's career within the Caribbean. The effect of this marginalization has been tragic both for Naipaul's career and West Indian literature. For Naipaul's best writing is on Caribbean subjects, and especially Indo-Caribbean ones. One only has to look at his later fiction on African and English subjects, or his nonfiction works on India and the Middle East, to notice their reduced accuracy, conviction, wit, humour, gaiety and satiric edge compared with the Caribbean books. If we compare the deeply wounding truths of *The Middle Passage*, for instance, with the almost mischievous generalizations and pallid stereotypes in *Among the Believers*, we shall see that Naipaul's personal experience of diasporic exile is no different from that of Ramgoolam in Bissoondath's story "Security:" one of material comfort or professional success that is severely tempered by inner estrangement from his most familiar (Indo-Caribbean) sources of satisfaction and inspiration. At any rate, neither Naipaul's achievement nor its repercussions are unique, for prophets are not generally honoured in their own countries, and we should not be surprised that Naipaul had to endure the hell that Patrick White endured from his fellow Australians, Mordecai Richler from fellow Canadian Jews, and Wole Soyinka from fellow Nigerians, most notably his own Yoruba brethren.

It was too much to expect West Indians to cherish Naipaul while, with his unsparing insider's eye, he blazoned their worst vices to their worst enemies in the developed world of Europe and the US. Yet such is the Indo-Caribbean virus that Selvon, who endeared himself to Caribbean and Third World critics, never got a university appointment in Black Studies like several of his Afro-Caribbean fellow writers. Perhaps his non-African ethnicity automatically made him ineligible. Selvon's desperate wanderings in his final years drive home the argument both of a deep-seated diasporic impulse in Indo-Caribbeans, and of its disruptive spiritual effects. Dr Jagan's twenty-eight year sojourn in the political wilderness, from 1964 to 1992, is another example of Indo-Caribbean diasporic marginalization in which Afro-centricity had a far more visible hand, because of the overtly political issues; and although Alvin Kallicharan is too coy to be explicit about it, Rohan Kanhai, greatest of all Indo-Caribbean cricketers, also felt circumscribed by Afro-centricity when he was replaced by Clive Lloyd as West Indian captain in 1974.

As already mentioned, the Indo-Caribbean diaspora is one of several that sprang ironically from the attainment of freedom and Independence by Caribbean nations in the 1960s. A volume like the present one could be composed about the Afro-Caribbean diaspora, or the Chinese-Caribbean diaspora, for example. While it is invidious to fully compare the relative victimization of groups, it is doubtful that the feelings of other groups can match the intensity of Indo-Caribbean victimization, alienation and loss; for none of these other groups, except the Africans, were large enough to have invested their labour on a similar scale in the soil; and none but the Africans could have entertained political expectations that would have produced similar awareness of injustice and political loss. Besides, since Afro-Caribbean parties ruled Guyana and Trinidad and Tobago almost continuously since Independence, it is possible to regard some Afro-Caribbean diasporic grief as self-inflicted or partly deserved. The difference with the

Indians is that since the 1830s, they remained virtually "en bloc" on the land. Their political frustrations, combined with this sense of uprooting from the land, confer a unique intensity on their sense of marginalization and make their second migration more grievous than that of other Caribbean groups.

One might expect that a common pattern of victimization shared by Caribbean groups would serve to unite rather than separate them. It would be ironic if Caribbean nations, after Independence, were to continue the process of fragmentation and division that they had to endure when they were colonies. These nations are too small in geographical size and numbers, too short of natural resources, and too insignificant in world affairs to survive division. Undoubtedly, to some extent the racial polarization and political disorder that followed Independence in Guyana and Trinidad and Tobago may be partly blamed on greedy and unscrupulous politicians. But the truth is that the behaviour of these politicians flourished because of a deep-seated colonial legacy of hierarchical patterns, like those of master and slave, governing social and personal Caribbean relationships. Indo-Caribbean marginalization and homelessness are direct products of these patterns, however global or universal they may also be. Still, as Walter Rodney showed in his magnificent study, *A History of the Guyanese Working Class 1881-1905*, a common pattern of victimization did produce solidarity between the two major racial groups in Guyana in colonial times. Through its documentation of Indo-Caribbean experience, the present volume throws light on the process by which this solidarity became unravelled during the postcolonial period in Guyana and Trinidad and Tobago.

Before it can be transcended, this process of post-Independence unravelling must be seen as a partial result of Afro-centricity, which itself is the product of a peculiar history of slavery/indenture and the plantation system. In this sense, although Forbes Burnham may be regarded as the villain of the piece, so far as the Indo-Guyanese diaspora is concerned, his role is not entirely self-willed. This is true for most protagonists in the drama, not least Indo-Guyanese quislings who served Burnham's regime. The unsavoury morality of quisling roles should not blind us to their crucial importance in the unfolding of the plot; for these quislings lent the Burnham regime exactly the aura of multiracialism that it needed to achieve plausibility as a national government. Yet the "brahminist" motives of self-assertive greed, supercilious egoism and benighted ignorance that inspired Indo-Guyanese quislings, are produced by slavery/indenture and plantation values, and these motives remain "brahminist" whether the protagonists are Hindu, Muslim or Christian.

The motives of most of the players here originate in the hierarchical feudal patterns, and brutal, social conditions bequeathed by slavery/indenture and the plantation system. In his autobiography, Albert Gomes describes social conditions in Trinidad that are typical of the feudalistic and brutal patterns that prevail in the Caribbean:

> It was this ubiquitous cruelty—of man to animal, of man to woman, of parent to child, of white housewife to Negro domestic, of almost everyone to the scorned and ostracized "coolie," of the ruling classes to the masses—that fouled the spiritual climate of the community, and overcast my sunlit childhood.

This has the ring of truth, and it applies to Guyana and Trinidad and Tobago at least until about the 1950s. The humiliation and degradation of such conditions were part and parcel of Indo-Caribbean experience, and inevitably induced despair. Merely to survive such conditions would have been enough. For Indo-Guyanese to have found as well, resources of body, mind and spirit to triumph over despair is one of the still unsung epics of resistance to British colonialism in this century. In the closing comments of his interview, Robert Janki praises the triumphant heroism of Guyanese "coolie" workers in overcoming despair through their labour and, in the process, pioneering the growth of a new nation:

> They [Indentured Indians] suffered in the mud. They worked day and night. Rain came and wet them; the sun came and dried them. They would get up at four o'clock in the morning, and walk miles to the backdam without any transportation to take them . . . It was they who built Guyana prior to 1964. Future Guyanese of all races and groups should know this.

Such heroic and unrelenting toil did succeed; it did defeat despair; and, as Janki implies, it deserves to be recognized as a glorious example of self-sacrificial struggle waged by all colonized people to resist oppression everywhere. Janki's words serve as an imperishable epitaph both to this universal struggle and to the heroic role played in it by Indo-Caribbean labour. That such glorious heroism should be shunted by post-Independence insecurity into escape, exile and regret is the ultimate tragedy of the Indo-Caribbean diaspora.

As a collection of book reviews, literary essays and interviews, this book is not a conventional work of history, sociology, anthropology or literature. It seems too improvised or random for that. But this seemingly random structure reflects the incoherent and fragmented nature of Indo-Caribbean experience, which begins with cultural deracination from India, passes through economic exploitation in the Caribbean, and emerges in feelings of disorientation and exile that Indo-Caribbean immigrants experience in alien cities of North America and Europe. Instances of so-called "repetition" may emerge because related subjects and issues are considered from different angles; for this collection functions less by frontal logic than by the sort of lateral or circular reasoning that Shakespeare's Polonius advised Reynaldo to employ, when he sent the latter to spy on Laertes and his associates in Paris: "by indirections [to]find directions out". In other words, despite a surface appearance of randomness or repetition, a connected and comprehensive argument does emerge when all sections of the volume are taken together.

An example of this is seen in references to Forbes Burnham. Burnham is first mentioned in this Introduction; and his career is considered in Part One in reviews of Chase's book *Guyana: A Nation in Transit: Burnham's Role*, and Norma de Haarte's novel *Guyana Betrayal*. These books present contrasting but interdependent portraits of their subject. And there are differences between both these books and Shinebourne's novel *Timepiece* (Part Two) which also reflects on Burnham's regime. Then, in Part Three, almost every Guyanese who is interviewed comments on Burnham, each in his or her own way.

Would it have been preferable to employ a more concise, and firmly structured statement of the effect of Burnham's regime on Indo-Guyanese? Perhaps. Perhaps too it would fail to capture the complexity of interaction between racial, ethnic, psychological, social, political, religious and economic forces that prevailed during Burnham's time. Admittedly, if each repetition of Burnham's doings yielded identical insights, they too would fail to capture the complexity of these forces. But if each instance of so called "repetition" yields fresh insight into Burnham's personality and career, or throws new light on aspects of

Introduction

his regime in Guyana, the result could be a many-sided, multivisioned record that incorporates, among other things, a political study of dictatorship, an analysis of postcolonial disorder, and an investigation of motives that prompted Indo-Guyanese to migrate for a second time. Thus the random appearance of the methodology of this volume is deceptive: it facilitates both the structure of an anthology in which each item can be savoured independently, and an analytical study in which all items and sections collectively serve to advance an argument about the essential homelessness of humankind, and to reinforce the view that Indo-Caribbean people have been driven from pillar to post in their formation of a new diaspora.

This volume owes much to past executives of OSSIC (The Ontario Society for Services to Indo-Caribbean Canadians) and, in the early stages, to Michael Latchana when he was secretary of the organization. For a grant to complete the volume, I am especially grateful to the Dean of Arts at York University. I am indebted to several individuals for word-precessing skills: Maureen Principe, Janice Pearson, and Tessa Chakkalakal. Grateful thanks to Lisa Salem-Wiseman and Odette Denton for word-processing and editorial help. I am also grateful to TSAR for publication. Most of all I wish to thank those who were interviewed, for their cooperation, generosity, and kindness; and I include those whose interviews were not included due to lack of space.

Part One

The Caribbean

Ayube Edun
London's Heart-Probe and Britain's Destiny
London: n.p; n.d.

As the first full-length prose work by an Indo-Caribbean author to be published in England, Ayube Edun's *London's Heart-Probe and Britain's Destiny* is of unique historical interest. Although it gives neither its publisher nor year of publication, we may assume that *London's Heart-Probe* appeared shortly after 1928 because it is an account of a visit that the author made to England in that year. Edun was well known in Guyana as the founder/president of the Manpower Citizens' Association (MPCA), a trade union which represented workers in the sugar industry. Even before the formation of the MPCA, Edun was seen to represent the rights of sugar workers in articles which he wrote firstly for the *Tribune, Guyana Review* and later the *Labour Advocate*.

In *London's Heart-Probe* we learn that robberies, murders, drunkenness, prostitution, pubs, and drug—and gambling dens exist in London's East End which the author calls "a benighted environment of hopeless moral leprosy" (p. 31). Since these are all symptoms of the Great Depression, there is much talk about economics—three million unemployed in Britain—exploitation, and social problems of one kind or another. Edun evidently is not one to mince words, and nothing misses his roving eye, from pavement artists to scandal-mongering newspapers. The result in *London's Heart Probe* is a richly varied mixture of observations, comments, opinions, suggestions and forecasts in which Edun expounds on all manner of subjects including his dislike of drinking, smoking, lawyers and religion, his advocacy of birth control, and his view of the backward opinion of the Roman Catholic church on this last subject. He believes, for instance, that English people have bad teeth because they eat meat, and since the struggle for Indian home rule was then in full swing, he is in no doubt that the British should leave India. As a Muslim himself, he cautions that Indian Muslims should not side with the British during this Indian struggle. Inevitably, these comments have a quaint ring today, when India has long ceased to be a British colony and Pakistan has existed for half a century.

Despite its negative or critical judgments, *London's Heart-Probe* should not be taken as an attack on British society or institutions. On the contrary, amidst its gratuitous hodgepodge of concrete observation and random speculation, the book offers something of a rationale of the author's point of view in an introduction in which Edun twice states that he is a "Britisher," that he has: "probed with the lancet of Rational-Practical-Idealism into the heart of British Civilization," and that he has written with "sincerity, honesty of purpose, and affection towards Old England, the centre of every Britisher's thought". Here, clearly, is an ambivalent view of Britain, one which nowadays may seem ignorant or lunatic until we recall that at the end of the last century and well into the present one, many informed or "progressive" people in British dominions and colonies held similar views inspired by a rather old-fashioned faith in Imperialism as a benevolent ideology. Some of these people agitated for federation of various parts of the British empire. Influential Canadians, for example, supported the Imperial Federation League which advocated federation between Canada and certain Caribbean territories as a benign imperial union that would provide economic prosperity and military security to all its partners.

Like those Imperial Federationists, Edun saw British dominions and colonies as virgin territories with "vitality and virility" which, through an improved, federal form of imperial union, could reinvigorate "an old race" like the British, and promote economic progress, social stability and world peace. This point of view is identical to that expressed in one of the best known Canadian novels, Sara Jeannette Duncan's *The Imperialist*, which was written at the turn of the century, and asserts stout faith in Britain's benign imperial destiny. In an historical context, therefore, despite their random, surface appearance, critical stance, and sometimes hectoring tone, the observations and opinions in *London's Heart-Probe* are neither ignorant nor lunatic: they belong to a particular period of history, and represent the considered views of a responsible, public-spirited and well-informed, if self-taught individual who achieved distinction as one of the first Indo-Guyanese authors of note.

Gobin Sawh, ed.
The Canadian Caribbean Connection
Halifax, Nova Scotia: Carindo Cultural Association, 1992.

In addition to its subtitle "Bridging North and South: History, Influences, Lifestyles," *The Canadian Caribbean Connection* carries an introduction which states that its purpose is: "to provide readers with relevant information about the Caribbean West Indian islands, its peoples, and the Canadian Caribbean Connection." This information covers a broad range of geographical, historical, social, economic and political details about West Indians in Canada. The book's coverage is comprehensive although it deals only with the English-speaking Caribbean, and only with island territories, not with Guyana or Belize.

The information in *The Canadian Caribbean Connection* is not exactly new; the aim of the volume is not fresh information or original research: it is rather in the collection and gathering of varied Canadian/Caribbean materials into one volume, where they are classified, organized, and presented so that they can be: "understood at the grade ten level whether you are a student, a traveller, a business person or a curious reader." For example, the chapter "Concerning the Geography of the West Indies" provides excellent, up-to-date, statistical information on each English-speaking island, while chapters such as "Women of the West Indies" and "The Social Milieu of the Caribbean" deal with related but different areas of Caribbean experience. So far as relations—"the connection"—between Canada and the Caribbean are concerned, they are comprehensively chronicled in two chapters—"Canada and the West Indies" and "Canada and the Commonwealth Caribbean"—which trace Canadian/Caribbean history from the earliest period of colonial settlement to the present day. Some of the most interesting information is contained in these two chapters which illuminate darker areas of the relationship between Canada and North America. It was the loss of Britain's North American colonies in the American War of Independence, for example, which unintentionally struck the first decisive blow for the British emancipation of slavery by reducing the number of British plantations and the need for fresh cargoes of slaves from Africa.

After slavery was abolished in 1834, close ties continued between Nova Scotia and the West Indies. Trade flourished in fish, livestock, lumber, rum, molasses and salt. Commercial and cultural links between Eastern Canada, Nova Scotia in particular, and the West Indies stimulated interest in some form of political union between Canada and some West Indian islands in the second half of the nineteenth century. The interest waned in due course; but by the twentieth century, when long-established links had made it commonplace for West Indians to study and live in Canada, the Canadian Caribbean "connection" had become a "fait accompli."

Because the book was produced by CARINDO—the Caribbean East Indian Cultural Association—which is based in Eastern Canada, it includes a chapter on "West Indian Immigrants in the Maritimes." There is also some concentration on links between Canadian Presbyterian missionaries and the Indians among whom they mainly worked in the Caribbean; but this merely helps to emphasize the Canadian Caribbean connection and does not imply a bias in favour of Indo-Caribbean subjects. Guyana, for instance, the Caribbean territory of largest Indian settlement, is not considered in detail. In any case, each chapter in the book is written by contributors drawn from a mixture of racial and national backgrounds. Sir Philip Sherlock, Dr Brinsley Samaroo and Dr Sahadeo Basdeo are well known Caribbean scholars. Other contributors are Canadian or West Indian academics and university graduates or professionals, most of whom now live in Canada. It is a feat of successful editing that so many contributors, dealing with different aspects of their subject, can produce a uniform style that is simple and expository, and capable of reaching both the student and general reader. Questions at the end of each chapter are evidently intended for students, although they provide a rough summary of the chapters as well. Gobin Sawh executes his job as editor with deceptive ease.

Sawh recommends that *The Canadian Caribbean Connection* should be read in sequence, chapter by chapter, although he thinks it could also be read in sections. This dual approach necessitates some repetition, as Sawh admits, if each chapter is to be comprehensible in itself, and form part of a larger whole. Yet such is the richness of the information in *The Canadian Caribbean Connection*, and so accessible its format, that it remains a valuable reference work, a handy source to be consulted at will for all sorts of facts, figures, names, issues and details about the English-speaking West Indian islands and their relationship to Canada.

Henry Josiah
Makonaima's Children
Georgetown, Guyana: Roraima Publishers, 1994.

Makonaima's Children is a slim volume consisting of eight Guyanese folktales which, as the author explains in the Preface: "come from traditions passed on by word of mouth through descendants of the original Guyanese who lived on the land before the white man came." These original Guyanese are people such as Caribs, Macushi and Patamona, Wapishiana, Warrau and Wai Wai, Akawaio, Arecuna and Arawaks, aboriginals of the Americas and the Caribbean who survived in Guyana largely because they lived on the South American mainland with a huge forest in which they could seek refuge from European colonial invaders, during the period of colonization that began in the early sixteenth century. Their compatriots on neighbouring Caribbean islands were not so lucky: as islanders they had nowhere to run, and perished at the hands of the colonizers. But even if Guyanese aboriginals did survive, they were greatly damaged by European conquest, their very name—"Amerindian"—illustrating European dominance, since it perpetuates Columbus's error in confusing them with people from India. The real value of the folktales in *Makonaima's Children* is that they proclaim the resilience of contemporary aboriginal culture in Guyana despite the colonial damage of previous centuries.

Like most cultures, "Amerindians" have their own cosmogony by which they understand the origin of the universe and their place in it. The opening story of the volume—"Makonaima and Pia"—states that the Guyanese branch of "Amerindians" were originally called the Cariama and: "lived near the great spirit in the Place of the Sun above the sky"(p. 3). Makonaima and Pia climbed on a ladder down through a hole from the sky to the earth; but their ladder disappeared and they would have been marooned, except that their female classmates Mazaruni and Cuyuni had also come down the ladder to join them on earth. Makonaima married Mazaruni; and Pia, Cuyuni; and in time their progeny formed the Amerindian population of Guyana. As an aboriginal version of the birth of civilization, with evident parallels to other similar stories, for example, the Christian story of Adam and Eve in the garden of Eden, *Makonaima's Children* relates several anthropomorphic tales that account for the names of Guyanese mountains, rivers, trees, birds, fish, and animals; for example: Mazaruni and Cuyuni (rivers), Roraima (mountain), Kaietuk (waterfall), Perai and Arapaima (fish). Perai, for instance, was a woman who was turned into a flesh-eating fish as punishment for a curse she had put on her lover Arapaima.

The themes in *Makonaima's Children* are elemental and universal. In the tale "Kanaima-Dai-Dai," which illustrates the necessity of brotherly love and reconciliation, the village of the heroic Rima is unexpectedly attacked. Many people are killed, and Rima and her "yagon" (younger brother) flee into the forest where they are separated and frightened out of their wits; but they are safely reunited in their village where the villagers feel a natural instinct for revenge against the enemy who launched this utterly unprovoked attack. But the wise, old chief advises his fellow villagers to bury their dead, and forgive their attackers so that peace will be maintained. Since the theme of forgiveness or loving one's enemy is common in both folklore and religion, it strongly reinforces the mythic aspect of *Makonaima's Children*. Similarly, in "Kaietuk," when old man Kaie sacrifices himself during a period of famine so that growth will return to the land, he represents a scapegoat or martyr figure that appears in many cultural traditions that stress the need for individual sacrifice in the interest of the community.

Colonialism in the Americas and the Caribbean has not only destroyed or damaged aboriginal cultures: it has uprooted people from other cultures, for example, in Asia and Africa, and transplanted them in new environments across the Atlantic. Consequently, people in postcolonial environments such as Guyana suffer from cultural fragmentation and displacement, and face a formidable challenge to forge fresh, collective identity out of their mixed and broken colonial inheritance. The survival of a precolonial Guyanese cultural tradition is a powerful weapon in confronting this challenge, since it provides an example of cultural continuity that may serve not only as an antidote to raw feelings of colonial fragmentation and displacement, but as a mark of postcolonial identity in Guyanese people. This may not be as easy as it sounds because aboriginal cultural traditions have been marginalized during colonial times, when aboriginals were regarded pejoratively as "bucks," that is to say, crude or primitive jungle dwellers. The publication of *Makonaima's Children* is a welcome sign of rehabilitation that can help the development of a national culture in Guyana, by restoring continuity with the people who first inhabited the national landscape, and established basic patterns of humanizing it.

Because of its slim size, the claim of national significance for *Makon-aima's Children* may appear exaggerated. But the volume should not be seen in isolation. It comes in the wake of earlier volumes such as Rev. William Brett's *Legends and Myths of the Aboriginal Indians of Guyana* (c. 1880), Walter Roth's *An Inquiry into the Animism and Folklore of the Guyana Indians* (1915), Edwards and Hubbard, eds. *Folktales and Legends of Some Guyana Amerindians* (1979), and Sister Rose Magdalene's *Amerindian Stories for Young Guyanese* (1983). As a distinguished addition to this list, *Makonaima's Children* makes a more powerful impact. The folktales themselves capture much suspense and drama, and evoke the varied local colour of a tropical Guyanese landscape. Josiah's language is rich and poetic, as well as factual and down to earth, as in the following description of Rima and her little brother in the forest:

> They were afraid because they knew the jungle held not only tigers and the deadly labaria and bushmaster snakes and the camoodi which could coil itself around you and crush you to death and swallow you whole, but also there was kanaima dai dai, the vengeful bush devil who, unseen by human eyes, lured you away, put you to sleep and killed you horribly with a poison stick in your bowels. (p. 32)

This judiciously selected array of forest creatures and their deadly functions captures the fear of innocent, unprotected children at the mercy of natural and unnatural evils of the forest, and illustrates Josiah's skill in creating tales that can remain entertaining while they provide mythic and national significance to Guyanese readers.

Ashton Chase
A Nation in Transit—Burnham's Role
Georgetown, Guyana: Pavinkpress, 1994.

As lawyer and author, former politician and trade unionist, and someone who played a leading role in the pre-1955 People's Progressive Party (PPP) under the leadership of Dr Cheddi Jagan, Ashton Chase is well known in Guyana. He served as Minister of Labour, Trade and Industry in Dr Jagan's ill-fated government of 1953, and he has written such books as *133 Days Towards Freedom in Guiana* (1934)—an account of the 1953 PPP administration—and *A History of Trade Unionism in*

Guyana: 1900–1961 (1964). But, unlike so many other disillusioned politicians or professionals, and tens of thousands of his countrymen who emigrated from their homeland, Chase remained in Guyana where he still lives. This is a distinct asset to his writing, for it adds authority to his role as an informed, on-the-spot observer, and discriminating commentator on Guyanese public events, issues and personalities.

Nation in Transit was completed in 1989, and in a brief letter to the reader, Chase states that he resisted suggestions to update the manuscript. This might make the volume look like a record of the People's National Congress (PNC) régime while it was in power from 1964 to 1989; but this is not the case. *Nation in Transit* does consider the political career of the founder and leader of the PNC—Linden Forbes Sampson Burnham—who became Prime Minister in 1964 and remained in office until his death in 1985. Yet the volume is neither a biography of Burnham nor a history of the PNC; its scope is much wider, and as P.P. Dial says in his Preface, it: "presents a clear picture of the political life in Guyana over the last 40 years." (p. iii)

The main argument is that Burnham's unbroken rule in Guyana from 1964 to 1985 was a result of his insatiable lust for power. Chase allows that Burnham possessed a fine brain, a prodigious memory, unsurpassed ability at speech making, and a charismatic hold on the Guyanese populace; but he claims that these gifts were combined with a cynical, Machiavellian approach that led him inexorably to autocracy. Chase's impeccable research offers convincing facts, statistics, and revelations to support his claim. What is absent is a sense of outrage over the shocking nature of his revelations. Perhaps the author expects the horror of his revelations to be self evident; or a long legal career may have led him to distrust explicit emotion which might devalue either the integrity or the persuasiveness of his claim. Whatever the case, the calm, controlled air of his narrative is a little unnerving: his patience, sobriety and seeming equanimity contrast too sharply with the frenzied nature of the deeds that he reports. But that may be exactly the point—a contrast between the civility and decency of the author (or his countrymen) and the perverse nature of Burnham's deeds.

Chase opens by quoting from Jessie Burnham's pamphlet "Beware my Brother Forbes" which gives her brother's motto: "the personal ends of power justify ANY means used to achieve them." (p. 7) Jessie also states that: "His [Burnham's] bible is *The Prince* by Machiavelli."

(p. 7) In corroboration, Chase points out that, despite being a leading member of the PPP in 1953, Burnham deftly distanced himself from his party and colleagues when he realized that the PPP was discredited as communist. Later, Burnham exploited the British-American strategy of proportional representation and the support of individuals like Peter D'Aguiar and Richard Ishmael to win national elections in 1964; but once power was safely in his hands, he cynically jettisoned D'Aguiar, Ishmael, and later the British and Americans.

Burnham was a past master at manipulation and chicanery: he rigged elections with brazen regularity, and secured his power by creating and controlling paramilitary organizations such as the National Service, National Guard, and People's Militia. His chicanery is evident in his rhetoric about nationalization. According to the author:

> Nationalization . . . was portrayed as an act of statesmanship, a sign of political maturity and an index that we were converting our political independence in order to bring social justice to the masses. (p. 58)

The truth was the opposite: "capital resources were being drained and wealth was being transshipped to build other countries" (p. 58) Yet, by 1976 "He [Burnham] had brought the commanding heights of the economy both within State control and State ownership." (p. 67) Chase's summary of Burnham's political strategy is succinct: "The bottom line was personal power and personal glorification." (p. 51)

Less overtly political events are darkly suggestive, for example, Burnham's association with "rabbi" Washington, and Reverend Jim Jones of Jonestown notoriety. There is also possible government implication in the death of historian and politician Walter Rodney, the shooting of Dr Joshua Ramsammy, and the terrorizing of Dr Clive Thomas. Of psychological interest is Burnham's penchant for reenacting colonial authority:

> he [Burnham] would strut around on his horse, stirrup whip et al, from one field to another over the Estate, reminiscent of the old colonial overlord. In this overseer role, instructions were shouted to the unfortunates to do or do over this or that task. (p. 158)

There is Fanonesque pathology in this, but Chase refuses to court prurience by providing: "reports of extravagance of language, conduct and behavioural patterns of a nauseating type". (p. 160) Such virtuous restraint is dignified, although it lets Burnham off the hook. At any rate, Chase abruptly curtails reports of Burnham's excesses and concludes that his behaviour reflected: "contempt for society and humanity or at the most charitable level . . . schizophrenia." (p. 160)

If all this makes *Nation in Transit* seem like an anti-Burnham diatribe nothing is further from the truth. Many of Chase's revelations are echoed by numerous independent observers. Nor are his comments all anti-Burnham; he suggests, for instance, that some good did come from the international aid given to the (Burnham) régime—improvement of roads, and construction of the Demerara harbour bridge; and he admits that neither Burnham nor his régime can be blamed for the international rise of oil prices which wrecked their economic plans in the mid 1970s; but he also confirms that Burnham was not a good long term planner. Not one to save for a rainy day, he quickly used up income from sugar when the price of sugar was high, and became economically stranded when the price dropped.

How did Burnham turn an entire country into a personal fiefdom where his say-so commanded instant obedience? The secret is that, in addition to the police, paramilitary forces and economic structures which he controlled, he devised an intelligence network that brought him: "information from every hamlet in the countryside and every nook and cranny in the towns". (p. 49) This enabled him not only to forestall every move of Dr Jagan and the Opposition, but to win over Opposition members to his side. Perversely, Burnham's very cynicism gave him an advantage over Dr Jagan. When he touted socialist principle as his reason to amend the Constitution and speed up nationalization in the 1970s, Dr Jagan supported him out of genuine socialist principle. This merely increased Burnham's power and promoted his self-aggrandizement. He also used his power to help people with guilty secrets, then hold them to ransom for life; for instance, by making favourable revisions of income tax owed by prominent (mostly Indian) businessmen, he could command their financial and political loyalty ever after. But gradually, inevitably, the fatal acid of corruption began to eat into the fabric of Guyanese society:

The lazy and the indolent with the right connections were protected. Some people were permitted to be off their jobs away from essential production on his [Burnham's] party missions real or invented. In time, the work ethic was affected, and many of his [Burnham's] own supporters felt that they did not have to work hard, or perhaps, at all. (p. 91)

This structural unravelling at the very heart of Guyanese society is what reduced the country to shambles well before 1989.

Through a compelling array of facts and figures and a clearly argued, readable text, Chase unambiguously denounces Burnham. Yet the title of his book is optimistic in implying that Guyana's misfortune under Burnham and the PNC was a stage of transition which, by definition, could not last. Perhaps. But it is also possible that, out of patriotism, Chase turns a blind eye either to the scale of PNC destruction or its actual circumstances. However cunning, cynical, eloquent or charismatic Burnham was, he could not have done what he did without help and cooperation from a good many Guyanese, not all of whom acted out of fear or coercion. After all, Burnham was not the only one to profit from corruption. There were, for example, pro-PNC Indo-Guyanese who, in return for financial gain, professional advancement, or simple security, prostituted their Indian identity by supporting Burnham and allowing themselves to be used as window dressing to lend a multiracial look to his administration.

It is not possible that a whole nation would passively acquiesce to a hateful régime for so long without violent protest. If they did not protest, one must face the possibility that they did not all find the régime as hateful as Chase thinks. Vehement criticism of the current PPP/Civic government indicates that there are still people around who may be all too ready to serve another Burnham. In Chase's view, PPP/Civic was expected to prove that Guyana is a nation in transit from Burnhamite autocracy to genuine democracy. Maybe, after twenty-one years of autocracy, this expectation itself is too optimistic. We must wait and see. Meanwhile, whether it arouses optimism or pessimism, *Nation in Transit* contains a wealth of information, analysis and insight that makes it an essential text for understanding postcolonial Guyana.

Norma DeHaarte
Guyana Betrayal
Toronto: Sister Vision Press, 1991.

As its title implies, *Guyana Betrayal* is a novel about the failure of the political process in contemporary Guyana. It is a provocative title that lays down the gauntlet by promising revelations about possible culprits who "betrayed" Guyana, in the sense of reducing it from a British colony of some potential in the 1940s to the second-poorest nation in the western hemisphere by the 1980s. One of the main characters in the novel, Lucius Hoffman, is the chief culprit. Hoffman's biography is identical to that of Forbes Burnham who led the government of Guyana from 1964 to his death in 1985. Not only is Hoffman a lawyer and an exceptionally gifted orator, he is also given the African nickname of "the Kabaka" as Burnham was. The other culprit, although he plays a minor role in the novel, is Dr Chandra Ram Jattan who, like Dr Cheddi Jagan, the Guyanese opposition leader from 1964 to 1992, is a dentist whose main political support is drawn from the countryside of Guyana. There are other political figures as well. Through their activities and those of other characters, within an atmosphere of intrigue, violence, terrorism, bribery and corruption, the author creates a dramatic portrait of the political history of Guyana from 1947 to 1974.

Within this political background DeHaarte skilfully weaves a story about the romantic, domestic, professional and inter-family affairs of two women—Phyl (Phyllis) Martin and Pat Sandiford. Phyl works in Hoffman's office, from which vantage point she provides an authoritative, insider's view of her employer's corrupt practices. In one example, Hoffman gets two illiterate clients to sign over their inheritance to him. A more intimate example of Hoffman's villainy comes at the end of the novel when Phyl approaches him for legal advice, and is required to offer him sexual favours as his fee. Apart from all this, numerous electoral malpractices are attributed to Hoffman or his party.

In linking Phyl's personal fortunes with the career of a corrupt politician like Hoffman, the author hopes to heighten the drama in Phyl's life as well as the degree of corruption in politicians like Hoffman who may be said to "betray" Guyana. Unfortunately, neither the drama of the characters' personal lives, nor the depravity of the politicians' "betrayal" registers clearly. In the case of the politicians, Hoffman is obviously the most depraved. But he is too bad to be true. This, in spite of our knowledge of Burnham, Hoffman's real life model. If Hoffman's cunning, greed, cynicism, selfishness and lack of principle are presented as acknowledged facts, how can the Guyanese people be "betrayed" if they continued to reelect him while knowing these facts about him? The narrative neither asks nor answers such a question. Is it possible that an entire people could have been deceived for so long without public displays of resentment or revolution? The fact that such displays materialized neither in Burnham's Guyana nor in DeHaarte's novel suggests that there was more support for Hoffman/Burnham than DeHaarte is disposed to admit. Hence my sceptical reaction to the politics of the novel.

Pat's love affair with Ken Masterson arouses similar scepticism, with Ken leaving Pat pregnant in Guyana, while he goes off to study medicine in England, and returns many years later to find her sick in a hospital, but regaining consciousness in time to see him at her bedside. This improbable situation seems more contrived when we learn subsequently of Ken's conveniently loveless marriage in England, and his inevitable forgiveness by Pat. Phyl's relationship with her husband is equally unconvincing because it is described in somewhat stilted or sentimental terms reminiscent of Victorian melodrama. Lovers "swear" undying love to each other, with blood "coursing" through their veins. The effect of this archaic diction is compounded by repetition of many details to produce a narrative that delivers rather less than its provocative title promises. This is disappointing, for there are many promising revelations of scheming and skullduggery, which might produce suspense and drama were it not for the stilted language and style of the novel.

At the same time, *Guyana Betrayal* may be excused if it does not completely fulfill expectations of a dramatic narrative of social hardships and political villainy that add up to "betrayal" of a whole nation. Perhaps DeHaarte set her sights too high in her first novel. But there are compensations. Her reproduction of urban, Afro-Guyanese conduct and speech rivals a similar portrait in the novels of Roy Heath who has superseded Edgar Mittelholzer and Jan Carew to become the acknowledged master of this subject. The first two or three pages of Chapter 20, for example, illustrate a flavour of informality, outspokenness and relish for communal camaraderie that is recognizable as the hallmark of Guyanese life. There are several other passages and incidents like this in the novel, and they augur well for DeHaarte's future writing.

Albert Gomes
Caught in a Maze of Colour: Memoirs of a Colonial Politician
Trinidad: n.p. 1968.

In a Maze of Colour is the autobiography of Albert Gomes, a descendant
of Portuguese immigrants who came from Madeira[1] to Trinidad in the
second half of the nineteenth century. Despite early poverty the family
prospered so that by the time Gomes was born in 1911, he enjoyed
distinct advantages as a local, white, middle-class boy in a British Caribbean colony. Gomes was in turn a pharmacist, editor, trade union
leader, and politician; and in 1962, when he felt that his political career
had ended, he settled in England where he died in 1970.

Apart from telling the author's personal story, *In a Maze of Colour*
provides excellent sketches of conditions in Trinidad during the first
six decades of this century. The book was written six years after Trinidad and Tobago[2] gained independence, and contains valuable comments on the immediate postcolonial situation there and in the
English-speaking Caribbean as a whole. But this book is primarily
Gomes's own story, recording the process of his personal development
as a politician, and accounting for his ideas and actions.

Gomes's father was a shopkeeper and businessman who seemed so
totally preoccupied by his financial transactions that it was his mother
who provided the dominant influence on her son's education and attitudes. Through the example of her own father, Mrs Gomes maintained
warm, personal relations with her black servants, despite the feudalistic, hierarchical mores of early twentieth-century Trinidad. No doubt
her outlook was more paternalistic than egalitarian, but it may have
helped to engender in her son passionate sympathy for the largely
black working class in urban Trinidad.

This sympathy led Gomes and a colleague to take over the leadership of the Federated Workers Trade Union in the early 1930s. In 1938
Gomes was first elected to the Council of the City of Port-of-Spain; he
became Deputy Mayor three times. In 1946, in the first general elections held under adult suffrage in Trinidad and Tobago, Gomes won a
seat in the Legislative Council that governed the whole country. From
there on, as a member of the Executive Council and as a government
minister, Gomes held public office until the early 1960s when the cause
of West Indian Federation, on which he had staked his political future,
failed to win support from the electorate. By that time Gomes had lost

popularity and credibility; he even feared for his safety. Hence his migration to England.

The society which Gomes describes in *In a Maze of Colour* is typical of a region in which the most dominant historical forces were the British plantation system and African slavery. The population consisted mainly of descendants of former African slaves and European slave owners, together with descendants of other groups—Indians, Chinese, Portuguese—who were brought to work in the plantations after slavery was abolished. In social, cultural and political terms, Gomes sees the Trinidad of his early years as "infested" (p. 12), or "abscessed" (p. 28). Where he does not employ disease imagery, he speaks of Trinidad as a "jungle" (p. 5) and of the "lopsidedness" (p. 109) of the island's personality.

Gomes unambiguously attributes these adverse characteristics to political causes. He sees Trinidad as "politically inchoate" (p. 109), and he thinks of himself as living in an era of "political makeshift" (p. 13). The root cause of Trinidad's problems is what he calls the "colonial trauma" (p. 109): the continuous exploitation and repression of her people which eventually produced a "log-jam of imprisoned waters" (p. 28) and erupted in the riots of 1937, only to be followed by further political agitation until Independence was achieved.

Gomes's recollection of Trinidad is of a society that so lacks the most elementary niceties of communal (civilized) behaviour that brute force becomes decisive in a grim struggle for survival. Physical strength is admired, and weakness either ridiculed or eliminated:

> The society was infested with beggars, vagrants and misfits of all kinds—filthy, lice-ridden scarecrow shapes, with the everpresent sores that discoloured their skins and the fitful throaty coughing that convulsed their frames. This human flotsam met ridicule, even violence, in the streets. And to merit such punishment, the mere fact of looking different seemed to provide sufficient offence. The ragged, the ugly, the idiotic—deviants of every kind—were uniformly punished for this singular nonconformity. Wherever they ventured gangs of boys and girls relentlessly pursued them with jeers and taunts—and stones. Shamefully, even the adults indulged in the collective sadism. (p. 12)

There is little difference between what Gomes calls the "farmyard ethos" surrounding his childhood in Trinidad and the picaresque world described by V S Naipaul in *The Middle Passage:*[3]

> This was an ugly world, a jungle, where the picaroon hero starved unless he stole, was beaten almost to death when found out, and had therefore to get in his blows first whenever possible; where the weak were humiliated; where the powerful never appeared and were beyond reach; where no one was allowed any dignity and everyone had to impose himself; an uncreative society, where war was the only profession. (p. 79)

What both Gomes and Naipaul describe is the legacy of three centuries of the plantation system and slavery that allowed white masters absolute power over black subjects.

Although the conditions described by both authors are almost identical, Gomes is less detached. When he first runs for elections he is appalled by the corrupt practices involved. He is shocked to learn that his supporters must impersonate potential voters who are not likely to cast their ballots, and he can only laugh when told that "even the dead vote" (p. 35). But such things are no laughing matter in a region where as recently as the 1960s and 70s, the late Mr L F S Burnham[4] is believed to have won elections in Guyana partly through votes cast in the names of dead people. In any case, even if Gomes disapproves of unsavoury electioneering practices in Trinidad, he turns a blind eye to them in subsequent elections. His approach is like that of C L R James in his *Life of Captain Cipriani.*[5] Gomes and James provide equally damning insights into the history and culture of Trinidad, but they treat them as symptoms of political problems that need to be solved. On the other hand, Naipaul either does not contemplate solutions or considers them too difficult.

Gomes's comments on the vexed question of West Indian identity confirms his political commitment. In a society of mixed ethnic and cultural inheritance, he is alert to the danger of social fragmentation if narrow, ethnic loyalties should prevail. Since different racial groups were brought to Trinidad to satisfy the needs of a colonial plantation economy, it is this political factor—colonialism—which must be removed before a truly integrated West Indian culture or identity can emerge.

Gomes believes that the new West Indian identity would be substantially African, because poor, working class Blacks, who form the bulk of the population in urban Trinidad have made the most enduring contribution to West Indian culture:

It was the illiterate and semi-illiterate Negroes who kept the ancestral fires burning; who remained active in the Shouters during the difficult years of proscription; who continued to worship the dark gods of the Shango in the face of middle-class indifference and contempt; who filled the Calypso tents with song and music in the early days before this Aristophanic art form became a tourist attraction, favoured by British and American alike and so won at long last the approbation of the middle-class educated Negro; who invented the steel band and fought and died to keep it alive so that it would become eventually a status symbol proudly adorning the drawing-rooms of the same middle-class, who during its embryonic period joined forces to stamp it out as another culturally retrogressive influence. (p. 82)

Gomes's close political association with working-class people convinces him that their culture should prevail regardless of its quality or status in the eyes of the outside world.

Breadth of political commitment adds objectivity to Gomes's comments. On the question of superstition, for example, he professes to adopt a rational attitude. But he acknowledges that superstition is rife in Trinidad, and feels it is impossible to completely reject the claims of those "who profess supernatural powers" (p. 94). His own daughter is cured by supernatural means after medical specialists in the US could not help her, and he himself gives up a thirty-year addiction to smoking through similar means. Gomes is therefore neither sneering nor dismissive on the subject of superstition, although he does not advocate it either.

His is a realistic, pragmatic point of view, well illustrated when he reflects on his Madeiran ancestors:

They were a robust lot, these immigrants from Madeira. They possessed all the animal cunning, concupiscence and penchant for the obscene of the peasant. Their manners were appalling and their general deportment almost totally lacking in the graces of restraint or refinement. Much of what they said and did in public,

wise custom reserves for the lavatory or bedroom. All their appe-
tites were large and unrestrained. A misfortune for both their
health and morals. (p. ll)

Gomes can scarcely be more candid about people whose cause he may
be expected to champion. He is a nationalist, after all, concerned with
the welfare of all his countrymen rather than with the fate of his own
ethnic group. When he says, "My search has been for identity with the
West Indies" (p. 81), it is a simple, fervent statement of nationalism.

His political commitment, nationalistic fervour and candour are evident in his account of the development of steel band music. He rejects
middle-class opposition to the steel band as mere "puritan humbug"
(p. 95). Instead, he sees the steel band as an "innovation in musical
expression and a social explosion in Trinidad" (p. 95). While he admits
that no one can be certain about the exact origin of the steel band, his
own explanation tells us much about his preferences:

> I prefer my own version namely, that the steel drums brought
> forth music because the youth of the slums were determined to
> rise above the depravity and despair of their surroundings; that
> it is just another instance of the triumph of beauty over ugliness,
> of the forces of life over the forces of death. (p. 96).

If this analysis appears somewhat forced, it is consistent with Gomes's
penchant for seeing everything in social or political terms that are profoundly nationalistic.

As the distilled reflection of one who played a leading role at many
levels of government, for almost twenty-five years, *In a Maze of Colour*
gives a rounded report on Trinidad up to Independence. The book is
memorable in the first place for this commentary, an achievement it
shares with reports by other authors, for example, C L R James, Eric
Williams, the Naipaul brothers, Arthur Calder Marshall, Samuel
Selvon and Merle Hodge.[6] What is even more memorable is Gomes's
commentary on postcolonial Trinidad and Tobago, the Caribbean, and
indeed the whole world; for it is not until Independence that he realizes there is no place for him in the land of his birth. The sense of
bitterness and insecurity produced by this realization make us see a
side of Gomes that is hidden by the buoyant optimism and political
hopes of his more activist years. This sense of ungrateful rejection by

countrymen to whom he has dedicated lifelong service, passionate solidarity and nationalistic loyalty dominates the final pages of the book and endows it with unique interest, substantially different from books on Trinidad by the authors mentioned earlier.

Gomes is in no doubt about the racial nature of the feelings against him. His use of such phrases as "the lineaments of black nationalism" (p. 158), "negro emergence" (p. 160) and "Black workers of the world unite" (p. 162) are heavily ironic. As a Trinidadian of Portuguese origin, Gomes sees his position as follows:

> It was a foreboding of the apprehension that increasingly gripped me as the society I was helping to transform underwent changes that ultimately entailed dispensing with the services of persons like myself.
>
> For I was destined to be the main architect of my own downfall, not unwittingly, however, but by conscious and deliberate choice. I must have known what risks would be involved when I entered a career of public life in a country where both Negro emergence and my eventual supersession were fairly predictable: the 1937 crisis certainly did not lack prefiguration in this aspect. (pp. 159–160)

Although he does not mention his Portuguese origin, the phrase "persons like myself" clearly indicates people who are not black. His gallant attempt to blame himself for lack of foresight does not hide his feeling of victimization.

If the signs of his eclipse were so clear, since at least 1937, why did he persist? He attributes persistence to vanity and the challenge of proving that "Trinidad was as much my country as the Negroes' or Indians' " (p. 160). But he claims that by the time Eric Williams entered politics (1955–56), his days were numbered:

> For my complexion—skin not political—qualified me for participation in the West Indian national movement only until such time as in its natural effluxion it became an assertion of black nationalism. And as it happened, this merely awaited a "deus ex machina." For when Dr Eric Williams appeared on the scene he fulfilled all the requirements for which the movement had waited, and the rest should have been predictable. But I was too

deeply involved at the time to see this way and illumination only came later as so much hindsight. (p. 173)

Gomes accepts his victimization philosophically, realizing that racism was always there, and that when it became exploited by politicians, only those representing major racial groups could win.

The future will tell whether Gomes's vision of West Indian federation will materialize. As we have seen, he considered West Indian nationhood to be synonymous with West Indian federation, a view shared by many of his contemporaries. Although it seems impractical nowadays, there are structures of inter-Caribbean association which still exist and illustrate the potency of the federal vision. But Gomes dismisses insular loyalties too easily. He recognizes the: "basic incompatibly of two ambitions, namely the desire for insular independence on the one hand and the urge for federal fusion on the other" (p. 120). And he speaks with almost prophetic certainty of the political independence of each West Indian territory as: "a parochially undesirable goal, a geopolitical miscalculation" (p. 120).

Gomes's uncompromising faith in federation places him in the paradoxical position of an ardent West Indian nationalist who also admires the British connection with the Caribbean, for Britain has often advanced federation chiefly to alleviate the dislocating effects of her colonial policy in oversea territories that are no longer economically useful to herself. In this sense, federation is a largely synthetic theory advanced by the British to instil political validity into postcolonial fragments whose very political identity is defined by their connection to Britain. No wonder this federal solution failed not only in the West Indies but in Nigeria, Central Africa and South East Asia, among Britain's former colonies; and where it has succeeded, as in Canada, it needs to be propped up, more than one hundred years later, by endless conferences and compromises. This view of federation benefits from hindsight which Gomes could not have possessed in the 1950s.

At any rate, despite his fulminations against Britain's "alien authority" in the Caribbean, it is not surprising that Gomes also refers to British rule as an "otherwise benevolent overlordship" (p. 77) or that he "can recall no deliberate repression in British rule" (p. 79). Gomes expresses admiration for British institutions such as an independent judiciary, the civil service, and a police force free of political pressure and influences. His admiration is not unqualified:

I realize that, although the moments of revolt are inevitable and endlessly will recur, it is the social tidiness of the Anglo-Saxon world that attracts me—despite its joylessness, its parliamentary humbug and its sexual stupidity. But the tidiness of its public life, of its courts and even of its restraint of the individual desire in the widest possible sense—these far outweigh its shortcomings. (p. 109)

This ambivalent attitude towards Britain is not uncommon among colonial leaders of Gomes's generation who were influenced by British models in education, politics and much else. Such men—Nehru, Kenyatta, Kaunda, not to mention Grantley Adams and Norman Manley—could be anglophile while remaining nationalistic. At the same time, since Gomes finds ordinary English people indifferent to issues of colonialism, his dislike of the actions of the British government does not necessarily contradict his admiration of British customs and institutions.

For a British colonial politician to show ambivalent feelings towards Britain is one thing; for him to criticize the process of decolonization itself is another. Yet, in his assessment of the postcolonial world, Gomes expresses distinct regret over the emergence of so many "micro-nations" (p. 200) which he feels has turned the colonial "dream of liberation" (p. 200) into a postcolonial "nightmare" (p. 200). There is even a trace of gloating in the following:

I signally failed to anticipate the time when colonial policy, in particular British policy, would ostentatiously invest microscopic and unviable colonial entities with the trappings of political independence (i.e. a constitution, a flag and an anthem) and send them barefoot into the world of international politics. However, history is fast vindicating the view I expressed seventeen years ago. The dream of liberation, for so many of the new micro-nations, has already begun to seem like a nightmare. (p. 200)

Whatever problems they may have experienced—including civil war—it is unlikely that the leaders in Africa and Asia would express regret about their decolonization and liberation. By suggesting that the method of decolonization was either not correct, or too quick, Gomes comes dangerously close to adopting a well known argument used,for example, by white South Africans to defend the obscenity of apartheid. The argument is one of gradualism, of grooming colonial subjects for eventual liberation, and it has been used by many imperial rulers in Vietnam, Indonesia, and elsewhere as a ploy for maintaining their colonial authority for as long as possible.

That Gomes should be associated—even remotely—with apologists of colonialism is ironic, because his whole life was devoted to fighting colonialism. Nothing in his career, not even his love-hate of the British, impugns the sincerity of his feeling against colonialism. It is rather the insecurity of belonging to a Portuguese minority in an Afro-dominated Caribbean that induces his vehement advocacy of federalism. The fact is that a larger interterritorial or federal structure offered better hope of safety and security to ethnic minorities since it would make them less vulnerable to ethnic rivalries or petty tensions emanating from within their own territory. This is why Gomes can say: "I never once visualized an independent sovereign state of Trinidad and Tobago except as part of a federated West Indies" (p. 200).

In its final pages, *In a Maze of Colour* successfully captures the essential tragedy of postcolonial displacement and alienation in the Caribbean. Gomes's grudging remarks on the postcolonial world are tragic in import and should not open him to charges of hypocrisy or racism; for he was neither a racist nor an imperialist. His assessment of decolonization is tempered by the insecurity of his displacement and alienation in a Caribbean context where his ethnic minority status deprived him of political credibility after Independence. His bitter experience is a poignant example of the mixed aftermath of colonialism that followed the dissolution of European empires in many lands after World War II.

In a Maze of Colour consists of brilliant character sketches, illuminating descriptions of the Caribbean social milieu, racy anecdotes, coherent analysis, and sustained commentary on all aspects of history, culture and politics in Trinidad and Tobago. Rather than a considered autobiography, the book is more a collection of memoirs, slow paced and indulgent, but rich in variety of incident and vigorous in its exposition of ideas and explanation of public policies and events. The style is old fashioned, often solemn and ponderous, almost Victorian in formality and stateliness; but these qualities are happily relieved by the frequent introduction of informal West Indian imagery and colloquial idiom. The confessional tone is persuasive, the product of Gomes' high maturity, reflecting a lifetime's experience of thinking, travelling, reading and participation in public affairs. One is persuaded by his frankness in revealing his love-hate for the British, his disillusionment over Independence for Trinidad and Tobago, and his deep regret over the breakup of the West Indian Federation. Even if it provides an assessment of the postcolonial world that differs from that of most colonial leaders, it collects a wealth of information about the inner workings of colonial government in the Caribbean, about the social and intellectual life in a British colony, and about individuals of importance in Caribbean history. Gomes is a skilful raconteur and fluent writer, and his book is a valuable contribution to the literary history of the English-speaking Caribbean.

Roy Heath
The Shadow Bride
London: Fontana 1988.

The chief interest in Roy Heath's *The Shadow Bride* is its study of Indo-Guyanese society. As Heath's previous novels show, his experience comes almost entirely from the Afro-Guyanese community but, surprisingly, *The Shadow Bride* offers abundant details about Indo-Guyanese domestic, religious, cultural and social activities. This is what is notable: apart from its purely artistic merits as a novel, *The Shadow Bride* presents the inner workings of an Indo-Guyanese family that probably come as a total revelation to Afro-Guyanese readers in the same way that, thirty years ago, according to George Lamming, V S Naipaul's *A House for Mr Biswas* revealed an Indo-Caribbean world almost entirely unknown to Caribbean people of African descent.

The central character of *The Shadow Bride*, Mrs Singh arrived in Guyana from Kerala, India in the early 1920s. She herself was not indentured as most Indo-Guyanese at that time were: she was the bride of an Indian who had come to Guyana as an indentured labourer, then returned to India to marry before settling in Guyana again. Mrs Singh is a strong-willed matriarch in the manner of Naipaul's Mrs Tulsi—another Hindu widow who exhibits the strength, intelligence, self interest, practicality and cunning that Hindu widows are not supposed to possess. Mrs Singh presides over a household as ramshackle and crumbling as Mrs Tulsi's and, with an equal combination of ingenuity and will power, establishes some sense of order over competing interests, rival personalities and rebellious subordinates. At one time or another, apart from her son Dr Betta Singh, her household includes Mulvi Sahib (a Muslim teacher), a Pujaree (Hindu priest) who later marries Mrs Singh, and a host of hangers on such as the two girls Rani and Lahti, and Lahti's lover Sukrum, together with Bai and Aji who also depend on Mrs Singh's charity. The following conversation with her daughter-in-law, Meena, illustrates Mrs Singh's iron will and the complicated power relations prevalent within her family. Mrs Singh confronts Meena head on:

"That's why I don't like you Meena."
"But why?"
"Because you stole my son." (p. 369)

Marriage to Mrs Singh's son automatically turns Meena into an enemy of her mother-in-law who, because of her greater power and prestige, forces Meena into humiliating submission and compels her to say:

I beg forgiveness for not coming to ask your advice in all important matters and for being a bad daughter-in-law. You are my husband's mother and I dare not call your name (p. 369).

Mrs Singh derives perverse pleasure from this ritual recitation of obsequious submission and frightens Meena by telling her the story of a young woman who stood in such fear of her mother-in-law that she walked into the sea of her own will and was never seen again.

Mrs Singh's domestic tyranny reflects an elaborate network of intrigue, rivalry, jealousy, deceit and connivance between various factions of her household which vie with each other to obtain favours from her, the ruling deity. Heath's grasp of Indo-Guyanese domestic routine is as sure as his handling of aspects of Indo-Guyanese religious belief, ritual and devotional practice. Here, for instance, are the thoughts of the Pujaree relishing the success of worming his way into Mrs Singh's trust and getting her to expel Lahti and Sukrum from her household:

They [Lahti and Sukrum] were gone and now Mrs Singh could embark on a new life, guided by him [the Pujaree]. Lord Krishna created the world with the sound of his flute, the fertilizing element from which all thought arose, like bubbles from a stagnant pool. The storehouse had become a surgery, which was later transformed into a room of depravity. If life was change then he would change everything around him beyond recognition.

The Pujaree decided there and then to install in the centre of the drawing room a glazed earthenware model of Shiva, Parvati and Ganesha, garlanded with wreaths of vermilion flowers. (p. 295).

Heath does not only show the Pujaree as a successful schemer who is expert in intrigue, he endows him with the authentic consciousness, mannerisms and concerns of a Hindu priest.

Heath produces a similar portrait of Mulvi Sahib whose Muslim rituals are as accurately observed as the Hindu ones of the Pujaree. When Mulvi Sahib visits Dr Singh his host knows that he prays five times a day, and advises his wife to keep the Mulvi adequately supplied with water for his ritual ablutions. Other social or cultural aspects of the Indo-Guyanese community that are recorded include *tadjah* ceremonies, musical instruments such as the tabla, sitar, mridangam, and Indian women labourers described as: "unbrassiered women walking along earth dams with their two tiered enamel saucepans swinging at their waists" (p. 101). Compared to Edgar Mittelholzer's *Corentyne Thunder*, *The Shadow Bride* gives an altogether fuller, more rounded portrait of Indo-Guyanese society. The characters are portrayed in all aspects of their social, cultural and domestic relations. Their intertwined lives form an Indo-Guyanese social panorama of vivid density, variety and colourfulness.

Throughout the dense weave of this panorama, Heath expertly threads a theme that is quintessentially Caribbean to the extent that it reflects standard Caribbean responses to displacement, exile, adaptation, cultural mixing and the emergence of fresh identity. Very early in the novel the theme is introduced during a conversation between Dr Singh and the Pujaree:

"You think East Indians should go back to India?"
Betta reflected for a moment before answering.

27

"I don't know. Probably they have no choice."

"A third of them already gone back."

"As many as that . . . ? I bet nearly all of them were first genera-tion though. The young people won't go."

"True," the Pujaree agreed. "But should they?"

"I think you could make out as good a case for them going as staying. The death rate among them is high, so they should go. On the other hand the young people wouldn't want to, so they shouldn't" (p. 26).

Although the system of indenture did hold out an option of return to India, historical records suggest that almost three-quarters of Indian indentured immigrants did not take it up.

The indenture system stopped in 1917, and up to then some Indian indentured immigrants regarded the Caribbean mainly as a place of temporary residence before returning home to "Mother India". But Mother India became an increasingly elusive attraction as time went on. Mrs Singh herself harboured dreams of returning to India:

Was it not possible that she might return to die in India, in the south where the ashes of her parents and grandparents had been scattered? No, she could not, for she had given birth here [in Guyana]. And as she was saddened immeasurably by the reali-zation of her exile she was heartened by the belief that one day Betta would come back to her. (p. 101)

Mrs Singh's thoughts catch the ambivalence that tormented many first generation Indo-Guyanese in whom memories of India were fresh. But as these memories began to fade, they were gradually replaced by new interests and loyalties in their place of settlement. Of these, as Mrs Singh admits, the parenting of children who had no experience of India was one of the strongest factors against return. Another factor was the inevitable loss of Indian cultural traditions, especially of language and religion. Dr Singh himself is tempted to convert to Christianity, and more creolized Indians, or Indians who had risen in the economic or class structure "are ashamed to speak Hindi because it is the language of estate workers" (p. 178).

When we realize how important it was to become creolized or west-ernized in order to achieve social prestige or economic prosperity, we understand why Hindi (the Indian language), and Hinduism or Islam (the Indian religions) had to lose out. There is simply no question that, in time, both in actual history and in Heath's novel, creolization proved irresistible. Mulvi Sahib confirms this in his comments on Sukrum's claim that he is Guyanese rather than Indian:

> When most East Indians still see themselves as Indians and not Guyanese Sukrum shouts he's Guyanese. Don't underestimate Sukrum. The cane fields can be a great educator. You've never heard him speak of the past, have you? No, he wouldn't tell you. But mark my word, you should show great respect to those who come to town from the sugar estates and survived, the Bais and the Sukrums (p. 303).

This is as accurate a summary of Indo-Caribbean experience as one can get anywhere: of deracination from India, indigenization in the Caribbean, and acquisition of a new or fresh Caribbean identity.

Although notable fiction on Indo-Caribbean subjects has previously been produced by creole writers such as H G Delisser (*The Cup and the Lip*), Edgar Mittelholzer (*Corentyne Thunder*), Merle Hodge (*Crick Crack Monkey*), and Wilson Harris (*The Far Journey of Oudin*), these works do not always offer the richness of detail and sympathetic understanding of their subject found in *The Shadow Bride*. In the case of Guyanese writers, Harris's novels tend to be too philosophical, and Mittelholzer's too sensational, whereas Heath strikes a better balance between a detached outsider's point of view and an insider's subjective accumulation of detail that could have a largely documentary effect. His method is naturalistic to the extent that he does accumulate an extraordinary amount of detail about food, clothes, flora, fauna, history, geography and everything else. What was said of *A House for Mr Biswas* many years ago can be said of *The Shadow Bride*: that it reflects an encyclopedic knowledge of its subject. This is evident particularly in the references to diseases such as diabetes, Bright's disease, blackwater fever and the historic contribution of Dr Giglioli to the treatment of malaria in Guyana. As Heath explains, Dr Giglioli identified a mosquito, "anopheles darlingi," as the carrier of malaria (p. 191), and his treatment, which achieved spectacular success, was directed towards killing the mosquito rather than curing symptoms of the disease. *The Shadow Bride* is a veritable compendium of medical conditions and treatments, both orthodox and alternative, within a Guyanese context—tuberculosis, anemia, narah, and mad blood. It is interesting, for instance, to know that "mad blood" is merely the common Guyanese term for an allergic reaction, and that "teh teh" carries the medical name "leishmaniasis".

One implication of Heath's focus on the Indo-Guyanese community in *The Shadow Bride* is that after one hundred and fifty years of continuous residence in Guyana, Indians have become more Guyanese than Indian, and are likely to become more so as time goes on. At the same time, the novel does not completely neglect Afro-Guyanese characters such as the Merriman family and Mr Chapman the sicknurse dispenser. Nen Merriman's neighbourhood court is attended by Africans as well as Indians. In the so-called court, Mrs Merriman settles disputes in her local community without recourse to lawyers or legal expenses. It is a prime example of community self-help and self-management. She listens to both sides of a dispute and offers impartial advice based on common sense and deep knowledge of community affairs. Mrs Merriman's court illustrates the multicultural reality of Guyanese society and confirms that although the central focus of *The Shadow Bride* is Indo-Guyanese culture and society, it also projects possibilities of a genuinely multicultural society in Guyana.

Part Two

The First Migration

Ron Ramdin, Ed.
The Other Middle Passage
London: Hansib, 1994.

"The Middle Passage" was the middle or second stage of a three stage voyage which British trading ships made, between the sixteenth and nineteenth centuries, firstly from Britain to West Africa, secondly from West Africa to the "New World" of the Caribbean and the Americas, and thirdly from the New World back to Britain. The main purpose of the voyage was trade, but the second stage or "middle passage" became notorious because its cargo consisted of slaves, human beings taken from West Africa to be sold as labourers on British-owned sugar plantations in the Caribbean. Many biographical, historical and fictional works attempt to capture and record the outrage of the "middle passage" although it is doubtful that they could ever capture its full toll of human pain, suffering and loss of life. Another outrage, however, in curiously similar circumstances, has scarcely been recorded at all. It is what Ron Ramdin calls "The Other Middle Passage": a voyage made by so called "coolie ships" to the Caribbean, from 1838 to 1917, bringing Indian indentured immigrants to replace the Africans who had provided enforced labour on British Caribbean sugar plantations for more than three centuries. *The Other Middle Passage* reproduces the journal of Edolphus Swinton, the British captain of one such "coolie ship", the *Salsette*, which left Calcutta with 324 Indian immigrants on March 17, 1858 bound for Trinidad. The text of Swinton's journal is only sixteen pages, but it is supplemented by Ramdin's Introduction which is twice as long and which provides a lucid explanation of the circumstances of the *Salsette's* voyage and the mixed fate of her human cargo.

Slavery turned human beings into mere property and completely dehumanized them, but as Captain Swinton's journal shows, Indian indenture was not much better. Even if Indian indentured immigrants were not property, they were in a situation of powerlessness and vulnerability not very different from African slaves. Their voyage from Calcutta (or Madras) went down the East coast of India around the Cape of Good Hope and across the Atlantic, and was longer than the route plied by slave ships directly from West Africa to the Caribbean. The *Salsette* took three and a half months to reach Trinidad. Ramdin describes the crew on "coolie ships" as follows: a British contingent consisting of captain, surgeon-superintendent (doctor), third mate and engineer; and an Indian contingent consisting of compounders (mediators), sirdars (disciplinarians), bhandarries (high caste supervisors) and Topazes (cleaners).

Captain Swinton's journal is one of only two first hand accounts of the voyage of a "coolie ship" to Trinidad, and it is the only captain's journal; the other account—of the voyage of the *Delharee* in 1859—is by the ship's doctor. Captain Swinton's opening entries are as follows:

> **March 17th, 1858.** Left Calcutta for Trinidad; several coolies sick.
> **18th.** An old woman died of cholera; she was rejected on coming on board but eighteen men would not come without her.
> **19th.** Several coolies sick.
> **21st.** A little girl, six years of age, died of dysentery in its mother's arms.
> **24th.** An old woman died of diarrhea.
> **26th.** A little orphan girl, four years of age, died in a state of great emaciation.

When we consider that Captain Swinton's prime motive was to deliver immigrants who were alive, his curt mention of frequent deaths is prompted less by sentiment, than by his desire for factual accuracy. Ironically, these factual, laconic entries evoke all the more poignantly the plight of people victimized by an elaborate system of enforcement through poverty, deception, coercion, and family breakdown of one kind or another.

Part of the entry for 28th March runs: "Coolie died from fear, seeing so many die" (p. 47). It is bad enough to die from starvation and disease, but to succumb to fear suggests a degree of desperation that is difficult to contemplate a century and a half later. It suggests conditions of cramped passenger space, unsuitable or inadequate diet, limited medical care, squalor, frailty, and unrelieved or unrelievable misery. People died daily of debility, dropsy, diarrhea, dysentery and cholera, not to mention neglect and a sense of moral isolation that sapped their basic will to live. But such misery was less the result of cruelty or neglect by the ship's crew than the product of a system that was ramshackle and chaotic, open to abuse and manipulation, and beyond adequate regulation or supervision. It is always difficult to pinpoint a single culprit in such systems. It seems too vague and inadequate to assign blame to something as abstract as capitalist greed, although, undoubtedly, greed was at the bottom of it. At any rate, out of the *Salsette's* original complement of 324 emigrants, 120 died at sea, and 4 died after arrival in Trinidad.

This large number of casualties prompted the government-appointed Agent-General or Protector of Immigrants in Trinidad, Dr Mitchell, to carry out an investigation. He found no deficiency in the care of the immigrants, although he attributed the high percentage of casualties to the fact that many immigrants came from swampy, jungle areas, and had sickly constitutions; he also found that a biscuit diet, inferior dhal and inadequate accommodation and ventilation were contributory factors on the ship. He recommended recruitment of a better quality of immigrant and improved housing conditions at the depot in India before boarding ship. Further recommendations were that the Surgeon-Superintendent should speak the language of the immigrants and have two Indian assistants. Woolen clothing was also recommended for cold weather. These recommendations eventually led to provision of a hospital on the ship's deck, a nurse, purified water, improved diet and more Indian assistants. By providing all this information, *The Other Middle Passage* helps to fill a gap in the historical consciousness of Indo-Caribbean people, and illuminate a dark area of Caribbean history.

Ramdin's well-researched and lucid introduction includes "Remarks" by Mrs Swinton, the captain's wife. Since it was unusual for a captain's wife to travel on such a ship Mrs Swinton's insights are of rare value: they add a personal and emotional flavour lacking in her husband's laconic comments. She states that most of the immigrants did not know where they were going and therefore "were entrapped" (p. 54). She also states that "Some emigrants hide what they cannot eat, and before they eat it, it turns sour, and brings on diarrhea"(p. 55). The fact that Mrs Swinton did not like the immigrants—she refers to their "dirty habits"(p. 55) and "immorality" (p. 56)—adds conviction to her comments. She observes, for instance, that on arrival in Trinidad, the emigrants made "the best appearances" (p. 57) when they were being selected by the planters; and she adds: "It looks very like slavery"(p. 57). This is objectivity rather than sympathy, and it adds poignancy to the narrative of *The Other Middle Passage*. Unfortunately, after she left Trinidad to return to England the *Salsette* and crew sank in bad weather. Shortly before the disaster, they had stopped in New York from where Captain Swinton had advised his wife to travel to England by mail steamer. It is fortunate for Caribbean history that he did so and entrusted her with his journal.

Noor Kumar Mahabir
The Still Cry
New York & Trinidad: Calaloux Publications, 1985.

Although the vast majority of the population of the English-speaking Caribbean are descendants of slaves brought from Africa during the sixteenth to the nineteenth century, Walter Rodney shows in *A History of the Guyanese Working People, 1881–1905.* (Baltimore, 1985), that no historian of territories such as Guyana and Trinidad can afford to neglect Indian aspects of his subject; for Indians have settled in these two territories in larger numbers than anywhere else in the anglophone Caribbean, where today, they form a majority of the population in Guyana, and almost that in Trinidad and Tobago. If Rodney was not the first historian to recognize the importance of Indian indenture to Caribbean history, he was the first to study the effects of this system side by side with the consequences of the Atlantic slave trade in Guyana. The Foreword to Rodney's book by novelist George Lamming, contains this sentence: "There can be no question that Indian workers were now condemned to a history of humiliation almost indistinguishable from the memories of African slavery." (p. xxii). Those who doubt Lamming ought to read Noor Kumar Mahabir's *The Still Cry* which carries the subtitle: "Personal Accounts of East Indians in Trinidad and Tobago during the Indentureship (1845–1917)."

The Still Cry contains accounts by four men and one woman of their recruitment as indentured labourers in India, of their voyage by ship to the Caribbean, and of their subsequent careers in Trinidad. All came on ships that began their voyage at Calcutta, and sailed via Natal, South Africa, and Demerara, British Guiana, before landing in Trinidad. Since the accounts are presumably quite recent, and since indenture to the Caribbean stopped in 1917, all five participants must have been quite advanced in age when they were recorded. It is a pity that Mahabir does not provide more information about the participants in his short, perceptive Introduction. Perhaps he expected them to reveal themselves fully in their own narratives, and to some extent this happens, but more information about the process of each recording and the circumstances of the participants might have been helpful. Why, for example, are the accounts of Bharath and Sankar together twice as long as the accounts of the other three combined? Bharath's account is four times as long as Maharani's, although the latter seems the most incisive and articulate commentator of the five. Were the participants allowed to speak continuously, without interruption or prompting? Frequent repetition of details about food, clothes and living conditions suggest that Mahabir gave his participants free rein. It is more convincing to hear the same facts or situations described by different speakers. They tend to corroborate each other, and because of the particular type of facts and situations, they firmly drive home the limiting sameness and restrictive, exploitative nature of the whole indenture experience.

All five speakers agree on the broad pattern of the indenture system which entailed physical dislocation from India, economic exploitation, and cultural dispossession in Trinidad. Sankar gives the fullest account of the recruitment process in India while Fazal's comments are brief, to the point:

> dem muslims fellar fool me
> bring me dis country (p. 50)

We are told that some white officials spoke against the use of force or compulsion in recruitment, but the Indian recruiters were not above coercion, threats and trickery. In any case, once the immigrant was on board ship, the indenture pattern had already been set in motion. Crowded quarters, and a shared routine meant enforced assimilation. Whatever their religious or dietary preferences, immigrants had to eat what was available. A vegetarian, for example, would eat meat if necessary to survive. The Caribbean did not change this leveling tendency: whatever their caste or social or economic background, all Indians were united in the Caribbean by their common function of labour. They lived together, ate together, worshipped together, amused themselves together; above all they worked together. Bharath gives an excellent description of these conditions in the last two pages of the second section of his account:

> if a chatri [warrior caste]
> if a brahman [priestly caste]

37

if a naw [barber]
if a dhome [weaver]
if a kattik [teacher]
ha to come to ork (p. 103)

And again on the same page:

de brahman
 de chatri
de ahir [cowherd caste]
de kurme [farming caste]
he living one village
all a dem living one village
 de low nation nuh living one village
chamar bhai [leather worker, therefore outcast]
kattek bhai
now living one place
now living one village (pp. 103–104).

This is the general pattern. We may argue about the rate at which assimilation proceeded, or about the completeness of its effect, ending in cultural dispossession and eventual creolization: but there is no denying it. Sankar's final words sum the matter up:

i tell de man
write a letter for India
to family
an ley de letter come back
den i could know
e send three letter
three letter
an up to today
i eh get no answer (p. 183).

Prolonged separation from India had its effect, and Sankar responds with resigned acceptance. This does not mean that he has entirely lost the culture of India, but separation has meant some degree of loss, adaptation, and transformation by the reality of Caribbean experience. This will be even more true for Sankar's children. Altogether, *The Still Cry* comes close to presenting the totality of Indian experience in Trinidad when the effects of indenture were still fresh. We are told about the different labouring duties of the newcomers, about their wages, relations with other races, foods and amusements, marriage and funeral customs, medical problems, religious practices and much more. This information would be invaluable to anyone interested in social, economic, cultural and political issues in Trinidad during the last one hundred and fifty years. Equally valuable is the language in which this information is presented: it consists of a blend of the original Indian dialects, and the English acquired in Trinidad. Neither Mr Mahabir's Introduction, nor the equally useful Foreword by Selwyn Cudjoe fully explains this language. Perhaps it is now impossible to discover the original dialects on which it is based. Many words are neither Hindi, Urdu, Bengali or Punjabi. Most likely, they derive from the Bhojpuri-speaking dialects of Uttar Pradesh, India's largest province, and the area from which most people came to the Caribbean. To determine how the original dialects mixed with English to produce the texts in *The Still Cry* would be a fascinating linguistic challenge. Here again, one needs to know how much of Mr Mahabir's own translation has gone into each text. The speakers are unlikely to use words like "remain" and "cemetery." Perhaps such words were translated or supplied by Mr Mahabir to aid the reader's comprehension.

The fact that *The Still Cry* raises such questions is proof of its interest both for the scholar and general reader. A glossary is provided, but it too is inadequate, and needs to be greatly amplified with more information on the derivation and semantic history of words. All this is too much to expect from an editor working singlehandedly and apparently with funding from only one limited source. One can only marvel at the immense patience and energy that went into the recording and transcription of the accounts in *The Still Cry*. This is not to mention the pioneering initiative and zeal necessary to execute such a project as a whole. *The Still Cry* breaks new ground by providing a more complete and authentic account of Caribbean indenture than we have ever had. It is a work that can be read with profit alongside Walter Rodney's *A History of the Guyanese Working People, 1881–1905*.

An interesting feature of *The Still Cry* is the attitude it reveals towards people of African descent. It seems a minor feature, but in view of subsequent Caribbean history, it may be one of the most important revelations in the volume. We know that Indians were taken to the Caribbean to fill the labour vacuum created by the freed Africans. Yet none of the five speakers in *The Still Cry* had seen an African before leaving India. The stop in Natal was their first opportunity to set eyes on Africans, and Maharani's reactions are typical:

dem kirwal [African] an dem stand up watching
i say
wha kind ting dat
i never see da kind people (p. 82)

It is extraordinary to reflect on the scale of abuse of power by which British imperialism could freely transport large and less than willing populations to destinations half way across the globe, to live among people they had never seen before. The newly arrived Indians naturally regarded their new countrymen as alien, and if an African ventured into an Indian estate, he could be beaten or worse. It is easy to see how genuine unfamiliarity gave rise to conflict between the two ethnic groups, and how this conflict was exploited by British employers for economic reasons. No wonder this conflict between Afro- and Indo-Caribbean people remains a serious problem, at least in Guyana and Trinidad. *The Still Cry* illustrates the roots of the problem, and reveals both Africans and Indians as victims of colonial or imperial overlords, motivated predominantly by economic concerns that blinded them to more humane considerations.

Anthony De Verteuil
Eight East Indian Immigrants
Port of Spain, Trinidad: Paria Publishing, 1989.

In his preface to *Eight East Indian Immigrants*, the author states that his aim is to tell the story of Indian immigrants: "how they were recruited, the voyage to Trinidad, the labour on the estates, and the life after indenture" (p. xiii). In order to achieve this, Father Anthony de Verteuil, a Trinidadian Catholic priest of French creole stock, adopts a format different from what he calls "the story of immigrants as an impersonal account of a faceless multitude" (p. xiii). His format consists of eight biographical sketches, each one chapter long, together with a prologue and epilogue.

Father de Verteuil's eight "protagonists" cover a cross section of experience which began with the arrival of the first Indian immigrants in Trinidad, in 1845, and ended with their last voyage back to India about seventy years later. All eight are successful; some are famous. Gokool and Ruknaddeen are Muslims, the former achieving fame as a cinema tycoon, and the latter becoming such a distinguished leader of the Muslim community that elected members of the Trinidad House of Representatives took formal note of his death (at the age of 98). A third "protagonist," Soodeen, arrives as a Hindu orphan in Trinidad, and transforms himself into a renowned Presbyterian catechist, quite apart form achieving great wealth and prosperity for his family.

Sookoo, Capildeo and Bunsee are Hindus. Sookoo's biography, which is the briefest, appears in the volume mainly because of his leading role in the Hosay riots of 1884, when British colonial regulations prohibiting the Hosay procession from passing through San Fernando, led to death and injury among Indians in the procession. Capildeo acquired fame as a pandit. He visited India four times, and was the maternal grandfather of V S Naipaul. Partap Bunsee established a fortune through cocoa farming, money lending, and the oil rush that overtook Southern Trinidad in the early decades of this century. Beccani, a female "protagonist", came as a child from India and married an Irish plantation owner. Despite her illiteracy, she was able to manage the family's affairs successfully after her husband's death. Vailama the other female "protagonist" is notable as the lone Madrassi in the volume, and as someone who came to Trinidad via Martinique, where she acquired skills as a French cook and masseuse. After her husband's death, she too successfully brings up her seven children and sees them properly settled.

Eight East Indian Immigrants pays tribute to the resilient spirit, dogged perseverance and business acumen of indentured Indians who arrived in Trinidad in a state of destitution, and within two generations, had begun to make an impact on the island's agricultural, commercial and professional life. They influenced religious, social and cultural affairs as well. At his death in 1940, Gokool left a bequest of over one million dollars to be used in service of the poor in Trinidad. If there is a prevailing theme in the volume, it is that of financial success exemplified in the Prologue's subheading "Coming in Search of Money." Father de Verteuil is evidently struck by this aspect of Indo-Trinidadian experience which, in his view, is crucial to our understanding the origins of Indo-Trinidadian society. Since the circumstances that immigrants left behind in India consisted of rapacious landlords, restrictions of the caste system (especially of untouchability), famine, disease, and family quarrels, it is quite plausible to claim that people fleeing such circumstances might place undue value on quick acquisition of land and money.

This claim is invested with a critical tone in the chapter on Partap Bunsee, and an epilogue that carries the subheading "The Curse of Too Much Money." More evident towards the end of the volume, this tone seems inspired by a familiar idea in Christian apologetics: "radix maolrum cupiditas est"—love of money is the root of all evil. Father de Verteuil expresses admiration for the first generation of Indian immigrants who worked extremely hard and valued the money they earned: it is the inherited wealth of their children and grandchildren that worries him. He sees "something almost obscene" in Partap Bunsee's oil wealth which he describes as follows:

> One has simply to sit down and do nothing but let more and more money flow in from royalties—and then spend it. This money may ruin the soul of a man, engender family quarrels among the recipients. It can conceive cupidity, jealousy and crime in the hearts of those who see wealth acquired without effort, while they themselves struggle in vain to escape from their poverty; and finally (as we now know too well) the whole group may be corrupted. The Partap family, in particular, were to be cursed by this oil wealth. (pp. 258–259)

The corrupting effect of inherited wealth is illustrated by an horrifying accident which kills Partap Bunsee and fifteen other people including family members and friends. The stark drama of this accident—an explosion on Bunsee's Dome Oil Field—is wholly absorbing. Father de Verteuil calls the tragedy "a sacrifice to the god of money" (p. 282), and, as if this tragedy were not sufficient confirmation of the corrupting effect of inherited wealth, he ends the volume with an Epilogue outlining the heavily guarded lifestyle of Bunsee's heir Sobran, who desperately attempts to protect his wealth and his own life at the same time. The attempt fails, despite his retinue of servants, and a bodyguard who is apparently lured away one night, when Sobran is shot dead in his own house. His murder is never solved.

As a seasoned author of seven books on biography and social history, mostly to do with Trinidad, Father de Verteuil exhibits diligent research, and considerable organizing skills in *Eight East Indian Immigrants*. The volume contains a wealth of information about Indian history, geography, politics, economics, religion and culture, not to mention as full a portrait of Trinidad as could be desired. Every incident or character in the volume is located in context, and rounded out in lavish, generous detail. For example, we are not just told that Ruknaddeen was a Sufi: we are given a lucid two-page commentary on the history and theology of Sufism. But *Eight East Indian Immigrants* is not a conventional work of scholarship. The preface expresses a wish to avoid an "impersonal account" with "faceless" people in it. This presumably, would result from a strictly scholarly or academic approach. Instead, Father de Verteuil adopts a style that is richly evocative, even flowery. He speaks of "the mighty Himalayas" (p. 24), and of famine that "stalked the land" (p. 3) in India. When young Capildeo's delicate brahmin sensibilities are offended by the indignity he suffers in cleaning animal dung, his probable reactions are suggested with melodramatic and speculative plausibility: "What bitter tears he [Capildeo] might have shed or prayers he said, we do not know" (p. 123). Similarly, hyperbole is not spared to convey Beccani's virtues as "the calmest, gentlest, lovingest grandmother that anyone could have" (p. 179).

It appears that in spite of its formidable historical research, *Eight East Indian Immigrants* is not primarily concerned with literal truth or factual information. When he is uncertain about the motives of his protagonists or about their exact circumstances, Father de Verteuil is not above embroidery and reconstruction through the use of introductory phrases such as "we may expect" (p. 33), "we may presume" (p. 212), or "we can hazard a guess" (p. 125). The orphaned Gokool (then called Modhoo) is abandoned as a child in India, and the author adds: "perhaps it is not too imaginative to think that at this time the child had some sort of religious experience which affected his future" (p. 30). This is not factual; but it is plausible; and far from damaging accuracy such reconstructions enliven reality, giving it a touch of romance that guards against the narrative impersonality and blandness that the author wishes to avoid.

Eight East Indian Immigrants is an informed, coherent and reliable (if not literal) account of Indo-Trinidadian indenture and its consequences. It compares well with Noor Kumar Mahabir's *The Still Cry* which assembles five Indian indentured immigrants who describe their journey from India and their settlement in Trinidad. *Eight East Indian Immigrants* captures similar feelings of loss, exile, resistance, and struggle that we see in *The Still Cry*. What differentiates *Eight East Indian Immigrants* from *The Still Cry* is its special critical tone of the corrupting effect of inherited wealth. But this tone is neither accusing nor mocking. It seems more one of gentle moralizing rather than sharp criticism, allowing the author to expose human weakness in his subjects while maintaining a stance that is largely benevolent. No doubt this tone has to do with Father de Verteuil's secure, patrician, social status and distanced religious vocation which does run the risk of conspiring to produce a patronizing narrative. But charity is not patronage. Charity, as St. Paul says, is the greatest of virtues, greater even than faith or hope; it is a welcome asset in *Eight East Indian Immigrants*.

Clem Seecharan
India and the Shaping of the Indo-Guyanese Imagination 1890s–1920s
Leeds, England: Peepal Tree Press, 1993.

When Indian indentured labourers first arrived in Guyana in 1838, most of the population consisted of descendants of Africans who had already worked on the colony's Dutch and British-owned plantations for two and a half centuries. By the 1920s, as more Indians continued to come, a well-known Indian leader (Ayube Edun) spoke of Indo-Guyanese as forming forty-two percent of the colony's population, and therefore of being in a position "in the near future" to "dominate the political situation." This represented an astonishing transformation in people who, on their arrival in Guyana, found themselves in an environment alien to them in every way. It was natural that Indo-Guyanese should react strongly and intimately to India—their motherland. But not all their reactions were based on historical reality: some reactions were based on myths of religious significance, and yet others on the idea of a motherland that was, ambivalently, both an object of sentimental longing, and a convenient counter weight to be wielded defensively against encroaching social, cultural and political obligations in Guyana. In the space of ninety-eight pages, thirty-four of which are appendices, Clem Seecharan's *India* provides an account both of the socio-intellectual background out of which these mixed reactions evolved, and of their impact on the Indo-Guyanese imagination.

Dr Seecharan's research is meticulous and his analysis penetrating, which is why, despite its specific Indian focus and slender look, *India* offers much insight into the broader history of Guyanese society as a whole. In the first place, by the early 1900s, after a century and a half as a British colony, India herself was going through a period of cultural rediscovery and renewal inspired partly by Indian reformers such as Ram Mohun Roy, and by European scholars like Max Mueller, who drew attention to a common Aryan ancestry that was shared by Indians and Europeans. To impoverished Indo-Guyanese living in humiliating circumstances as mere plantation labourers or "coolies", rediscovery of an illustrious Indo-Aryan past was enthusiastically embraced as a welcome source of new-found racial dignity and cultural pride. The Ruhomon brothers—Joseph and Peter—played an important role in articulating this new, uplifting sense of Indianness which was also fostered by social and cultural activities, and by visits from prominent Indians, for example, Pillai and Tivary, Kunwar Maharaj Singh, and Rev C F Andrews (an Englishman, but a close associate of Gandhi), all of whom came to Guyana in the 1920s.

In this climate of rekindled Indianness, an East Indian Cricket Club was founded in 1915, and an East Indian Young Men's Association in 1919. In 1916, J A Luckhoo became the first Indo-Guyanese to enter the legislature. In 1922 the Hindu Society was formed, while a new Hindu temple was built in 1923, and a dharma sala (home for the poor) established in 1929. It is possible too, that the formation in 1927 of an East Indian Ladies Guild with a woman president owed something to the example of Mrs Sarojini Naidu being elected as president of the Indian National Congress. In fact, the whole Indian movement towards swaraj (home rule) and the nationalist agitation of Gandhi and the Indian National Congress helped to transform traditional Indo-Guyanese attitudes of loyalty to the British empire and infuse them with a measure of political militancy.

Through analysis of such facts and events, and evidence of numerous statistics and quotations, Dr Seecharan conclusively proves that Indo-Guyanese opinions and attitudes were profoundly influenced by social, cultural and religious ideas, and political events and personalities emerging out of India from the 1890s to the 1920s. Evidence of this shaping effect on the Indo-Guyanese imagination is also provided in extensive Appendices and Notes packed with rich details, anecdotes and observations drawn from an impressive variety of sources, including books, periodicals, official documents and rare publications like Joseph Ruhomon's *India: The Progress of her People at Home and Abroad, and How Those in British Guiana May Improve Themselves* (Georgetown, C K Jardine, 1894). All this only confirms the exhaustive research that went into *India*. The scholarly penetration of the book is best illustrated by its last chapter "In the Shadow of Mother India: The Limitations of Indo-Guyanese Politics," where the author states that Indo-Guyanese identification with Mother India:

> prolonged a sense of ambivalence towards the colony, even among creolized, Christian Indians. It delayed the emergence of a comprehensive, unmediated loyalty to British Guiana ... Above all it encouraged the Indo-Guyanese leadership to ignore the feeling of the Afro-Guyanese, and the political, economic, and cultural space this group was also demanding.

Since Afro-Guyanese formed a majority in the colony when Indians first arrived, it is not difficult to imagine their feelings of apprehension, resentment and sheer fright when Indians came to surpass them in numbers, and looked like they were moving ahead in agriculture, commerce and the professions. In the Angel Gabriel riots of 1856 and the Cent Bread riot of 1885, Afro-Guyanese had already shown themselves frightened by the Portuguese who, like Indians, began to arrive in Guyana as indentured labourers in the 1830s.

This insight into the potential for ethnic conflict in Guyana is perhaps the most signal achievement of *India*, for this potential was later exploited by an unholy trinity of conspirators—L F S Burnham, J P Lachmansingh and Jai Narine Singh—who, in 1955, engineered a split in the People's Progressive Party, while it was still a glorious movement of national solidarity led by Dr Cheddi Jagan. This split inflicted grievous damage on Guyanese national and political development. And when, in 1964, the same potential for ethnic conflict was again exploited, this time more cynically, by L F S Burnham and a new conspirator—Peter D'Aguiar—to form another unholy political union, it precipitated Guyana into a dark age of domination by the People's National Congress, lasting for twenty-eight years and subjecting Guyana to even more grievous damage. *India* does not comment on these later events because they fall outside of its purview of the 1890s to the 1920s. But nothing illustrates the merit of this deceptively slender volume more than its ability to illuminate crucial events in Guyanese history that fall well outside its declared scope.

Noor Kumar Mahabir
East Indian Women of Trinidad and Tobago:
An Annotated Bibliography with Photographs and Ephemera
Chaguanas, Trinidad: Chakra Publishing, 1992.

East Indian Women—to use a short title—is yet another of Noor Kumar Mahabir's efforts in documenting Indo-Trinidadian culture. Mahabir's previous books include *The Still Cry* (1985) which gives verbatim accounts by indentured immigrants of their experience in coming from India to Trinidad and Tobago; *A Dictionary of Common Trinidad Hindi* (1990); and *Medicinal and Edible Plants used by East Indians of Trinidad and Tobago.* The main difference between *East Indian Women* and the author's previous works is its focus on women. Perhaps this makes *East Indian Women* more valuable since women have been neglected as a subject of Indo-Caribbean studies.

The book is divided into three parts: the bibliography; plates or photographs; and a third section strangely called "Ephemera." The bibliography, consisting of 218 items spread over 100 pages, is itself divided into eight subsections, each dealing with subjects such as law and politics, education or religion. Each item consists of an article, essay or similar piece of writing, quoted from mainly Trinidadian newspapers and journals, such as the *Trinidad Guardian, The Sunday Guardian, The Bomb, The Tribune, TnT, Mirror, People Magazine,* and *The Black Woman.* Most pieces were published in the late 1980s and early 1990s, although some go further back. The author's method is to quote the title of each piece in bold print, then give the name of the author and details of publication. This is followed by a summary of principal ideas in the piece. Item 24, for example, is about "Women of the Past Year" published in *The Express* on January 3, 1986. Mahabir gives the gist of the article, namely, that the author, Deborah John, looks at nine "outstanding" women in Trinidad and Tobago, only two of whom happen to be of Indian descent. There is no analysis or comment, but the information provided can be quite interesting. It is interesting, for example, to learn that in 1921 only 6.2 percent of Indo-Trinidadian women were literate, and only 30 percent in 1946, whereas in 1946 the literacy rate among other Trinidadian women was 75.3 percent. We also learn that Stella Abidh who died in 1989 at the age of 86 was the first Indian female doctor in Trinidad and Tobago and that, up to 1973, Senator Margaret Lucky-Samaroo was the only known Indo-Trinidadian woman in politics. Such news, taken from newspapers, inevitably has a topical, journalistic tone that reports rather than analyses facts. This is why, as the author himself says, *East Indian Women* is "informative rather than critical."

The second part of the book consists of 130 photographs showing Indo-Trinidadian women as lawyers, scholars, beauticians, musicians, housewives, farmers, artists, dancers and practitioners in other professions or vocations. Some pictures from the nineteenth and early twentieth centuries add an historical flavour which illustrates how far Indo-Trinidadian women have come. The third part of *East Indian Women* consists of a motley assortment of pictures, advertisements, statistics, paintings and news items. There are twelve pen pictures (with photographs) of "Some Prominent Indian Women 1845–1945," and essays by Judy Diptee and Phoolo Danny on the hardships of Indian women agricultural labourers, and their efforts to organize themselves by forming Women in Rice (WINRE), the women's arm of the Trinidad Island-wide Rice Growers Association.

The main achievement of *East Indian Women* is to gather assorted information into one volume, and present it in accessible form. The author has done well to provide indices which make his information more easily accessible. As he writes in his preface: "The main objective of this bibliography is to provide simple, inexpensive access to information on Indo-Trinidadian women, particularly for those who wish to examine the available material before initiating a research study or policy program." *East Indian Women* will serve best as an aid to scholarship rather than as a work of scholarship itself. "Ephemera" will become a "new" analytical tool for the study of gender in Trinidadian society. This claim, like Mahabir's general style, may appear slightly inflated; but this is probably due to the excitement of collecting so much interesting information. The information is certainly interesting; it is well classified, and it is very likely to promote further studies on Indo-Caribbean women.

Trevor Sudama
The Political Uses of Myth or Discrimination Rationalized
San Fernando, Trinidad and Tobago: Battlefront Printer's, 1993.

In *The Political Uses of Myth or Discrimination Rationalized*, Trevor Sudama has collected 90 of his articles, 87 of which were already published, one each week, between January 1990 and December 1992, in the Trinidad newspaper *The Express*. Sudama is a member of the United National Congress (UNC) and represents the constituency of Oropouche. As he explains in his preface, the main theme of his articles is: "an elucidation of the condition of citizens of East Indian descent in Trinidad and Tobago and the myths and misconceptions which surrounded their presence here." The main myth or misconception is: "the perception of non-Indians . . . that the Indians as a group had taken enormous economic strides and achieved an envious level of national self-sufficiency and security." Sudama's argument is that this perception of Indian or Indo-Trinidadian economic dominance promotes a defensive reaction among Africans or Afro-Trinidadians who believe that such dominance creates an imbalance that places them at a social disadvantage. In order to redress the imbalance and avoid any threat of being disadvantaged, Africans entrench themselves in state power—government jobs—a process which entails excluding or discriminating against Indians.

The Political Uses of Myth begins by offering observations and statistics about discrimination against Indians in Trinidad and Tobago; it then produces the arguments and analysis used to justify or rationalize this discrimination. Hence the second half of the title of the book. In his article, "Public Service Bias," Sudama gives statistics that confirm a deliberate attempt to exclude Indians from employment in the government or public service of Trinidad and Tobago. In 1980, for example, Indians accounted for 30.8 percent of workers in the public service, whereas in 1989 they accounted for 29 percent. During this period, when Indians had grown to more than 50 percent of the population, and had become both more educated and more interested in public service employment, this decline clearly suggests discrimination. (The social scientist, Selwyn Ryan, who provides Sudama's statistics, later objected to the interpretation placed on them in *The Political Uses of Myth*; but Sudama rejects his objections.) So far as fear of Indian economic dominance is concerned, articles such as "Big Business Control,"

"Sectors and Statistics," and "Control Banking" suggest that the belief that "Indians own everything" is an illusion encouraged by the fact that a few Indian families happen to be rich. Sudama provides facts and figures which prove that most Indo-Trinidadians are less well-to-do than other social groups and confirm that the belief in Indian economic dominance is largely a myth. But whether it is mythical or not, this belief persists in Trinidad and Tobago. The author quotes former Prime Minister, A N R Robinson, for instance, who refers to Fiji, Uganda, and Guyana as places: "where business activity was restricted to sections of the national community." Robinson's veiled attribution of economic dominance to "sections of the national community" defensively appears to justify withholding political power from "these sections"—Indians—either through expulsion, as in Idi Amin's Uganda, or through political thuggery and ethnic discrimination as in colonel Rebuka's Fiji and Burnham's Guyana. Writing in this vein is naturally controversial, and not surprisingly, it has provoked adverse criticism including charges of racism against the author. To his credit, Sudama reports some of these charges accusing him of invoking: "ethnic passions and divisiveness in the society in pursuit of a political objective which . . . would incite violent conflict."

As it happens, in the process of rebutting such charges, Sudama deploys some of his best writing. He is particularly good in using invective to defend himself against critics, one of whom he describes as: "an ostensibly anonymous member of the notorious ragtime band of sleazy, semi-cesspools of the weekly press." Such combative zestfulness is entertaining, and helps to relieve any tedium in a general style of writing that can sometimes betray elements of solemnity. In the end, Sudama denies being a racist and claims that his writing is that of a patriotic Trinidadian nationalist advocating a truly democratic, pluralist society in his homeland. He writes:

> The critical task as far as forging a soundly-based nationalism is concerned is how do we appreciate, respect and give recognition to the diverse backgrounds, heritage and traditions of the various ethnic groups which comprise the society and, at the same time, inculcate a sense of unity, common purpose and belonging which is necessary to promote national solidarity and nationhood.

Even if it runs the risk of encouraging divisiveness, this vision of ethnic diversity within national unity seems preferable to what Sudama calls the "facile and fatuous assertions" of "national unity" advocated by his critics, for it is precisely such assertions of national unity in post-Independence Guyana and Trinidad and Tobago that alienated Indo-Guyanese and Indo-Trinidadians in the 1970s and 1980s.

Whatever his critics may think, Sudama should at least be credited with publicizing a genuine contradiction between ethnic diversity and national unity in postcolonial societies. India and Nigeria, for example, not to mention former Yugoslavia, provide tragic examples of this problem. The question is whether Sudama's writing is likely to promote or prevent similar tragedy in Trinidad and Tobago. Some readers have already answered this question negatively. I disagree. Unless his statistics are doctored, Sudama offers open discussion of a potential for ethnic conflict which was swept under a carpet of selective democracy and nationalism during the long régimes of Forbes Burnham and Eric Williams. By warning against repetition of the undemocratic and spurious nationalism of governments in these two countries, *The Political Uses of Myth* vindicates both itself and its author.

Rooplall Monar
Estate People
Georgetown: Roraima Publishers, 1994.

Ian McDonald claims in his Foreword to *Estate People* that Rooplall Monar: "has succeeded in establishing himself as a leading, perhaps the foremost, interpreter of sugar plantation life in the West Indies" (p. iv). *Estate People*, Monar's third collection of stories follows his earlier volumes—*Backdam People* and *High House and Radio*—and his novel *Jhanjhat*. It is strange that there are few fictional studies of life on West Indian sugar plantations. One reason is that most West Indian writers have little direct plantation experience. The two best-known Indo-Caribbean writers, Selvon and Naipaul, pay relatively little attention to plantation aspects of Indo-Caribbean experience, while Monar, who grew up among Indian plantation labourers in Guyana, makes them the life and soul of his art. His stories recreate Indo-Caribbean plantation society more accurately and vividly than has ever been done in fiction.

In *Estate People,* as in his previous work, Monar's subject is the manners and mores of the Guyanese sugar plantation and its environs. A majority of his characters are descendants of labourers who first came to the Caribbean from India under a system of indenture in 1838. For the last century and a half, these labourers and their descendants have sustained Guyana's sugar industry and fostered a subculture, part Indian and part Caribbean, within an environment of harsh working conditions and basic emotional and psychological relationships. This is the subculture of Monar's fictional world.

In "Money Can't Pay," an aging Indian shovel man recalls an incident in which he and his fellow labourers confronted the estate administration over their starvation wages. Before they know it, police are called in, shots fired, and one labourer—Nankoo—is killed. The British governor promises action and the estate manager is put on trial, but he is acquitted and the story ends with an empty threat of defiance from the narrator: "Me been swear, if me foot been strong me would take policeman gun, shoot policeman, manager, overseer bladam and take brukneck in jail" (p. 15). This threat is empty because at the end of the story nothing has changed and Nankoo is the only casualty. What the narrator says earlier is more reliable:

> And all-yuh know how tings been ruff-and gruff in estate. Manager, overseer, driver and doctor, uses to knock one head. Estate people—coolieman and blackman—uses to knock other head (p.14).

The sharp division of power relations on Guyanese sugar plantations does not allow for accommodation or change.

But despite continuing exploitation and victimization many of Monar's stories create humour by exposing personal weaknesses of the victims, and illustrating their strategies in circumventing victimization. Big-mouth, for example, is a dexterous manipulator, whose adroit use of deviousness, connivance and obsequiousness help him to obtain favours and attain a level of comfort well above that of his fellow workers. As the author puts it, Big-mouth is: "colleaguing with estate against the people" (p. 19). One of Big-mouth's more notorious schemes is to steal estate funds and dole it out to female workers from whom he can then extract sexual favours. The author's exposure of Big-mouth's ruthlessness is deft and succinct: "Big-mouth is not only bully, he inside like rockstone" (p. 18). It is a resounding technical success that Big-mouth's flaws—hypocrisy, duplicity, bullying and cowardice and insentivity —should appear amusing within conditions of oppression and injustice that cry out for reform. Monar's comic treatment of his characters enables him to avoid sentimentality in presenting them as victims of oppression without lamenting over their conditions of oppression.

Much of Monar's success is also due to the well tailored structure of his plots. "Big-mouth," for example, opens as follows:

> Estate people say, whatever bad things a man do, he bound to suffer dearly for it before he spirit leave his body. Big-mouth, who been feel he could bribe God, was no exception (p. 16).

Since proverbial wisdom virtually assures us that Big-mouth will pay for his wicked deeds, we can laugh at his doings and treat them as misdemeanours rather than serious crimes. If his victims suffer, we still laugh because we know that comeuppance is in store for Big-mouth. Humour is also produced by farcical elements. For example, when his victims threaten violence and force him to flee for safety, Big-mouth's misdeeds are seen as high jinks, uproarious escapades, rather than shameful exploitation of kith and kin who are already exploited by a brutal plantation system. All this is confirmed in the end when the protagonist is afflicted by flu, bad kidneys and stomach ulcers all at once. Pain causes Big-mouth to moan and groan, but his distress is as comical as his mischief-making, for it represents one stage in a fixed moral pattern, whereby wicked or immoral actions lead inevitably to retribution. Big-mouth's story thus becomes an old fashioned folk tale that asserts the elemental power of good over evil.

Whether it is through Big-mouth's intrigue, Banga's obeah-working schemes, attempts to save Jamilah from a Hindu suitor, or Lil Boy's life of crime, the stories in *Estate People* portray a subculture in which people are forced to resort to nefarious plots, devious stratagems, crude violence and similar measures in the context of their everyday lives. Yet the harshness of their lives is miraculously relieved by a vibrant comic sense that transforms *Estate People* from a solemn record of social protest into a tragicomic extravaganza, unique in West Indian literature. One would need to combine the comic inventions of Samuel Selvon with Roger Mais's unsparing documentation of Jamaican urban slums to come up with a West Indian fictional text similar to *Estate People*. Even then, the largely Afro-Caribbean linguistic and urban context of Selvon and Mais would contrast sharply with Monar's rustic Indo-Caribbean speech and milieu.

The distinction of Monar's fiction is precisely its beguiling reproduction of Indo-Guyanese speech within a rural setting. The special flavour of this speech is caught in many proverbial sayings in *Estate People*: "But don't matter how much time you burn a dog mouth, he still can't able stop suck fowl egg" (p. 20); "People not fall down from tree-top yuh know. They come from somewhere as me daddy been say" (p. 36); "One-one day bucket bottom going lef' in well pipe"(p. 48); and "smart fly does en-up in cow-behind"(p. 49). The flavour of such speech places Monar's fiction within the main tradition of Guyanese prose writing that begins with Edgar Mittelholzer and runs through Jan Carew and Wilson Harris to Roy Heath. While Monar belongs to this tradition, he more specifically represents its Indo-Guyanese element that includes older writers like Rajkumarie Singh, Sheik Sadeek, Lauchmonen, and younger ones like Cyril Dabydeen and Sasenarine Persaud. All these writers share similar subjects, milieu, atmosphere and characters, but he rises supreme among them, largely because of his ability in accurately reproducing the finest nuances of thought and feeling, as if by magic, in the speech of his characters.

Janice Shinebourne
Timepiece.
Leeds, England: Peepal Tree Press, 1986.

Timepiece is a first novel by Jan Shinebourne, who was born in Rosehall, Canje, Guyana, but now lives in England. While most Guyanese writers come from either of the two major ethnic groups African or Indian, Shinebourne's father was Chinese and her mother part Chinese and part Indian. This feature of her biography may be relevant in helping her to project a perspective in her novel that is mixed and genuinely Guyanese in the sense of being multiethnic, nonpartisan.

Timepiece tells the story of June Lehall who leaves Pheasant, her fictional village, to work as a trainee reporter on *The Daily Mail* in Georgetown. The time is 1965, and Forbes Burnham has merely begun to set up the administrative machinery of the dictatorship that would

keep him or his party in power for a whole generation. Although Burnham does not appear in the novel, his presence and that of his government are felt everywhere. It is certainly felt among June's newspaper
colleagues who work in such an insidious atmosphere of rumour and
suspicion that they have to be careful about who may be within ear-
shot, when they are speaking among themselves. If this is not exactly
censorship it is not far from it. While it is true that reporters on *The
Daily Mail* are not told what to write, they know they should not write
anything with which their editor disagrees. A senior reporter, Clinton
Persaud, who is foolhardy enough to ignore this unwritten regulation
is abruptly fired. He is later jailed for a short period, before going to
Barbados in "voluntary" exile. Persaud's experience of harassment,
persecution and eventual flight will ring a bell for thousands of Guyanese who, similarly, took flight to face the unknown risks of "voluntary" exile abroad.

Timepiece captures the flavour of life in Guyana in the mid-1960s.
The novel fits into a documentary "genre" a literal "roman à clef" in
which Guyanese readers will recognize not only Burnham, but *The
Daily Mail* (*The Daily Graphic*), Clinton Persaud (Rickey Singh) and
numerous other thinly disguised personalities or details. Yet *Timepiece*
is not overtly political. By concentrating on the everyday lives of June's
professional and social associates, the author illustrates how, without
having to endure official discrimination or explicit persecution, ordinary Guyanese become so frustrated and desperate that they simply
want to escape from their native land. Shinebourne appears primarily
interested in this type of authentic social document which she successfully achieves in *Timepiece*. She tells us what people are doing and
thinking, but sternly refrains from passing judgement, or from analyzing what is being done or thought. It is as if she does not wish to run
the risk of giving offense to readers who might recognize either themselves or events in which they participated.

This apparent self-censorship may rob *Timepiece* of force and conviction, but not accuracy. Here, for example, is one character's account of
riots in Guyana in the early 1960s.

> All them poor people were beating up each other and looting
> left, right and centre. Men on East Coast chop up each other.
> Women get raped all over the place. The politicians call each
> other names. The civil servants show their true colours and

behave like a herd of idiots: A lotta people were more worried about their property than who get killed, beaten or raped.

This is excellent documentary writing. But the outrageous events that are reported are robbed of full impact because they form part of a conversation among discontented colleagues whose passionate elaboration of their discontent does not match their inability to do anything about it.

The strength of *Timepiece* is less in its ideas or action than its descriptions. Shunning the lyricism of Edgar Mittelholzer and the magic realism of Wilson Harris, Shinebourne gives concretely detailed pictures of familiar Guyanese scenes that are wonderfully evocative:

The lorries took barrels of pickled meat, crates of salted fish and cheap wares to the village. Grocer's children, still in school uniforms, helped clear the counters of sacks of sugar, salt, rice, grain, in half-dark, dank wooden shops, putrid with the scent of aniseed, chocolate, garlic. At the roadside, the men's cries had rung round the lorries as they yielded cargo brutally to each man's back: one hundred pound sacks and thunderous barrels of oil rolled up wooden slopes of bridges.

This is powerful, nostalgic writing which conjures up familiar sights, sounds and scents to recreate an era that has all but vanished, although it is still remembered by "voluntary" exiles living in alien surroundings in London, New York and Toronto. This alone is sufficient to win interest and admiration;for such descriptions will draw the reader back to *Timepiece* again and again, to taste, relish, savour and enjoy Shinebourne's recreation of life which, for all its colonial hardships and injustice, was invested with a rich, tropical mixture of bustling variety, energy, flexibility, cheerfulness and hope.

Lakshmi Persaud
Butterfly in the Wind
Leeds, England: Peepal Tree, 1990.

This first novel by a Trinidadian living in England focuses on Indo-Trinidadian experience, territory well traversed by literary sojourners that include members of the Naipaul clan, Samuel Selvon, Ismith Khan, and non-Indian Trinidadians such as Ian McDonald, Michael Anthony and Merle Hodge. But no sojourner has given the detailed and sensitive study of female childhood and adolescence, observed specifically from a woman's point of view, that we get in this novel.

In *Butterfly in the Wind* the narrator Kamla Maharaj describes her career through primary and secondary school to the time when she prepares to leave Trinidad for university in Northern Ireland. Kamla's father is a small businessman, a rum-shop owner and grocer, and what we get from his daughter's narrative are sharply etched vignettes of day-to-day living visible in household routine, incidents in the shop, business dealings, functions at church and school, and relationships with family, neighbours, teachers and officials. It is astonishing that the author can remember so much in such detail. Her book is a densely illustrated catalogue of memories, reminiscences and commentaries that form a warm tribute to the mixed blessings of a colonial upbringing in Trinidad. While the tribute is directed primarily towards the Indian community, it spills over to the larger community which is multiethnic and cosmopolitan in every sense, as illustrated by shared religious festivals, Catholic schools attended by Hindu pupils, and mixed social practices of all kinds. This is perhaps the most successful feature of the novel: the accuracy of its observation in catching the mixed atmosphere of a pre-Independence Caribbean society with different races, classes, and religions vying for survival under the imposed tutelage of British institutions, manners, values and standards.

Kamla's earliest memories are of people such as her first teacher, Miss Medina, who had a passion for straight lines. She also remembers Renée who did the family's washing, and who after a hard week's work could find solace simply by greasing herself with candle wax, "wrapping up" herself against possible draught, swallowing a drink of local rum, and smoking a cigarette. There are teachers like Mr Brathwaite who "had a secret desire to be a proper Englishman," and Mr Skinner whose theory of education began and ended with corporal punishment: "When we were confused we were flogged, when we were frightened we were flogged, and the dull were flogged daily" (p. 65). Since she belongs to a Hindu family, Kamla celebrates Hindu festivals and receives instruction from the *Ramayana* and *Mahabharata*, but because of the mixed nature of her society, she also celebrates Christmas. A sinister implication of living in a multicultural society is the discrimination the narrator suffers when she is told that she will not be sent on to St Joseph's Convent because she is not a Catholic. Religious discrimination suggests that a potential for discrimination lurks in other areas as well. But *Butterfly in the Wind* is notable for its concentration on more positive features of the narrator's life and her social milieu. Her parents seem paragons of virtue; and in a society noted for drunken brawling and the ill-effects of colonial exploitation, it is striking to read that drunks "would sing all the way home, becoming over-friendly to anyone they met." Yet these features fit the narrative of a young woman whose indulgent nostalgia over her early experiences allows her to dwell lovingly on a familiar landscape, remembered customs and ceremonies, and social practices evoking a colonial way of life that is obsolescent if not already obsolete.

The accuracy of terms used and of actual place names and institutions, together with the autobiographical structure and the sociological coverage of Indo-Trinidadian culture define *Butterfly in the Wind* as fictionalized autobiography or autobiographical fiction which devalues its achievement neither as autobiography nor fiction. After all, a novel like Merle Hodge's *Crick Crack Monkey* is not devalued by being placed in the same genre. In both books the main appeal is one of aching nostalgia for people, places and customs which indelibly shaped the narrator or author, but which have succumbed to the irresistible ravage of time, history and political change. In the following passage the narrator remembers an Indian Independence Day ceremony in which a little boy sang:

> Before me, this slender grain of rice, with the sun and wisp of hair in his eyes, sang with such youthful assurance that I wept for the supreme courage of the weak; and I wept too for those daring dauntless runaway slaves who never made it; and for the heroism and valour of the Red Indians of North America who did not have India's good fortune. Not for the first time in my life, as this stanza of Tagore's song came to an end, I felt a deep kinship with the courage of the vanquished. (pp. 186-7)

If there is any temptation to regard these brave words as mere rhetoric or wishful thinking, it is discouraged by the novel's superabundance of realistic detail and its authentic chronicle of growth, self-development in a British Caribbean colony. The chronicle establishes solidarity with colonized peoples everywhere, especially with women, a group who were doubly colonized. As such *Butterfly in the Wind* seems all the more intense, poignant, tender and eloquent.

Neil Bissoondath
Digging up the Mountains
Toronto: MacMillan, 1985.

The literary dynasty established by Seepersad Naipaul in Trinidad in the 1930s, and continued by his sons Vidia (V S) and Shiva in the 1960s and 1970s, appears confirmed through *Digging up the Mountains* by Neil Bissoondath, grandson of Seepersad, and nephew of Vidia and Shiva. The volume consists of fourteen stories most of which deal with the Caribbean—either with people living there, or with Caribbean people living abroad. While the fiction of his grandfather and uncles considers Indo-Caribbean experience mainly as a matter of reconciling ancestral Indian memories with Caribbean actuality Bissoondath's stories virtually eschew such memories, or any need for reconciling them with the Caribbean environment. Instead, Bissoondath's stories portray the Caribbean as a temporary stopover for one branch of a diaspora which spread out of India during the nineteenth century to diverse parts of the world, including Fiji, Mauritius, Africa, and territories in and around the Caribbean sea.

"Insecurity" is set on an un-named Caribbean island that is obviously modeled on Trinidad. The story focuses on the circumstances of Ramgoolam "an exporter of island foods and crafts" (p. 71). Ramgoolam already has one son in Toronto, and plans to send up another to study. But whereas such sons would have been expected to return to their home island as skilled professionals in his father's or grandfather's time, Ramgoolam now has second thoughts about his sons and their return home as skilled professionals. His father or grandfather would have regarded their native island as their home, and a returning son with professional qualifications as a sign of prestige, confirmation of success. But although Ramgoolam has no doubt of his success, he is overcome by worry, frustration, and insecurity.

He sends enough money to Toronto for his son to buy a house which could serve as a refuge: "should flight (from his home island) be necessary, and the more time passed, the more Mr Ramgoolam became convinced it would" (p. 72). The author sums up Ramgoolam's situation as follows:

> He could hope for death here but his grandchildren, maybe even his children, would continue the emigration which is grandfather had started in India, and during which the island had proved, in the end, to be nothing more than a stopover. (p. 72).

This idea of the Caribbean as a stop-over for Indians may have been mentioned before by other writers, but never discussed so explicitly in fiction as a feasible, indeed the only practical option. It is an option considered important enough to provide the theme of the title story in Bissoondath's volume.

"Digging up the Mountains" is also set in a Caribbean island like Ramgoolam's, except that currency restrictions, armed robbery and political terror make the hero Beharry even more insecure than Ramgoolam. When Beharry's friends Rangee and Faizal are found dead, the official police explanation that they were killed by robbers is obviously insufficient, if not entirely false. Beharry himself is robbed by an armed gang, and is lucky to get away with his life. As with Ramgoolam: "flight had become necessary, and it would be penniless flight. The government controlled the flow of money" (p. 20). Thus Beharry is faced with the possible prospect of leaving all he has worked for behind, if it would ensure his physical safety. It is not an entirely far-fetched prospect when we consider other branches of the Indian diaspora, for example, those who had to flee from Idi Amin's Uganda, or Rebuka's Fiji.

In some stories, especially those dealing with West Indians abroad, Bissoondath implies that his characters' experience of insecurity and flight is not simply Caribbean. In "Veins Visible" there is the idea that: "everybody's a refugee, everybody's running from one thing or another" (p. 222). But whether flight is Caribbean, or universal, or both, there is the fear that "the next stop . . . would prove temporary in the end" (p. 223). While the stories about expatriate West Indians do not show them in foreign lands beset by the same anxiety and terror as Ramgoolam and Beharry, the expatriates are far from content. Indeed, there is every indication that they could very well come to regard their new-found havens in North America as unbearable as their native Caribbean. "The Christmas Lunch," for example, exposes the suppressed frustration of immigrants forced, unwillingly, to conform to an alien,

North American lifestyle, and "There Are a Lot of Ways to Die" describes the predicament of Joseph, a successful West Indian immigrant in Toronto, who despite his outwardly comfortable life, remains inwardly unfulfilled like most of his fellow immigrants. He returns to the Caribbean where decay and disorder are so oppressive that he has no choice but to return to Canada. Joseph's story speaks for most of the Indo-Caribbean characters in *Digging up the Mountains*: when you come down to it, they have nowhere to turn to; their original dispersal from India entails permanent homelessness.

It would be misleading to leave the impression that *Digging up the Mountains* deals only with Indo-Caribbean experience. "Dancing" gives a sympathetic presentation of a black Trinidadian's preparations to come to Canada, and of her bemused, first reactions upon arrival. "Man as Plaything, Life as Mockery" provides a very moving study of the tragic effect of East European totalitarianism on the lives of ordinary people; and "The Cage" shows much insight into the inner struggles of a Japanese girl to achieve self-awareness. These stories illustrate the range and versatility displayed in *Digging up the Mountains*. It is rare for a writer, in his first volume, to display control over such a wide range of subjects, such insight into character, and close observation of so many varied details. Undoubtedly this is a promising first volume, and perhaps its most promising feature is its mastery of concrete, everyday detail, whether in describing a scene in a Toronto apartment or an act of violence on a Caribbean street. The sharp vividness of these physical descriptions combines with good control of character and dialogue to produce fiction of compelling authenticity.

Bissoondath's theme of homelessness corresponds exactly with the main theme of his uncle V S Naipaul, who portrays homelessness as a contemporary phenomenon, and not only a product of postcolonial Caribbean experience. This is the main difference between uncle and nephew: that Bissoondath's best stories are linked to a history of Indo-Caribbean expatriation, whereas V S Naipaul's Mr Biswas, for example, is both a Trinidadian and a modern man who is homeless. But it is invidious to compare a first volume with the established work of a major writer. Bissoondath's stories represent an impressive beginning. They also represent the theory of a literary dynasty, the first to appear in the Caribbean. For, in addition to his theme of homelessness, Bissoondath reveals an aloofness to his material which is reminiscent of the disdain in some of V S Naipaul's early writing. The coldly, objective presentation of an aggressive chauvinist in "A Short Visit to a Failed Artist," and the merciless exposure of the student's shallowness and hypocrisy in "The Revolutionary" match V S Naipaul's clinical detachment in such books as *The Mystic Masseur* and *The Suffrage of Elvira*. Consider this sentence from "Digging up the Mountains":

> It was not a matter of political miscalculation; it was simply the plight of a small country: nothing went as planned, the foreseen never came into sight, and possibilities were quickly exhausted (p. 6).

V S Naipaul's essay "Power to the Caribbean People" is only one of his pieces that records the same weary, though not unsympathetic dismissal of the futility of Caribbean disorder. The real promise in *Digging up the Mountains* is in the implied sympathy for the sense of futility felt by the main characters in stories such as "Insecurity" and "Digging up the Mountains."

Part Three

Indo-Caribbeans

CHHABLALL RAMCHARAN

Chhablall Ramcharan was born in 1918 in plantation Albion,[1] Guyana. Both his parents came from India; he was one of three brothers and three sisters. He lives in Toronto. The interview was recorded in Toronto, on 1 February, 1992.

Q: Do you know about your parents' circumstances when they left India?

A: The people responsible for the recruitment of indentured immigrants went into the country areas and told them of a glorious life in Guyana where they could earn 12 cents a day, "bit and a half"[2] as it was called. That was a lot of money at that time in India. The youths, who were attracted to material wealth were told of free housing and health care, etc. My mother told me that these were some of the things that prompted her and my father to leave.

Q: Which area did your parents come from?

A: From Benares.

Q: How old was your mother when she came?

A: About 16 years old.

Q: How would a young girl from Benares get to Calcutta to take the boat?

A: The people who were recruited as indentured labourers were more or less from provinces such as Bihar and Uttar Pradesh and cities like Benares, Delhi, and Bombay. I can only assume that the recruiting agents *arkhatis*[3] —went out to places like Benares—a holy city—because they thought that they could get a lot of people there. I think they knew how to get the best recruits.

Q: Were your parents married before they left India?

A: In India, in those days, there was no legality in marriage. For a man and woman to say they were married was considered enough proof that they were married. So my parents were registered in Guyana as "married on arrival".

Q: Where did your parents go on arrival in Guyana?

A: I think they went straight to Albion Estate.

Q: Did your mother say anything about their shipboard experience?

A: Yes. There was medical attention, but not the very best. They were given the right type of food—dhal, rice, fish, pumpkin and other vegetables, and made as comfortable as possible—but many immigrants could hardly eat, since they were seasick most of the time.

Q: What was life like for your parents in Albion?

A: Their services were exploited. There was no labour legislation geared to the well-being of indentured immigrants. Working conditions were not conducive to good health. But one thing the authorities made sure of was that when a person got sick, he or she had to be hospitalized: they wanted that person to regain health quickly and return to work. There was also what was called "Compulsory labour", which required both a man and his wife to work. My father came from a business family in India. He told the manager that he would go to New Amsterdam[4] to buy groceries, and bring them back by donkey cart to Albion. He considered that he was doing a service to his people by supplying them with groceries, and he asked to be released from labouring in the fields. He and his friends would join carts together in a procession to travel at night on the Albion road which had no street lights.

Q: It's very enterprising. How long did he do that?

A: For a long time. Periodically, the managers would threaten to terminate his work on the estate, or say that they would take away his house and expel him and his wife. But he continued to argue and, perhaps through advice from someone, threatened to report the managers to the Crosby Immigration Office,[5] which was well respected. After that, I guess they just let him go.

Q: For the rest of his life?

A: Yes. So he escaped the full hardship of the sugar estate.

Q: What about schooling?

A: My sisters were not sent to school, since in those days [Indian] parents did not send girls to school. My brother did not have much education either. He worked at the mess house or overseers' dining hall, and later as a butler in the manager's house. I passed the Primary School Certificate, or "School leaving" exam, and later took the Pupil Teachers' Examination.[6] I then taught for a few months at Albion School in 1934. Afterwards, I took a job as a weighing clerk in the estate. While there, I sat for the Hindi Interpreters' Exam.

Q: How was you Hindi when you took the Hindi Interpreters exam in 1944?

A: All the children in those days used to go to the *matia*[7] to learn

Hindi. I learnt from a gentleman named Rampersaud who had passed the Interpreters' Exam, and was working in the Immigration Department. He advised me to take the Interpreters' Exam and, in 1944, I passed with the top mark of about 94%. My performance impressed the Chairman of the Board of Examiners who was the Commissioner of Local Government as well, and he suggested that I should apply to join the Immigration Office in Georgetown[8], on a probationary basis. There was a Great Fire in the main Post Office in Georgetown in 1945, and many people who used to deposit their money in the Post Office Savings Bank lost their savings. The Government put out a notice in English assuring members of the public that they could bring forward claims which would be fully investigated to ensure that depositors were reimbursed and no one incurred loss.

Q: Were all records destroyed in the fire?

A: I would say all. They had to reconstruct records, and the Government wanted a Hindi translation of the notices already sent out in English. My translation was selected, and helped to confirm my appointment in the Civil Service. At the same time, I improved my proficiency by taking the London Matriculation exam with Hindi as one of my subjects in 1948. As a civil servant I worked in all three counties[9], and later in 1955, when the last ship was leaving Guyana to take repatriated immigrants to India, the Government selected me to accompany the immigrants.

Q: These were immigrants whose period of indentureship had ended decades earlier. The Government was obliged to send them back to India as part of the terms of their indentureship?[10]

A: Yes. I was sent as the repatriation officer, or "Crosby Baboo"[11] as the immigrants called me.

Q: What was your function?

A: My function was to look after the well-being of the returning immigrants. If they were sick, I made sure they were properly cared for. I also ensured that they got the type of meals they wanted. I was authorized to issue orders to the kitchen of the ship. We employed people from amongst the immigrants to do the cooking, and paid them.

Q: Did the ship carry immigrants only?

A: Mainly. There were about 375 immigrants. But we had space for a few first class passengers who paid their fare and traveled as tourists.

Q: The immigrants did not pay?

A: When immigrants were recruited in India, they came on condition that their full return passage to India, or one half or one quarter of it would be paid by the government. In 1955 the government used $60.00 as the basic figure to calculate the cost of a full return passage (the actual cost was about $400.00).[12] Those who were to receive half a passage had to pay the other half.

Q: It must have been quite a job to check out the terms for each immigrant.

A: We knew from our records which ship they arrived on. But the trip was very heavily subsidized by the government in Guyana.

Q: This return trip was being made in 1955, whereas the last ship came from India in 1917: that's a difference of nearly half a century. Where would these people be going back to? Did they keep in touch with relatives whom they had not seen for more than fifty years in some cases?

A: I do not think the people on the ship believed that they were going to India. It was only on the morning of departure, as people were going on board, that they realized that they were leaving for India. When I went into the ship, many immigrants were weeping. One of them walked off the ship before it sailed; after we reached to the beacon, where we had to wait for police clearance before sailing out to sea, if immigrants were given a chance to opt out of the trip, I believe a few of them would have returned to shore.

Q: They had no real knowledge of what was involved?

A: The Government of India had written to the Government of Guyana to discourage immigrants from returning. India was still in the process of repatriating people displaced by the partition in 1947. For example, people were leaving East Pakistan for India. The Government of India asked immigrants in Guyana to stay and make a contribution to Guyana. But some immigrants felt it was all a sham, and that it was the Government of Guyana that was discouraging them. When they went to India, it was a different story.

Q: How were they received?

A: A lot of Indians showed up at the port of Calcutta to meet the returning immigrants. I remember Chanchal with whom I had gone to school in Guyana. He had returned to India twenty-five years earlier. He and his sister showed up, but he was mentally deranged. I asked Chanchal's sister if she knew me, and she said, "Yes," but she didn't know me. She was merely trying to get some help from me. She knew my brothers and sisters. I was nevertheless happy to see people like Chanchal and his sister. But the Government of India couldn't settle them. I met about forty or fifty others, like them, who had returned earlier and were living in terrible conditions in Calcutta. The Government of India was very helpful in settling the immigrants whom I took. For example, if the immigrants were entitled to twenty rupees, the Government gave them two, and sent the other eighteen to their area office. I had to ensure that they reached the areas that they wanted to go to. We bought their tickets, and the Government of India arranged for a special coach to take them to the train station. To my surprise, a few days after I had seen them off, about forty immigrants returned to my hotel and held on to me weeping. For about ten days, I had to be at the Immigration Office in Calcutta preparing reports on these immigrants. They all wanted to go back to Guyana. The conditions they encountered in their villages were unbelievable. Their parents and relatives had moved.

Q: How did they know where to go?

A: They relied on memory. But things had changed. From India, I informed the Government of Guyana that some immigrants wanted to return to Guyana. Relatives in Guyana then collected money and gave it to the Guyana Government to be used as return fares. This money was then forwarded to the Protector of Immigrants in Calcutta to negotiate passages with the shipping company. In that way some immigrants were able to return to Guyana.

Q: That sums up the experience of Caribbean indenture under British colonialism: a pitiful end to an enterprise that may have been successful for the British in economic terms, but was tragic for Indians in human terms. Of course, the large majority of immigrants stayed in Guyana. Yet there was still that feeling for India.

A: Some people undoubtedly had that sentimental attachment to India. They just wanted the satisfaction of going. They did not care what suffering they would have to put up with. They only wished to die in India.

Q: The ancestral homeland! But the hard fact is that once they had left to come out to the Caribbean, they were separated from India. For most of them, whatever illusions they may have had, there was no turning back: they had come to a new life. I assume you returned from India to your job in the Immigration Department?

A: Yes. I was promoted to different departments over the years, until I retired as Personnel Manager in the Ministry of Housing, in 1975.

Q: You lived in Georgetown for a long time, and I take it you remained a Hindu. Did leaving Albion and coming to Georgetown affect your religion?

A: My mother was a strong devotee of Hinduism. I cannot tell you very much about my father's religious views, since he died fairly young. But through someone on my plantation we heard about the Arya Samaj[13] and our house became the centre of this movement in our district. Around 1943, I became secretary of the Samaj there, and it was because I felt that the secretary of the Samaj should know Hindi as well as English that I decided to take the Interpreters' Exam. Had it not been for my association with the Arya Samaj movement, I doubt that I would have been interested in Hindi. That is why I feel a lifelong debt to the Arya Samaj movement. It kept me from alcohol and meat, and it helped me to meet my wife. My future father-in-law heard me speak at a Samaj function and the matchmaking came out of that. I got married in 1942.

Q: Was there any friction between Arya Samajists and Sanatanists?

A: When the Arya Samaj movement first started in Albion, the Sanatanists did not take too kindly to it, because, unlike them, Samajists do not believe in the caste system and idolatry. Also, the Sanatanists believed that you have to be born into a Brahmin family to officiate in a ceremony whereas Samajists regarded you as acceptable if your conduct and education were good. In the beginning, even my mother felt that we were doing something that was probably sinful. But she was very understanding, and gave in to us.

Q: I assume that the Arya Samaj movement originated in India. How did it come to Guyana?

A: It came from Surinam to Skeldon, Albion, and Rose Hall, Canje—these were the centres—and it spread further across the country.

Q: Does this sectarianism still exist?

A: The conflict has waned. Now Sanatanists and Samajists live well with one another. In terms of worship, there is not much conflict, since we are worshipping the same God, but on the question of the caste system we are still apart.

Q: What about politics? As a civil servant, of course, you could not engage in politics?

A: No.

Q: But you were in Georgetown at a time of great political change and upheaval.

A: Under the British, the working conditions and the wages did not permit a good standard of living in Guyana, but I think there was some change after Dr Jagan[14] raised political awareness in the late 1940s. Before that I think the Man Power Citizens' Association under Ayube Edun[15] also had a good effect. The sugar estates began making changes, and I think the rate of those changes would have been faster if Dr Jagan had not shown his communist side. His communistic tendency militated against him, and affected the life of the people adversely. It allowed the authorities to "buy over" Burnham:[16] Burnham played the game with them. If Dr Jagan had played the game with Bookers, conditions for workers on the sugar estates might have been better.

Q: Were you in Georgetown in 1962–63, when the riots occurred?

A: I was beaten in 1963, not for any political reason. Africans were beating Indians at random. It happened the day the crowds entered the Deeds Registry, and broke an Indian girl's back. They picked up a typewriter and struck her. They were then about to strip her, when a judge rescued her. He took off his jacket and covered her. I was cycling along to work on the same day, and was beaten. I couldn't remember the beating. I just found myself in the hospital. But three years later, I met the individual who had called the police to get the ambulance when I was beaten

Q: You were left for dead?

A: Yes. My spectacles were broken, as were two of my teeth; two ribs were fractured.

Q: You suffered no permanent injury?

A: No. Before that day I used to travel all over the city without anyone bothering me. But this day, Africans were beating all Indians indiscriminately. This is the time that Jagan's influence started to weaken. His opponents began to erode his influence by fanning racial flames.

Q: But when you grew up in Albion, a heavily Indian area, race relations were not bad?

A: No. Indians and Africans used to get along nicely. The plantation managers respected Indian culture. They had formed a special area for the masons and engineers who were mostly African. It was called the "Bajan Quarter."[17] This enabled Africans and Indians to live in close association, without friction.

Q: Do you know how the term "Bajan Quarter" came about?

A: African people from Barbados were originally the engineers, I believe, in the sugar estate. Cooks for the managers and the mess house were also African since they knew how to cook for the Whites. The management provided a special range [living quarters] for these people nearer to the mess house. The "Bajan" engineers also lived closer to the factory. Our teachers were African. In the hospital, the nurses were African. So, there was a good relationship between Africans and Indians. In those good old days people used to believe in "bush medicine," and if you had a fever, Africans would come and do things for you that our own mother would not know to do.

Q: Up until 1953 racial relations were relatively good?

A: It was when Burnham severed connections with Jagan, that people started to become aware of racial differences. Even then, some Blacks ignored it, for example in Cane Grove, a sugar plantation where Africans and Indians lived well together. It was the politicians who fanned the flames of racism, and Burnham and the PNC were most responsible. B S Rai[18] saw that, and asked Dr Jagan to include more Indians in the Police force. Rai was also responsible for appointing the first Indian Commissioner of Police. The sugar estates were changing too: some Indian drivers were made overseers, and my nephew became the first Indian manager of Blairmont estate. The estates also brought in the eight-hour shift, and better wages and working conditions. There was all round improvement. But when Jagan and Burnham severed connections, all the problems started.

Q: What about the British Guiana East Indian Association?[19]

A: I think that C R Jacob[20] and Dr J B Singh[21] played a role. But their role was limited. Dr Jagan and Ayube Edun must be credited with bringing about labour legislation. Later on, for political awakening, it was Jagan and Burnham, when they were together.

Q: Dr Jagan was in power from 1957 until 1964. The elections in 1964 were won by Burnham, with help from D'Aguiar.[22] The PNC has been in power ever since, and the country has declined.[23]

A: People lost interest in what was going on after a while. Burnham infiltrated the Hindu pandits and gave them a beautiful building in Georgetown. They became his stooges. The pandits had a lot of *chelas* [disciples] who regarded them as their gurus and used to submit to them. Some Hindus believe it is a great sin not to do whatever their guru says.

Q: But the fact is that Burnham held unbroken power for twenty one years, in a country with numerous factions, sections, races, groups, and classes.

A: When elections took place he won, because they were all rigged. Inwardly, people never liked Burnham.

Q: But they submitted?

A: Yes, because some people felt that his influence might be necessary if they needed help economically, or had to find a job for their child. So they joined the government.

Q: I can see how they would do that out of expedience. But it still seems a little surprising that Burnham could have remained in command in a country where so many people disliked him.

A: You see, Burnham used pressure groups. He was a very wise man; a good crook. He knew the pressure points, and used to press them at the right time. He made one pandit a minister, and this pandit capitalized on the discipleship of his father who held many *chelas* and was known in the temple as a *puruhit*—a priest who cared about the well-being of everyone. (This is all Hindu custom, and the modern mind may not accept it). Once I attended a function where this minister pandit's uncle said to me: "My brother died and Burnham and all of them [PNC officials] came with a plane and they fetch my brother coffin. It make me feel great." These are the kinds of strategies Burnham employed to command loyalty. And they were combined with the rigging.

Q: As you said, the communist scare meant that external powers such as Britain and the US were not inclined to question or challenge Burnham?

A: If Dr Jagan had suppressed his communist tendencies, he might have gotten support from America. People wanted employment and money. If they had work, and the comforts of life, they would have supported Dr Jagan because he was never a racist. When he was in power, he tried to help everybody, regardless of race.

Q: Now lots of talented and skilled people have left Guyana. What do you see as the prospects for Guyana, with this large population abroad?

A: If there are fair elections, and Dr Jagan gets into power, the damage that has been done would take a very long time to be repaired. The new government will have to pressure people by way of taxes or something, and that will make it unpopular. If I were Dr Jagan, I would let people understand that they shouldn't allow their expectations to rise too high.

Q: How have all these social and political changes affected Indo-Guyanese culture?

A: I see young people adopting a sort of East-West cultural blend. In modes of dress, something like the *shalwar* is worn merely for fashion not as cultural observance. Even Canadian people are wearing it. We cannot say now that the *shalwar* is an article of Indian dress: only that it originated in India. Circumstances and conditions are causing people to move away from the orthodox code in what to wear. I was shocked in India, in 1955, when I heard people singing Hindi songs to English tunes. And in the large cities like Bombay and Delhi, people dressed in English fashions.

Q: What future do you see for Indo-Caribbean people in Canada specifically, where they are intermarrying and becoming more integrated in mainstream society?

A: I do not see much wrong with getting into the mainstream, but when it goes to the extent that it looks immoral, like someone having very little clothes on, I think that is going too far. Moral values must be preserved. I recall attending a reception in Toronto where I had to move a toast on behalf of the bride's parents. The person speaking before me said that they wouldn't like to hear that marriage was a sacred institution. That is going too far. Marriage is the oldest institution in family life which is the basic unit of human society. If we depart from that, what is human society going to become!

RAHMAN B GAJRAJ

Rahman Gajraj was born on 11 May, 1910, in Georgetown, Guyana. He had a highly successful business career in Guyana before serving in various government appointments. He now lives in Toronto. This interview was recorded on 27 May, 1992, in Toronto.

Q: Could you tell me about your family's connection with India?

A: The date of my paternal grandparents' indenture was 17th December, 1872. They got their certificate of exemption on the 29th December, 1877.[1] On my mother's side my grandfather also came from

India. He was one of three brothers whose parents had died. According to my grandfather, his uncle and aunt took them in; but they had their own children and there was confusion. As a result, my grandfather and his brothers decided to get away from their uncle and aunt, and go to Calcutta. There they met an "arkhati"[2] who encouraged them to put their names down to emigrate. Since their uncle was a sergeant of police, and might be able to find them from the immigrants' list, they decided to change their names. As Muslims, however, they considered it best to pick Hindu names: Gajraj, Manraj, and Nisbet. It was with these Hindu names that they arrived in Guyana.

Q: Since indentured Indian immigrants were taken to work on sugar estates, how did your family move out of the estate to establish a business in Georgetown?

A: Towards the end of their indenture on Enmore[3] estate, my grandmother would buy coconut oil and trade by moving about the estate to sell it. In this way, my family accumulated a little money that enabled them to come to Albuoystown in Georgetown,[4] where they bought a plot of land with a logie[5] that had several rooms. They converted one of the rooms into a little shop, and started a business. Then they moved into Water Street[6] in Georgetown about 1900.

Q: So your father grew up in his father's business in Water Street

A: Yes. My grandfather had seven children—six boys and one girl, and the business became too small for them. So the children moved out. My father moved to Carmichael Street, where he bought and sold plantains and eddoes at Stabroek market.[7] Then he moved into a little store and began to import small items. Gradually, he built up a business. Then, he went on his own about the end of World War I. I remember the time because it wasn't easy to get flour and other imported foodstuffs.

Q: Your father was not just a businessman though. He was a member of the Georgetown Chamber of Commerce. How did that happen?

A: He was a thorn in the side of some distributors of imported foodstuffs, because he used to import goods on his own. He seemed to have built up a good name for himself with people abroad, and received foodstuffs like potatoes and onions on consignment from Canada. He couldn't buy them: he received them, sold them, took out his commission, and remitted the rest of the money. That was a big portion of his business. He also had contacts in the West Indies, in Dominica, for instance, from where someone used to send him oranges, grapefruit and avocados to sell in Guyana. So far as the Chamber of Commerce is concerned, it was the Managing Director of Bookers[8] who put the idea in his mind.

Q: The Chamber would have been all white at that time?

A: White and Portuguese.[9] The Bookers' Director must have supported my father's application for membership on the grounds that he would represent Indians. Then Francis Kawall and Mahadeo Panday[10] joined. These were the first three Indians to become members of the Georgetown Chamber of Commerce. My father was later a member of the Council of the Chamber rather than just an ordinary member. Then Mahadeo Panday became the first Indian councilor in the city of Georgetown. But he got into difficulties with his business and had to give up membership of the town council. My father was then substituted for him. My father and Panday were both nominated councilors: they were not elected. According to the constitution, in those days, the city council consisted of nine elected members and three government nominees. My father remained a councilor until I became an elected member of the council in 1951.

Q: Your father was also a leader in the Indian community. He was active, for instance, in the British Guiana East Indian Cricket Club, of which he was president from 1926 to 1934.

A: My father came in later. In the beginning, the important people in the club were J A Veerasammy and Thomas Flood. Veerasammy[11] was a magistrate and cricketer, and was interested in having a cricket ground. He got Flood to put a downpayment on four lots of land which they built up into a ground that was less than regulation size. That was about the end of the First World War. In trying to find money to pay their mortgage, they brought in my father and his group, and others interested in the project. It was around that time too that indentured immigration from India came to an end. The planters [plantation owners] objected to this because they needed fresh labourers for their plantations. They therefore put pressure on the Indian government, who sent a delegation to observe the conditions of Indians in Guyana and other West Indian territories where Indians had gone. Later, the Indian government also sent a commissioner, Kunwar Maharaj Singh,[12] to hold meetings with Indian people [and] plantation owners.

Singh liked cricket, and was invited to the small East Indian Club ground, where he was clean bowled first ball. Since he was the centre of attraction, our umpire thought quickly and called "No Ball" so that

Singh was given not out. Singh then went on to play very well, and make some seventy odd runs. After the match, we explained to him that we had applied for a lease of land by the sea wall, and were told that it was imperial war property, which couldn't be touched. We asked him if he could use his influence to get it released to us. He did, and eventually we took possession.

Veerasammy then got Thomas Flood to donate a Cup for competition between Indians of the three counties: Berbice, Demerara, and Essequibo.[13] It was an annual competition through which Indians were able to show that they knew the game. There were two cricket competition Cups in those days: the Garnet Cup for junior players, and the Parker Cup for senior players. At first, Indians were not even allowed to field a team for the Garnet Cup. Eventually, however, they were allowed into the Garnet Cup competition, and another ten or fifteen years later they could play for the Parker Cup.

Q: Who controlled these competitions?

A: The Georgetown Cricket Club(GCC)[14] — all whites. The top men in the GCC would have been firstly, the British whites, then the local whites, and at the bottom you had the Portuguese.

Q: How did the British Guiana East Indian Cricket Club develop?

A: After we got the new ground, we began correspondence with Indians in Trinidad, and were invited to send a team of our cricketers to play Indian cricketers in Trinidad, and vice versa. We had to find money for travel and equipment. This is where my father's knowledge and contacts helped considerably. We were able to raise money, book passages, send people out, and bring them back. The first team we sent over was in the 1920s. My father and my wife's uncle went on that tour. I myself went on the second tour, although not as a player.

Q: Your father also took an interest in his own Muslim community?

A: He was quite active in Muslim community affairs, and helped, financially, in the rebuilding and extension of the Queenstown mosque. He was also chairman of the mosque's Board of Trustees until his death in December, 1963.

Q: Was your father not involved in the British Guiana East Indian Association,[15] formed to promote the welfare of Indians?

A: Yes. He was president of the East Indian Association for a few years. One of the big men in the East Indian Association was Dr J B Singh.[16] He was president for a number of years. Others who were involved were Arnold Seeram and Francis Kawall.[17] In those days,

Indians were beginning to feel that unless they did something on their own, others would keep them down. They felt they had to work on the political side. When there was a strike of sugar workers at Ruimveldt, Francis Kawall became a spokesman for the strikers.[18] At that time, the Man Power Citizens' Association[19] did not exist, so the British Guiana East Indian Association was really acting as a trade union for the sugar workers.

Q: What were relations like between the British Guiana East Indian Association and the League of Coloured People (LCP)?[20]

A: The LCP's attitude was that Guyana should belong to the descendants of slaves (Africans).

Q: Because the slaves had suffered for three hundred years?

A: Yes. They blamed Indians, saying if we hadn't come as indentured labourers, they would have taken over the country.

Q: No doubt, the arrival of Indian labourers reduced the bargaining power of the freed slaves, because the plantation owners could use the Indians as an alternative source of labour. In this situation, the freed Africans perceived Indians as scab labour.

A: Yes, although at that time I don't think the freed Africans were well enough organized to be able to bargain effectively with the plantation owners.

Q: At any rate, in the structure of colonial society, the Whites had the greatest power in commerce, the professions, and government. Then Creoles or Africans were next in line as the most likely group to replace Whites. But, from what you are saying, by the 1920s and 30s, Indians were organizing themselves.

A: We were getting organized and moving up the social ladder.

Q: Africans would have seen that as a threat?

A: Yes. Dr T T Nichols was president of the LCP in the 1930s, while Dr J.B. Singh was president of the East Indian Association. When elections were approaching, an attempt was made to reach an agreement whereby the two groups would not compete against each other; but Nichols and the LCP would not agree and, as a result, neither side got a majority in elections.

Q: As a boy growing up, you obviously got a very good grounding in public affairs, from observing your father's involvement in so many organizations. Where did you go to school?

A: I did my primary education at St Thomas's Scots School, then went on to Queen's College[21] on a scholarship. I won the scholarship in 1921 and attended Queen's College until 1926.

Q: The teachers were all white?

A: Mainly, but we had some local people as well.

Q: While at school, do you remember what were your horizons? Did you think of going into business or getting a profession?

A: I didn't think of business at all. I wanted to be a lawyer. I kept saying this at home, and I took an interest in legal matters that were reported in the newspaper. But my father had in mind that I should join him in the business. That is why I left school without sitting for the Cambridge Higher School Certificate exam. I wasn't happy about leaving school at all. During my time at Queen's College, I used to have to leave school at the end of the day, and ride on my bicycle to the store to relieve my father if he had to go somewhere. During the August holidays even, I was in the shop all the time.

Q: Did you not go abroad later to study for your B A?

A: I didn't study abroad. I did the degree by correspondence. It took a number of years—longer than if I had gone full time as a student to college. It was an American college—McKinley Roosevelt University.

Q: Meanwhile, the business was growing all the time?

A: Yes, it was becoming more important. I specialized in finance and accounting which became very useful in the business.

Q: How did your entrance into public life come about?

A: Since I was a teenager I had an interest in public life. The first time it seemed to stir me was during a mayoral election in Georgetown, when the contestants were Percy Wight and Nelson Cannon. Those were the days before motor cars, when the candidates hired cabs carrying flags with their own colours. You could tell which was a Wight or Cannon cab coming. It was great fun. The second thing I remember was Seeram going up for his seat. My father was anxious to see Indians in these positions and supported Seeram, who won; not because of my father, but my father's involvement in the victory caught my interest. I also took an interest in affairs in the city [Georgetown], and used to write letters to the editors of local newspapers. On one occasion, in fact, the editor of the *Daily Argosy* referred to my letter in his editorial! I felt as if I had reached the very top.

I waited some years before entering an election for the Town Council. There were a majority of Portuguese names on the voters' list[22] and my opponent—Eddie Gonsalves—was Portuguese. However, we put up a fight. I rented the Town Hall for an election meeting and was asked many questions, but I was able to hold my own. Then election day came, and I lost by only seven votes? I thought it was a marvelous ending. I couldn't have asked for more. Eddie Gonsalves eventually became mayor too, because he was with the Wight group—Percy Wight, Vibart Wight, and Eddie's brother John Gonsalves—who had a majority on the Council.

In the next election, I decided to run in the ward in which we lived, because we had more Indians, although they were not a majority. I found myself opposed again by Eddie Gonsalves, who was already a member of the council and mayor. He gave up his Charlestown ward to come and fight me! He, of course, would capture the Portuguese vote, while Eric Stoby, another candidate, would capture the coloured vote;[23] so my chances did not look good. But I won by three votes! That was my first public office.

Q: We are now in the early 1950s, and in 1953 the Jagan government was thrown out by the British and the Constitution suspended.[24] You were not involved in politics then?

A: No. I came in after the suspension. Because of my work on the Town Council, I was well known and was asked by the governor to serve in the Interim government[25] between 1953 and 1957. I was a member both of the Interim legislature, and the Executive Council. I preferred to serve without portfolio. I assisted others in presenting their bills. The once-a-week Executive Council meetings were an interesting experience for me. The governor presided over the meetings, but the real power in the Interim government was E F McDavid, the Colonial Treasurer.

Q: What were his politics like?

A: I would say that he certainly was an imperialist. Now and again he expressed views that were a little socialist. He would give a little but take plenty! He was very clever. He had in his portfolio the Rice Marketing Board, the Rice Producers Association, and the sugar interests. He was also chairman of the Public Library Committee.

Q: On the whole, the Interim government was just marking time between 1953 and 1957?

A: It was marking time, and endeavouring to create economic conditions which would sway the people away from the socialist bent of the Peoples Progressive Party (PPP).

Q: It was also during this Interim period that the PPP split into two parties. Were you involved in that?

A: No. I was never a member of the PPP. I've never been a member of any political party.

Q: What caused the split?

A: Nothing but racialism. Although, I must say that Cheddi [Jagan] did everything possible to create a cohesive nation between the Africans and the Indians. It was he who pushed Burnham into the leadership! He told me this, and I heard it from Burnham himself too, that when he [Burnham] was still a student in England, Cheddi wrote and encouraged him to come back and join the PPP, to take a leadership role.

Q: Cheddi always had the vision of a unified Guyanese nation.

A: I still think he has that vision, although he would know that it is harder to realize now than in the 1960s.

Q: The early 1960s was a crucial time in Guyanese politics. There was talk of independence, and the new electoral system of proportional representation was implemented in 1964, allowing Burnham and D'Aguiar to form a coalition government.[26] This is probably the most crucial single event in modern Guyanese political history. Why did Cheddi agree to proportional representation at the Constitutional Conference in London in 1963? As I understand Cheddi's argument, if he hadn't agreed, there would have been such chaos and destruction when he returned to Guyana that the country would have become ungovernable.

A: I think he is right. If there was a breakdown of the Constitutional talks in London in 1963, the opposition would have indulged in burning and destruction as they did in 1962 and 1963.[27] All the Indian business places would have been gone.

Q: You became Speaker of the House in Burnham's government and must have known Burnham and D'Aguiar well. What was D'Aguiar like?

A: He was a free-enterprise man, and was committed against communism. I wouldn't say he was in any way racial. For him, as long as you were not a communist, you were all right. He tried to win over as many Indians as possible to the United Force (UF) by putting them in positions of authority in the UF

Q: You say you never joined a political party, but you were appointed by Burnham as ambassador to the US?

A: It was in 1970 that I was approached to be ambassador to the US, and High Commissioner to Canada. At the time, I think Burnham wanted to have another Indian in the diplomatic service, because when we got Independence, the first two heads of missions were John Carter in Washington, and Lionel Luckhoo in London. Later, Burnham tried to get Lionel to go to Venezuela, but Lionel resigned instead. In the meantime, Burnham moved Carter from Washington to London, and Washington was vacant. Since Lionel was Indian, he wanted to replace him with an Indian so he could say he had Indian supporters. He asked me if I would go, and I agreed. I don't know if I did the right thing.

Q: How did you feel in that role, because you must have been aware that Burnham was using you as a figurehead, as an Indian who could make his government look (multiracial) abroad?

A: I felt as a Guyanese that I should take it, and I felt as an Indian that if being there enabled me to help my people, I would do so, if possible.

Q: Because of the flight of talent from Guyana during the Burnham years, the country is now depleted of intellectual and economic resources. I believe Guyana is next to Haiti as the poorest country in the hemisphere. What went wrong?

A: They had no experience, really, of managing an economy. Guyanese had a feeling that they were excluded from power during the colonial period, so when they got power after Independence, they wanted to make up, in a very short space of time, for all that they felt that they had been robbed of. So they went on spending money blindly, on themselves, on their groups, and on this and the other. Money was no object, as it were. They didn't realize that they had to use their resources to pay for their expenses. The result was that foreign exchange went completely flat, and some people say that individuals benefited from it. Personally, I don't know about that.

Q: The charges of corruption have always been there. But I like your general point that it was a matter of power without responsibility: they were so drunk with power, which at last they had obtained, after centuries of colonialism and exploitation.

A: Of course, power was also perceived as spreading to the ordinary man in the street who felt he should get something from Independence too.

Q: Was Burnham a Machiavellian type of leader who was concerned with his own power and nothing else? He could not have been unaware of what was happening. Why did he let it happen, or were there forces that he could not control?

A: I think he must have become aware of the desperate situation subsequent to its happening; not before hand. I don't think he deliberately set out to destroy the country. It just happens to be his bad luck that he goes down in history as the one under whose leadership the country broke up.

Q: In your own case, you had a successful business in Guyana as well as long public service. Yet you have settled in Canada. What about your business establishment in Guyana?

A: When I agreed to be ambassador in Washington, I stipulated that suitable arrangements should be made for the business. This led to discussions about the government taking over the business. Burnham told me that he was trying to nationalize the sugar and bauxite industries, and if a Guyanese firm could be taken over by the government, it would give them greater incentive to get the foreigners out. We agreed for the government to take over our business if they would pay for it, but they said they didn't have enough cash. They could only pay 5%, and give us bonds to pay the rest over a period of twenty years. The bonds were printed in Guyana dollars. At that time, the Guyana dollar was worth fifty cents US. Today, it is worth less than one cent US.

Q: In fact, you did not receive full payment for your business from the government.

A: We have not received the value; but they could still say that payment was made in Guyana dollars through these bonds.

Q: If that money is still in Guyana, what will happen to it?

A: I'll probably give it to a mosque.

Q: Do you feel bitter about all that has happened?

A: I wouldn't want to use the word "bitter." Disappointment, yes.

Q: Obviously, you would prefer to be in Georgetown now?

A: Oh yes. I would have loved to remain there. Life in Georgetown, as we knew it, was very happy. We knew so many people. We could just go for a drive in the country. We could stop in somebody's home without appointment. I still think if it was possible to live in Georgetown, I could be of some use to the country.

Q: It is sad that the promise of independence and freedom should lead to power without responsibility, and ultimately to decline in Guyana. Why did things turn out this way?

A: The real thing, I submit, is that Burnham never wanted Cheddi to be leader. He wanted to be leader: that is the big fight that they always had. He says that when he was studying in England, Cheddi promised that he [Burnham] would be the leader when he came home. I know that Cheddi wouldn't have done that.

MARGARET JAGESAR

Margaret Jagesar was born in Penal, a village in Trinidad on 15 December, 1928. She is the last of seven children although her family became much larger after her parents, the Laltoos, adopted several children from the orphanage. The interview was recorded in Kingston, Ontario, on 6 March, 1992.

Q: How many (adopted) children were there in your family?
A: Two when I was growing up.
Q: Does that mean that your father was fairly well to do?
A: He wasn't wealthy, but he had a big heart. He was a Pastor.
Q: I assume he came from a Hindu family?
A: Yes. My father was born in Farekhbad, Uttar Pradesh, India, on 10 May 1876. He went to Trinidad with his parents on a ship called *Foyle*, and they arrived in Trinidad on 3 May 1881.
Q: Do you know why they left India?
A: I think they were tricked into thinking they were going for a better life, not that they were going to work on the estates. They felt they were going to get good jobs. This is what I heard from my older brothers and sisters.
Q: What happened immediately after your father and his parents arrived in Trinidad?
A: They were sent to an estate in Wellington where my grandfather worked. At the time my father began going to school, a Canadian missionary called Miss Copeland saw that he had potential, and tutored him. He made rapid progress and in 1894 became a qualified teacher. Later, he became a headteacher who not only taught what was in the curriculum, but was also judge, lawyer, even dentist. I remember seeing the instruments which he used as a dentist on the villagers. He kept them and was able to pass them on to a qualified dentist later on. I guess it was through moving around helping people, that he was persuaded into joining the ministry. He had already been baptized on 26 November 1881. In 1901, he left teaching, and started preaching as a Catechist. Later he attended Naparima Theological College[1] in San

Fernando and graduated as a minister of religion in 1915.

Q: When did he get married?

A: He married my mother in 1911.

Q: So he was able to study for the ministry while he was married and having a family? Was he also working as a Catechist?

A: Yes. Even though he was a minister, my father went into other fields, agriculture and bee-keeping for example. He was conversant in about five Indian dialects. The dialects enabled him to move into Hindu and Muslim areas, and win souls for Christ. From my earliest recollection, my father was pastor in Princes Town, but he might also have to preach at four other services in neighbouring districts.

Q: Was a manse provided?

A: He lived in the Presbyterian manse at that time, but in 1937 he moved to Diamond village, where again he had about four other districts to visit on Sundays.

Q: Apart from Miss Copeland, did any other Canadian missionaries influence your father?

A: Miss Copeland tutored him, but he came into contact with several other missionaries whom he taught Hindi so that they were able to hold some Hindi services in the church.

Q: Can you describe your family life during the time you were going to school?

A: We had everything we wanted. During World War Two my older brother Ralph had come to Canada; some of my sisters were already married; and my brother who was two years older than me had left to join the Royal Air Force. We were all fully occupied. During the week we travelled to school—my father had arranged for a bus to pick us up—and we had a very nice family life. On Saturday, we would all go to music lessons, and on Sundays it was church. We had a very disciplined life with no time for anything else. In the weekday mornings we would have family worship before we left for school, and on weekends we had family worship before bedtime.

Q: Was there racial animosity in the communities you lived in?

A: Princes Town was an Indian area, and I recall just one Negro family on the street where we lived. Diamond village was a mixed area, but everyone lived in harmony—the Indians, the Negroes, the Spaniards.

Q: By the end of World War Two your father must have retired?

A: He had retired earlier but kept on working voluntarily. Then, my mother insisted that we move to a property that my father had bought in Penal. My father built a house on the property, and we moved into it in 1948. My father was able go to anybody's home regardless of their religious belief. He would go to a Hindu funeral, for instance, and explain what life and death was all about.

Q: Hindus, Christians and Muslims mixed quite freely?

A: They mixed freely, and my father had friends among all sections of the community. I still have a copy of one of his Ramayana[2] books, from which he used to read and draw comparisons to the Bible.

Q: What role did your mother play?

A: As a young girl, my mother grew up in the Iere Home for Girls[3] which was run by Canadian missionaries. She took part in activities like Sunday School, and helping the younger girls with sewing and baking. As a matter of fact, my father met my mother at the Iere Home, and they got married there. So she was perfectly suited to the role of a minister's wife. She was very much a live wire. My father never really went preaching or visiting without her.

Q: Your mother seems to have lived a full life in colonial Trinidad more than fifty years ago. She doesn't sound frustrated or dissatisfied?

A: She never had time to be dissatisfied, or frustrated. The little spare time she had was spent with the Women's Church Group.

Q: How long did your parents live together in their own home?

A: From 1948 to 1958 when my father passed away. My mother lived to be 81. She passed away in 1972.

Q: What about your own career?

A: I went to the Naparima Girls' High School[4] in 1941. I wrote the Cambridge Senior Certificate exam and graduated in 1946. My father wanted me to get married straight away as all my sisters had done, but I wanted to be a nurse. Eventually, I was persuaded to become a teacher, and I started teaching at the Presbyterian school in Penal in January, 1948. I stayed at Penal for a number of years and wrote my Teacher's Exam. I also got married in 1949, and lived close to the school and within walking distance of my parents' home. I continued with my studies, and exams, and in 1958, went to Training College.

Q: Where was the Training College?

A: The Presbyterian Training College did not accept married women, so I went to the Government Training College in Port of Spain. This meant that I had to live away from home, but my brother Ralph was in Port of Spain then teaching at Queen's Royal College. I was able to live with him. I spent one year at the Government Training College and became a qualified teacher. But then in 1961, my husband and I left for London, England, where I went to university. My husband's brother had migrated to London and was living there, so I felt that it was a good opportunity for me to go to university in London where we knew someone.

Q: How long were you in London?

A: From 1961 to 1962. I was on one year's leave to study Child Development at the University of London.

Q: How did you find London?

A: We met other Commonwealth people, and did not encounter any discrimination. Sad to say, whatever discrimination I encountered was at a West Indian cultural organization at London University. It was the end of the University year and we were putting on a play, in which all the West Indians were going to get together. But we just could not! The Trinidadians stuck together and put on the play with a few Jamaicans, but the others pulled out. Still, it was a very happy year. I was able to take back some of the methods and projects I observed, and adapt them to a Trinidad setting. I also contributed to several booklets on Infant Education, including a special article on reading; and when I became Vice-Principal I set up a model Infant School. I became Vice-Principal at a place called Jordan Hill in 1972. I was later transferred to another school closer to my home, and there I became Principal in 1981. Then I was again transferred to another school, and stayed there until I retired because of my husband's ill-health.

Q: Did you ever work in Government schools?

A: I worked with the Presbyterian Board all the time. In school we had a general assembly in the morning, and forty minutes religious education every day. Then the school would be broken up into different sections, the infants together, the juniors, and the upper classes.

Q: Were the teachers all Indian Presbyterians?

A: Yes. The majority would be Indians. Very few Negroes were Presbyterians and only Presbyterians taught in these schools. But we had Hindu and Muslim students.

Q: Did Muslim and Hindu students object to the religious education? Even nowadays I sometimes hear Trinidadians or Guyanese complain that they had to give up their Hindu or Muslim religion and become Presbyterians for the sake of education.

A: I knew Hindus and Muslims who did get baptized to go to the

Presbyterian Training College. Before Hindu schools opened, there were young Hindu men and women who got baptized, went to Training College, and became teachers in the Presbyterian schools. But when the Hindu schools were established, they left and went to those schools.

Q: How were Presbyterian schools funded?

A: Teachers' salaries were paid by Government, while repairs to school buildings were shared by the Presbyterian Board and the Government. School supplies were also provided by the Government. Appointments and transfers of teachers were done by the Board which consisted of Canadian missionaries until the Presbyterian Church in Trinidad became independent of Canada.

Q: Does this system of dual control in education still exist?

A: The Church Board is still running the schools, and they still have the Theological College which celebrated its 100th Anniversary this year. At first there used to be a connection between the Presbyterian Churches in Guyana and Trinidad, but it was broken. There was also a connection between the Presbyterian Church in Trinidad and Grenada; but now it is just the Presbyterian Church in Trinidad.

Q: The church was evidently a great influence in your life?

A: Yes, and in our coming to live in Canada, I have the opportunity to give back what I have received from the Canadian missionaries. Although we are supposed to be living in retirement here, I'm Superintendent of the Sunday School, and we are in various Church groups. It is strange that long ago we looked on Canada as a Christian country, but it is far from being so. In Canada today you cannot mention the name of Jesus, especially to younger people. I consider it to be a privilege to be able to do something about this.

Q: Why did you migrate here in the first place?

A: That I consider to be the hand of God. My husband fell ill in Trinidad in 1982 and was advised to come to Canada to have tests done. The hospitals in Toronto were booked up, and we decided to come to Kingston, because one of my nephews was here. My husband was admitted to hospital and had a tough time, but he recovered and I resumed work in Trinidad. But since he had to return to Canada annually for medical check ups,we decided to settle in Canada.

Q: You must have seen many changes in Trinidad over the years. Did political change affect you?

A: I was never active in politics, but when Eric Williams came on the scene and his People's National Movement (PNM) won the Elections in 1956, we thought that his promises were good. I must say that I benefited because it was the PNM Government that established an additional course for married teachers at the Training College, and I took advantage of it.

Q: Most people say that the PNM had good ideas in the beginning, but changed later on.

A: A lot changed with that party. As leader, when Eric Williams declared "massa day done," the Negroes felt that it was the Indians who were the "massas." Since the Indians owned land, properties and businesses, the Negroes felt that they were neglected and deprived, and they regarded Eric Williams as someone who had come to save them from the Indians.

Q: How did Williams become so unpopular later on?

A: From the time he started I think he was a dictator in certain things. But we cannot blame him entirely for it. It was the younger Negroes who joined the party and wanted something for themselves.

Q: What about Bhadase Maraj[5] and the Democratic Labour Party (DLP)?

A: When the DLP said they were going to be an Indian party, some people interpreted "Indian" to mean "Hindu." That caused division, because there were many Indian Christians who would have stayed in the party with Bhadase if it was not a Hindu party. That was very sad, I think.

Q: It's hard for the Indians. They've inherited divisions from three big religions: Hinduism, Christianity and Islam.

A: And within Hinduism they have the caste system.

Q: These divisions have all become a part of our culture. Do our children who grew up here feel that they belong to an Indo-Caribbean culture?

A: Our children who are brought up and educated here, know nothing of their heritage. Even when they go back to the Caribbean for a holiday, it is hard for them to fit in. When I was living in Trinidad, my sister returned from Canada with her granddaughter, and we were about to go to a movie at the drive-in cinema when some relatives dropped in unexpectedly. My niece was upset when I attempted to serve these guests some refreshments. She said they should have phoned to find out if they could come. I told her there was no phone in their village. She then said that they should have left anyway when they saw that we were dressed to go out.

Q: Her Canadian upbringing had made her an outsider to our more flexible customs.

A: Yes. We learnt from our parents always to cook a little extra food at meal times in case someone arrived with whom you could share.

Q: Must we relinquish such customs?

A: My brother has kept my father's indentureship papers. He was given a tabeej, a small metal container that you can attach to a chain. The early immigrants used to place a special prayer written by their priest, or pandit, in this container and wear it around their neck or waist, to protect them from evil. When the indentured immigrants went to Trinidad, they were given this canister, about eight inches long and one inch in diameter, and their indentureship papers were put in it. They had to wear it around their neck or waist so that if they were leaving their village or estate and going in to the town of San Fernando, the canister would serve as a type of passport of identification.

Q: For you the Indo-Caribbean story began when your father came from India. Did you think the story would end in Canada?

A: We did not think we would ever settle in Canada. My husband never wanted to live in Canada, but it just worked out that way and we are quite happy here. We are comfortable, and make an occasional trip back to Trinidad.

LILIAN BANKAY

Lilian Bankay was born in Station Street, Kitty, Guyana in 1924. She is one of six children who were raised by their mother after their father died. The interview was recorded in Toronto on 31 January 1992.

Q: Were you able to go to school?

A: Yes. I was a very bright girl in primary school. I went to fifth standard. Then I left school, and went to learn sewing. I was married at sixteen.

Q: How did you meet your husband?

A: You know how it is with Indians: once a girl was about fourteen, it was time to start looking for a husband for her. So when I was fifteen my mother told my uncles that she wanted to marry me off, and asked them to look for somebody. I was introduced to my future husband one day in Kitty market, in the drugstore. Then he came to see my mother, and she said that if he liked me, he should write a letter to her, since that was the formal thing to do. He wrote to her; then we got engaged, and married.

Q: You said you were a bright girl at school. Yet you got married at sixteen. Did you not have any ambitions about a career other than being a housewife?

A: I was equipped to sew, and to be a mother and a housewife. That was the goal. I do not think there was anything else for girls then, unless your family was rich and could afford to send you to high school.

Q: Did you have a Christian wedding?

A: My husband's family were Christians, from Bush Lot on the West Coast of Berbice. But my mother was Hindu, and wanted a Hindu wedding. Of course, we had to please her. I didn't care what type of wedding it was. I used to go to Sunday School which was held in the bottom houses[1] in the area.

Q: Did you convert to Christianity?

A: Yes.

Q: Where did you live after marriage?

A: We lived in a two-bedroom cottage in Station Street.

Q: What was it like for a housewife in Kitty, in the 1940s?

A: I looked after my children, and someone came in to help with the housework. I had three children by then—three sons in 34 months. I was all wrapped up with my children. It was a joy. We grew up together, since I was very young, and was learning too. My husband who was ten years older than me taught me, and I used to read a lot. I had a sewing machine and my sewing would contribute something to the family income.

Q: Were you active in Burns Presbyterian Church?

A: Yes. I attended service every Sunday; my children went to Sunday School; and I was a member of the Band of Love, which was a women's organization that met every Tuesday at the Church.

But in 1950 my husband was laid off from his job of managing a drugstore owned by his uncle Dr J P Latchmansingh.[2] My mother then bought a house for us, and we opened our own business. It was mostly a drugstore, but we had haberdashery, dry goods, hardware and so on.

Q: Was your husband a qualified chemist or druggist?

A: No.

Q: But he was able to set up as an independent businessman?

A: Yes. And we were able to put all our children through high school. The girls were on scholarships, but we paid for the boys, and soon, we had four children studying abroad. It was the business that did it. We continued to live there and operate the business from 1950 until 1975. Then we closed it down and decided to leave Guyana because of political harassment.

Q: It seems to me that your mother was extraordinarily successful?

A: My mother was a widow with six children. She worked and cared for all of them. She could neither read nor write. She would save her money and buy a house; rent it, and use that income to buy another one. By the time she died, she had four houses.

Q: In the 1950s as your business was growing and your children were getting their education, what did you do with your time?

A: I helped in the business. I did social work. I was a member of the Balak Sahaita Mandalee,[3] then president, and also treasurer. I was a member of the Cancer Society, of the Board of Governors of the Campbellville Government School (I was appointed by the Government), and I was also on the Board of Governors of the Progressive College in Kitty. In particular I dedicated myself to the Mandalee, because that was good work. We took care of children without fathers, and sent them to school. We had boys attending Queen's College.[4]

Q: Did you have a building to house these children?

A: No. They lived at home, but we gave them groceries every week. We'd also give them clothing to cover them for the year, and shop for their school books and get them school uniforms.

Q: Where did your money come from?

A: We had fund raising dances in Georgetown, and we had a few people who contributed.

Q: I take it the Mandalee helped only Indians?

A: Once the case came up, we'd investigate, and if we saw that we alone could not do it, we would contact the Poor Law Board and speak to them, because one of the men there was on our committee, Mr Frank Veerasammy. He would visit such people, and if they were in dire need, more than we could help, he would help them. Every Christmas we had a big party, where every child would get a toy. Every August we had a party and gave a big feast.

Q: Did you have an office?

A: No. We'd keep meetings at members' homes. Each member had a meeting once per month at their home.

Q: But how would people know where to contact you if they needed help?

A: People would know to go to the President, the Secretary, or the Treasurer. Then we would call a meeting and decide how much to give them. We had a Visiting committee—consisting of four women, each of whom had a car. This committee would visit and then we would decide how much to give. We even went into the countryside, not just Georgetown.

Q: Did you have black members in your group?

A: No, but we had coloured, Mr Cedric Figuera and his wife, and others. The majority of members were Indian though, and the majority of cases were also Indian. Remember that other ethnic groups had their organizations, so we became more or less supportive of Indians, some of whom were illiterate and didn't know where to go, or when or how to get help. Most of my time was spent with these people, and with fund raising. After I left Guyana, everything broke down. I went back in 1990. I had the Mandalee bank book with $22,000 in it. It was updated, and I found we had about $40,000 in the bank. I recalled all the members who were there and re-formed the group. They had two brunches and a dance, and they've started to raise funds again. We rekindled things, and got new members—mostly young people—and they're working very hard.

Q: When exactly was the Balak Sahaita Mandalee started?

A: It was started in the 1930s by Mrs J B Singh[5] and Mrs L Kawall. I joined in 1948. Mrs Singh was a wonderful woman, very talented. She was honoured by the Queen for her social and cultural work.

Q: How did your political activities start?

A: In 1948 I think my husband supported Dr J B Bissessar as a political candidate. He was our doctor, and his niece is married to my brother. We supported him because of the family relationship. There was a bill about adult suffrage. Women who stayed home and earned an income got to vote, so I got to vote because of my sewing. After that I supported the PPP, because I liked their policies. I sympathized with the underdog, and people who were poor. I sympathized because all my neighbours were poor. When Dr Jagan came to power in 1957 things improved. People had a good life. The poor people could have gone in the store and got so much sewing material for a dollar. The cost of living went right down. Stores like Bookers could not see with

Cheddi to bring in materials from the Socialist Bloc because it prevented them from making their big profits.

Q: What did you make of a man like Dr J P Latchmansingh?

A: He brought his family down from Berbice and opened businesses for them to run. In spite of his profession, he liked business. He saw how politics could help his business too. He wanted to be a big man, whether in medicine, business or politics. He was interested in his own ego, to get fame. His brother, Bally Latchmansingh, wanted to help the farmers and people in the country. But he died early.

Q: Do you have personal experience of malpractice in the elections during the Burnham years after 1964?

A: Yes, we worked in the Campbellville constituency and they would never let anybody go near the votes. The soldiers had full control; they rigged elections. Even people who were dead had their names on the list, and were voted for.

Q: What is your opinion of Burnham?

A: He was a ruthless and self-centred dictator. He went in there to destroy the Indians.

Q: Was he racist from the beginning?

A: Yes. He said, "You all didn't want me . . . I'm going to bring you down to your knees." He swore that, and he did: he brought the Indians down to their knees. He didn't help anybody. He destroyed the country. He and his friends went in there to have a good time, and that was it. They filled their pockets and made their bank accounts big. That's all.

Q: But how was he able to make people obey him?

A: Fear. Take a man like Steve Narine. He was a civil servant. He and his wife also worked with us in the Mandalee. He was president and she was treasurer. Burnham hauled him into the PNC. He didn't go voluntarily. He went because he feared for his job and his family. He was told he had to join the party and he said "Okay."

Q: Otherwise he'd lose his job?

A: Burnham didn't say "otherwise," but you knew.

Q: Did the Church play any role in politics?

A: The Church abstained from saying or doing anything. They felt that if they participated, or took sides, they would be vandalized. People were scared even to say the right things and to condemn wrong, because once you said it, and it got out, you'd have to look out.

Q: Since you lived in Kitty, did you know Mrs Mohan Ram?

A: She lived in the same street with me. I knew her very well. She was a Vedic missionary who came from Surinam. She was more or less associated with Dr Bissessar. They ran a Hindi school in Kitty, at the Hindu temple. He was interested in education and had given money but since she and Dr Bissessar were Arya Samaj, the Sanatanists withdrew their children.

Q: Kitty in the 1950s was a mixed place in racial terms. What were race relations like?

A: Race relations were so good, you would not believe it. The Indians and the Negroes lived like family. It was like we could not do without them, and they could not do without us. They were always in our homes, and would do things for us. We trusted them.

Q: How did things begin to change?

A: I recall one incident that hurt my feelings badly. We had a Negro maid in 1962. Anything she wanted, we would give it to her. She was like family. If she said she wanted to go to a party, I would let her choose the material from the store; then I would cut the dress out, and stitch it when I went on my break; then I'd hand it to her to go to her party. She was with us for almost four years. But the day the problems started in 1962, we both went to the window, and saw the riots in the street. I said, "Look at these people! They haven't got any shame! Look what they're doing!" And she was shouting, "Rape them! Rape them!" egging on the rioters—all Negroes. I was so shocked that I said to her "Get out."

Q: This racial hatred could not have erupted so suddenly. Something must have happened between 1953 and 1962?

A: You see, the Indians were getting richer and richer. The Negroes were not making any economic progress. They were looking on, and I think it bothered them. Also, Indians all over the country were winning elections, and getting political power; and some Indians were saying, "Awee deh pon top," and that sort of thing. It hurt, and Negroes started to react. I'll tell you one thing though, the people of Campbellville where we had our business, never attacked us. All through the disturbances they never touched us. In my mind, they protected us.

Q: You're talking about black people in Campbellville?

A: Yes. Blacks in Campbellville were our customers and we helped them with credit, when they couldn't pay. We lost a lot of money that way, because their debts were just written off. But the break-ins into my business every other night were a centrally directed thing, because we were Indian.

Q: How do you know it wasn't local people?

A: Because the break-in men would come in a car, and the local people did not own cars. That is what forced us to leave Guyana in 1976. We left our house, which had been rebuilt and fixed up nicely, because there was a political aim to terrorize certain people. We were evidently targeted, and made to feel insecure.

Q: You had never planned to leave Guyana?

A: I had no intention. And I can tell you that it contributed to my husband's death. He came here and sat in the apartment and died. He wanted to go back home. He was accustomed to his business and people, and felt it was degrading to come and just sit in this apartment. We couldn't bring anything that we owned out of Guyana. My husband took it very hard, and he died here in hospital—on Christmas day, 1983.

Q: It's very sad.

A: It's so lonely living in an apartment. At home people would pass by and drop in for a chat. I think the older Guyanese people in Toronto may still want to go back. But when they go back and they spend a month, they are dying to come back here.

Q: The lifestyle here is so different though. It can lead to cultural assimilation and intermarriage.

A: Both of my daughters are married: one to a white person, the other to a Pakistani. One son is married to a white Jamaican, another to a black Jamaican. The third son is now married to a Guyanese who has lived in England for 25 years—his first wife died; she was Trinidadian. That is how it is. I always thought I'd get a Guyanese daughter-in-law or son-in-law. Now I have one, but not Indo-Guyanese.

Q: What kind of future do you see for your children in Canada?

A: I don't think they have a future here. The competition will be so great, I do not know.

Q: Is racial discrimination a problem?

A: No. I don't look for it; I'm a bully myself. If they ask me, "Where did you learn to speak English?" I would say, "Excuse me? I come from an English-speaking country; I was born in British Guiana. I was ruled by Her Majesty the Queen, just like you."

Q: What do you see in the future for yourself?

A: I have to live here. I have integrated myself into this society, and I'm getting involved. I don't expect to go back home to live: but I will visit Guyana. I no longer have friends there. Who am I going to mix with? What I find now in Guyana is that the dollar is all that counts. Depending on how much money you have, you're that person. It's the car you're driving. It doesn't matter how you got it. And now it is the Negroes who have the money, because the cream of Indian society have left.

Q: As a woman who grew up in Guyana in the 1930s and 40s, do you think you had a hard time compared with young women today?

A: I think they have a harder time now. I didn't have to go out to work. Perhaps life in Third World countries is hard, but at least we used to get help from our families. So I think my life was quite easy in comparison to my daughter's and her girlfriends', because they have to go out and work, and then come back and work in the home as well.

Q: But they now feel they are liberated and have more control over their lives. In the 1930s and 40s you did not have similar control?

A: I think that I was quite liberated. My husband was a very free man who never stopped me from doing what I wanted to do. As I told you, I did a lot of social work outside my home, and I would help my husband too in his business. I don't know what women are fighting for today. I think they're liberated enough already.

Q: Don't you feel that your life might have taken a different turn if you were a man, and that perhaps you might have achieved things that, because you are a woman, you did not achieve?

A: Well, that's my mother's fault. She didn't send me for higher education, because the custom then was to get daughters married off quite young. But I learnt sewing and housework, and these are very useful to me now. I don't think I missed anything, because I enjoyed life then just as much as my daughter enjoys her life today.

DR CHEDDI B JAGAN

Dr Cheddi B Jagan, who died in 1997, was leader of the People's Progressive Party (PPP) and President of the Republic of Guyana. Up to its independence from Great Britain in 1966, Guyana, with an Atlantic coast and borders with Venezuela, Brazil, and Surinam, was known as British Guiana. Its two main political parties are the PPP and the People's National Congress (PNC), which was led from 1955 to 1985 by its founder Mr L F S Burnham. Dr Jagan had trained as a dentist in the

US and Mr Burnham as a lawyer in the UK. They returned to British Guiana after their studies, and Mr Burnham joined the PPP after it had been formed by Dr Jagan and others. In 1953, this party won the first national elections that offered universal adult suffrage to the people of British Guiana. Dr Jagan became leader of the government and Minister of Agriculture while Mr Burnham was Minister of Education. But after just over four months in power, the PPP was removed from office by the British governor, Sir Alfred Savage, who had the assistance of troops sent out from Great Britain.

After this débacle, an interim legislature of nominated members administered British Guiana until fresh elections were held in 1957. Between 1953 and 1957, political representation changed sharply in the colony. Mr Burnham and some prominent members of the PPP broke away and created a new party, the People's National Congress. The PNC and PPP were the chief contestants in the 1957 elections, which were won by Dr Jagan's party. Dr Jagan became the Minister of Trade and Industry and his government served its full term of four years until 1961. In 1961 the PPP won fresh elections and Dr Jagan became Premier and Minister of Development and Planning. But this third PPP victory led to hostile agitation from the PNC and other political and social groups. In 1962 there were widespread strikes and riots. Elections were held in 1964, under a new system of proportional representation, which allowed the PNC and another party, the United Force (UF), to unite and gain a majority of seats over the PPP Mr Burnham became Prime Minister, and his party has won all elections between 1964 and 1992, although the fairness of these elections has been disputed by local and foreign commentators. Mr Burnham led the government continuously from 1964 to 1985 and Dr Jagan led the opposition from 1964 to 1992.

While the PPP has traditionally relied for support from sugar plantation workers who are largely Indian, the PNC has drawn its support mainly from urban centres, where the population is predominantly African. Despite changes in population distribution caused by racial conflict, emigration, and political policies, this pattern of political support generally holds good at present.

The interview mentions several individuals who have been active in the political and social life of Guyana and the English-speaking Caribbean. Hubert Nathaniel Critchlow (African) and Ayube Edun (Indian) were trade union leaders whose main efforts preceded the establishment of political parties like the PPP and the PNC. Jai Narine Singh was an Indian lawyer who first left the PPP to join the PNC then went on to lead the small, unsuccessful Justice Party. Dr J P Latchmansingh joined with Mr Burnham to leave the PPP and establish the PNC, but he died before the party held office. H J M Hubbard was a minister in the 1961 PPP government. Ashton Chase was a minister in the PPP government of 1953, and became President of the senate in 1961.

Among the Caribbean leaders or public figures who are mentioned is C L R James, perhaps the first genuine man of letters to emerge from the English-speaking Caribbean. For more than fifty years James wrote and lectured on subjects such as Marxism, literature, cricket, and many other topics related to the experience of Caribbean and Third World people. James was born in Trinidad in 1901 but lived in England, except for brief interruptions, since 1932. For a time in England James supported the work of the Marxist George Padmore, a fellow Trinidadian who actively promoted the cause of African independence and pan-Africanism. Among those Caribbean leaders who held office, Dr Jagan mentions Sir Grantley Adams, who was Prime Minister of Barbados in the 1950s and 1960s. Norman Manley's party was the People's National Party, which was later led by his son Michael. Dr Jagan also refers to his wife Janet, née Rosenberg, an American whom he met during his early days as a student in the US. Mrs Jagan is active politically and has held ministerial positions in former PPP governments. Maurice Bishop was leader of the socialist New Jewel Movement, which ruled Grenada for three years until 1983, when he was murdered. American troops then invaded Grenada.

Frequent reference is made to Dr Jagan's autobiographical work, *The West on Trial* (London: Michael Joseph, 1966). The subtitle of the book is "My Fight for Guyana's Freedom." Dr Jagan is the author of other books, including *Forbidden Freedom* (London: Lawrence & Wishat, 1954) and *The Caribbean Revolution* (Prague: Orbis Press Agency, 1979). Dr Jagan has also written numerous speeches, articles and pamphlets expounding the policies of his own party as well as his opinions on imperialism, global capitalism, nonalignment, and the general relationship between industrialized and nonindustrialized nations. Dr Jagan has received many honours, prizes, and medals, including the Lenin Centenary Medal and the Pablo Neruda Medal from the *World Marxist Review*. This interview was recorded in Toronto, on October 24 1984. Dr Jagan died on 6 March, 1997.

Q: How did your political career begin? What situations at home inspired you? What intellectual influences did you come under?

A: Firstly, I grew up in a sugar plantation, and my parents had come with their parents as indentured labourers in 1901 [from India] to Guyana. Therefore my situation was one of great poverty. My father was a sugar worker; and growing up in that environment gave me a strong working-class bias as distinct, let us say, from Burnham, who was originally in our party and whose father was a headmaster. A headmaster, in those days, even as a black person, was a fairly high position. He [Burnham] came from the middle class, whereas my origin was working class. Now, the second factor which influenced me was the fact that after my father sacrificed everything and put me through Queen's College, I couldn't get a job. It was merely by accident, so to speak, that I went to the US to study dentistry, and I had to work my way through my studies. That was another experience that inspired my political thinking: that even though you had education, unless you had influence, you couldn't get a job. Thirdly, I went to a black university in the US, Howard, where I was able to experience what racism means in a capitalist society. I got to know the real America, not just superficial things about the US as a "Land of Opportunity" and everyone becoming rich. Another fact which helped me to become interested in politics was that in America people identified me with India because I was Indian. At that time India was very much in the limelight, through the independence struggles conducted by Gandhi and Nehru.

Q: What years are you speaking of here?

A: I was in the US from 1936 to 1938 at Howard University. I was in Chicago from 1938 to 1943. In those years the independence struggle got me interested in Indian politics. It was revolutionary politics—the fight for independence [from British colonial rule]. During this period I also came under the influence of an Indian professor, who was expelled from India because of his politics. That brought me more into the question of radical politics—American radical politics and Indian politics.

Q: I think that in *The West on Trial* you also mentioned Nehru's autobiography, as an influence.

A: I believe I must have read it at that time.

Q: Then you went back to British Guiana after your studies in America, and you were elected to the Legislative Council in 1947. What was it like in that legislature in 1947?

A: The legislature was then like a hallowed chamber, where gentlemen would sit and debate in leisurely fashion, without concern for the people at the bottom. The franchise was limited and generally only people from the business or professional class could become elected. So I was, let us say, a maverick in those days.

Q: You were up against everybody?

A: That's right.

Q: How successful do you think you were at that time? What do you think you achieved?

A: I achieved a lot. I was able to speak for the working people forthrightly for the first time. There were some people before me who had been nominated—Critchlow and Edun—but by that stage they were old and not very virile. I came into the Legislative Council as the youngest member from a working-class background, and I brought a consciousness to the Council which was never there before. I had got married in 1943, just before my wife and I went home from the US. My wife was a member of the Young Communist league and I was able, through her, to get Marxist/Leninist literature—Lenin's booklets and *Das Kapital*. The radical politics in which I was involved in the United States began to gain clarity from those books, clarity from a working class perspective. So my contribution in the Legislative Council was effective. I was elected as an independent member, but I joined what was called the Labour Party and became its spokesman. But the Labour Party was playing a dual role—some of its members were in the Executive Council, while some were ordinary members of the Legislative Council. So in two years the Labour Party collapsed, and that created the conditions for our party [People's Progressive Party] to be formed in 1950. Because of my work, which was done in the parliament from 1947 to 1953, our party was able to gain the big victory in 1953.

Q: You were able to lay a foundation for that victory by your work in the Legislative Council?

A: Yes, a foundation which led both to the formation of the People's Progressive Party and to the victory of the party in 1953. More importantly, it was a foundation that united the working people who were divided until that time. Burnham, incidentally, came back from London in 1949 and helped in the process of unity. But the foundation had already been laid by me in the parliament, as well as outside.

Q: The political awakening which was achieved in 1953 was, in fact, initiated before Burnham's return in 1949 from his studies in England?

A: That is right. I forgot to mention one thing. In 1946 we founded a committee called the Political Affairs Committee (PAC), with myself, Jocelyn Hubbard who was secretary of the Trades Union Council (TUC) at one stage (1941), and a Marxist, a young man called Ashton Chase who grew up in Critchlow's office, and my wife. Through this committee, whatever was done in the parliament was related in the streets. So that kind of thing brought about a tremendous awakening of working-class consciousness.

Q: That was the consciousness that took the People's Progressive Party to power in 1953. But the government which was then formed lasted only a short time—133 days, when it was forcibly removed by the British. This is one of the most turbulent periods of Guyanese history and will no doubt be discussed for a long time to come. But if we can pass over the main facts—that the British landed troops in British Guiana, to enable the governor to dissolve the democratically elected government formed by the People's Progressive Party, and suspend the new constitution which had given Guyanese the widest franchise they had ever enjoyed—we can come to a question people are always asking, especially younger people: after the People's Progressive Party received such solid support, based on cohesion and a unified consciousness among the Guyanese working class, why did the party split so soon after its victory in 1953? In *The West On Trial* you suggest that the split occurred because Burnham wanted power, not just to be a leader, but to be *the* leader. After almost thirty years, is that still your analysis?

A: It was sheer opportunism. Some people adduce racial motives here. This was not so, because both Blacks and Indians joined in the split. Jai Narine Singh and Dr J P Latchmansingh—Indians—joined with Burnham to form a new party, the People's National Congress. In fact, had Jai Narine Singh and Latchmansingh not split from the People's Progressive Party, perhaps Burnham would not have done so. There was no racial motive. It was plain opportunism. That opportunism is manifest now in Guyana where people are starving and their rights being taken away. Now, the black working people are linking up with us, the People's Progressive Party, again. In other words, we are coming back to the unity we achieved in 1953. It was the split within the People's Progressive Party in 1955 that precipitated racial divisions among the Blacks and Indians. Then, in the 1960s, the black people were further incited by those calling our People's Progressive Party government a "rice government" or a "coolie government" Burnham used the black people to come to power, and now he is attacking them, his own supporters, as well as our supporters.

Q: Which seems to confirm the point about opportunism.

A: Yes, it was opportunism, because many times, in the 1960s, we offered him [Burnham] the opportunity to come back into the government. But he preferred to satisfy his personal ambition to be Number One and to have a lot of wealth. That was his main motivation.

Q: So you stick with the analysis that you gave in *The West on Trial*?

A: Yes, that is still clear, and is now showing up to be true. A point which you should notice too is that Salvador Allende in Chile and [Michael] Manley in Jamaica had strong rightist opposition which pulled them down, just as Burnham pulled us down when we were in government in the 1960s. Burnham has now a situation where we are pushing him to go forward since he says he is a socialist. If he were genuinely socialist, and if there is an open door to move forward in the country and unite it, he would take it.

Q: Now a subject which has always interested me, and people in universities generally, is your relationship with West Indian intellectuals, especially those outside Guyana, for example, C L R James. James claimed to be Marxist long before the People's Progressive Party was formed, and he has written a lot about Marxism over the last fifty years. What support did you get from him?

A: We never had much contact with James. In fact, whatever he did in that period [the 1950s and 1960s] was in support of Burnham.

Q: Why?

A: James was one of the first people, along with Padmore, to study in the Soviet Union. They [James and Padmore] became Trotskyites. As Trotskyites, or as neo-Trotskyites later, they probably did not agree with our line. Our line was not Trotskyism but Marxism/Leninism in relation to the Soviet Union and other Communist countries. So for that reason he could obviously not have any close links with us or support us. So far as other West Indians are concerned, we had links with one of the main Jamaican parties [the People's National Party] for instance. My wife and I went there in 1949 or 1950 at their invitation, because at that time this party, led by Norman Manley, was the leading light in the Caribbean—the People's National Party. We took inspiration from them in a certain way. But the essential difference between us was this. In our party a majority of the leadership was Marxist/Leninist and revolutionary democrats, whereas in their party that faction was a minority. So when the Cold War started in 1947 and hit the Caribbean about 1949, they were coopted to the Cold War along with the whole Caribbean leadership. From then on they justified, for instance, the suspension of the [Guyanese] constitution [in 1953]—all the so-called intellectuals, like Norman Manley.

Q: Manley did too?

A: Yes—Manley, Adams, Bustamante—all those people, those who were in the political limelight at that time—they supported the British.

Q: It is interesting, looking back now at your career, that you received no support from supposedly like-minded people in the whole English-speaking Caribbean region.

A: That is right. They [Caribbean politicians] were taking an opportunistic position too. We did not see any reason for changing course. The Cold War was intended to stop not only communism, but national liberation. Why should we have joined the Cold War? The reason they [Caribbean politicians] joined was because they were right wing social democrats linked with the Labour Party in England; and the Labour Party had also been coopted to the Cold War.

Q: I'd like to consider a little more this point about regional unity in the West Indies, and the fact that your career has taken a particularly Guyanese course. C L R James sees the salvation of the West Indies in terms of federation. The argument is that the individual territories in the English-speaking Caribbean region are too small to survive or prosper as independent states.

A: We agree that the countries are very small and therefore we need a bigger unity, but we do not want unity just for the sake of unity. You can have unity on a capitalist basis, like the Common Market in Europe, or CARIFTA—the Common Market in the Caribbean—or the Central American Common Market. These are all failing. We want unity; but unity with content, that is, with democratic, anti-imperialist, socialist content. Otherwise unity would fail. That is the essential difference between us and them [Caribbean intellectuals and politicians].

Q: It is very difficult to persuade different peoples to unite.

A: But it was coming. In 1979 there was a declaration called the Grenada Declaration, supported by Maurice Bishop from Grenada. At that time there was a progressive government in Dominica, and the Dominican prime minister signed the declaration. There was also a progressive government in St Lucia in mid-1979. The declaration called for unity, but on a different basis—the basis which I have been calling for all along. That is why Bishop, on the first anniversary of the declaration, referred to me as the dean of Caribbean socialism.

Q: There was some hope then of Caribbean unity formed on a progressive basis.

A: That's right. That is why the United States moved to split the government and party in St Lucia, to destroy the government in Dominica, and finally to invade Grenada.

Q: In view of that fact—that the type of progressive political movement which you envisage for the whole English-speaking Caribbean region is up against American imperialism and power—how do you see the future? The United States with their money and guns are not going to go away. What is your strategy?

A: Yes, one can argue that the United states, with its guns and money, will not go away. But if we take that argument to its logical conclusion, we will have to join them.

Q: Perhaps for a time?

A: If you join them, then you will become like the [Grantley] Adamses and all the others in the Caribbean, and the whole of Latin America, which is exploding, at the moment, because that is the policy of accommodation. Mexico, Brazil, all these countries are up to their necks in trouble, and are now opposing the United States. Witness the Falklands war, when the United States supported the United Kingdom. All the Latin American countries in the OAS [Organization of American States] condemned the United States. The OAS was previously an instrument of the United States. The point which we have to see is that the United States is a great power. We recognize that. In the 1960s they destroyed our government; they destroyed the Brazilian government; they destroyed the Bolivian government, and later the Chilean government of Allende and the [Michael] Manley government in Jamaica. But, there is still Nicaragua. Let us remember this too. On the invasion of Grenada, the United States was condemned by even its own allies, including Margaret Thatcher and Pierre Trudeau. In other words, within their own camp, the Western alliance, there are serious contradictions because of the American methodology of maintaining control. Recently, the former West German chancellor Willy Brandt said that the United States must recognize that Cuba has a role to play, and stop their policy of just thinking that Cuba doesn't exist.

Q: So there is still some hope.

A: Not merely hope. They were able to destroy Grenada because of division inside the party and government. Similarly, they were able to take over in Guyana because of the divisions, the ratting of Burnham and others. If we have unity inside the country, and if we have unity on a world and regional basis, imperialism will not succeed, powerful as the United States is. They were beaten in Vietnam, and again in the Falklands war, when their traditional friends who backed them in the isolation of Cuba, mainly through the OAS, came out in condemnation of them. What I am saying is that we have this option: join them, or fight for what we believe in, principle.

Q: You have always done the latter.

A: Yes, because I feel that if you join them, you will go down in the end, and the people will curse and kick you. It is better to keep fighting. We are now uniting the people in Guyana. About three weeks ago, we took the Trades Union Council out of Burnham's control, which he had for twenty-nine years. Movement is developing in the Caribbean. We now have groups and support, parties and others in the Caribbean which we never had before.

Q: Acknowledging that your long political career of almost forty years is still unfinished, what would you like people most to remember you for? Undoubtedly, you have inspired political awakening in Guyana. But you have had disappointments too. What would you like history to see as your main achievement?

A: Simply that I have justified my existence in contributing to the struggle of people for social progress, both inside Guyana and outside Guyana.

Q: What, for instance, would you regard as your greatest regret over this period? What did not work as you had planned, or as you had hoped?

A: I have not many regrets, to tell you the truth. I am a revolutionary and I have confidence, revolutionary confidence in the future, because what I stand for is winning. It took a long time in Guyana, but it is winning in the world as a whole.

Q: You have been in opposition for a long time.

A: That does not matter, because I am not fighting only for the people of Guyana. I am fighting for the people of the world. I am contributing to that struggle. That struggle is winning. That is why the United States is so hysterical at this moment, because of that very fact, that what I stand for is winning.

Q: Let me finish with the last sentence of *The West on Trial*: "But win we will. History and time are on our side." Obviously, you believe that as strongly now as you did then.

A: Well, as I told you, we were able to unite the people in 1953. That accounted for our big victory then. Since then, Burnham carefully and cleverly manipulated the situation to divide and rule. He was able to stay in power that long. We could not do anything with that. We had to work patiently to achieve unity. and it is coming again.

Q: So it is something like what happened before.

A: Exactly. It is coming back to what we had in 1953. It is a question of time. It is a question of process.

ROBERT JANKI

Robert Janki was born in Helena, Mahaica,[1] on 9 December, 1913. His father was headmaster of the Helena Canadian Mission School, which he attended before moving to Queen's College. He then joined the civil service. The interview was recorded in Toronto on November 10, 1991.

Q: I imagine your father was born a Hindu?

A: His father was Hindu.

Q: How did the conversion take place? Did it just come from attending school?

A: I would think so.

Q: But your father became a Christian, and you were born into a Christian family?

A: Yes, as Headmaster of a Canadian Mission School, my father had to teach Sunday school at Mahaica. There he came under the influence of the Canadian missionary Dr James Cropper[2] who was appointed by the Government as Land Settlement officer for Helena, De-Hoop and surrounding areas. In 1905, it was a pioneer land settlement scheme.

Q: What was Dr Cropper's role as settlement officer?

A: After the abolition of slavery, the Anglicans, Methodists, Congregationists, and other mainline churches went into teach ex-slaves, in order both to give them an education and to convert them to Christianity. But Indian immigrants who started coming in 1838 were left, so to speak "unchristianized." That is why the Canadian Presbyterian

Church appointed Dr Cropper to work among the Indians.

Q: What was his function exactly as a land settlement officer?

A: I think a lot of Indians were beginning to come off the sugar estates at the end of their indenture contract and they had to be settled into the community.

Q: How was your father influenced by Dr Cropper?

A: Through his association with Dr Cropper and contact with East Indians at Mahaica, my father learnt to speak Hindi. So in 1917, when the Government decided to expand the immigration department and take on more interpreters, my father applied and was appointed as an interpreter. My family then moved to Georgetown. It was around 1915 or 1916.

Q: What about your schooling and early life in Georgetown?

A: I mainly attended the Queenstown Moravian School. I sat for the Primary Scholarship Examination in 1925 under Mr D J Richmond, the Headmaster. Of three candidates that year, two of us won Primary Scholarships from Queenstown Moravian School—myself and Lucille Campbell, who later became Principal of Bishop's High School.[3]

Q: The scholarship took you to Queen's College?[4]

A: Yes. At the time, Queen's College was a very prestigious school. To attend Queen's was an achievement in itself. Twelve scholarships were awarded annually: five to students from Demerara, four to Berbice and three to Essequibo.[5] The competition was very stiff.

Q: Did you have a particular ambition when you were at Queen's College?

A: I guess we all had big ambitions at that time, to become doctors. But I tried to concentrate more upon my work. I went from examination to examination, because we took an examination every year. First of all, we had what was called the Cambridge Preliminary, and then the Oxford and Cambridge Exams which consisted of the Senior School Certificate, then the Higher School Certificate.[6]

Q: So you took the Senior School Certificate and then the Higher?

A: No. In my day we did not take the Higher level. The Senior School Certificate examination which I took in 1932 was the competitive examination for the Guyana Scholarship, and I secured the highest percentage of marks in the country. On that basis, I should have been selected for the Guyana Scholarship that year. But there was some misinterpretation of the regulations, because of an impending change in the system. This caused many pupils at Queen's College to take seven subjects instead of eight, whereas a student from St Stanislaus College—Percy DeCaires—took eight subjects and got the highest aggregate of marks, although his overall percentage was lower than mine. I got around 71 percent while he got 66 per cent; he even failed one of the subjects he took. But his higher total in marks gave him the scholarship. Representations were made on my behalf, but the final decision rested with the Executive Council. The editor of the *Daily Argosy*[7] wrote an editorial on the subject and called it "Topsy Turvydom."

Q: It is an extraordinary story. Having failed to get the Guyana scholarship, what did you do after you left Queen's College?

A: I had to hustle around looking for a job, and it took me almost a year to find one. In those days, after you'd reached that level, if you didn't have the funds to go and study abroad, the options were teaching, the Civil Service, or as we say, "Water Street."

Q: Business?

A: Yes, business. But you don't go and start at the top in Water Street; you start as a salesman. I eventually joined the Civil Service and worked first in the Deeds Registry. Then I went into the Treasury, and later I joined the Audit Department where I spent almost all the balance of my career in the Civil Service. I had to study accountancy. In 1953 I was awarded a Fellowship which took me to the United Nations in New York, and to Ottawa at the office of the Controller of the Treasury. I observed various government departments, to see their systems, and I took a course called Public Administration, Principles of Auditing, and Accounting Principles.

Q: But this was after you had spent about twenty years in the Civil Service at home?

A: Yes. In 1957, I took the first course for Auditors in the office of the Auditor-General of the Overseas Audit Services in London. In 1961 I took the second course in London.

Q: So you were self-educated after Queen's College. You did all these exams on your own?

A: Yes. We had no university then.

Q: In the Civil Service, were you influenced by any particular individuals, or relationships?

A: You have to remember that I joined the Civil Service in the early 1930s, when almost all the heads and deputy heads of departments were European or British. Some chief clerks were coloured or what was called "high coloured."

Q: Closer to white would be higher up in the Civil Service.

A: Right. But they did their jobs. They were all aspiring, trying to make a living and going from grade to grade. In those days, there were six grades, and it took a man a whole lifetime to become a First Class Clerk.

Q: During that whole time in the Civil Service, was race a significant factor in your career?

A: I would say that civil servants of light skin colour had an advantage. The administration didn't actually show it, or say it, but they acted on it. It was there. Even in later years, all or most of the Permanent Secretaries were "high coloured" people.

Q: There would have been no Indian in a high position in the Civil Service in the 1920s and 30s?

A: No. As a matter of fact, Mr J A Veerasammy[8] who eventually was appointed a magistrate, acted for an interminable period of time before he was confirmed in his appointment. I think he has the record for holding an acting position in the Guyana Civil Service.

Q: Were there any Indian professionals like doctors and lawyers?

A: There were lawyers like J A and E A Luckhoo.[9] Dr J B Singh,[10] a medical doctor, was also very much on the scene then, and was very highly respected. He started what was called the Hindu Maha Sabha.[11] Indians looked to him as a leader, and he did much to give them a sense of national pride.

Q: Wasn't Mrs Singh involved in artistic activity?

A: Yes. Dr Singh and his wife had got a group of East Indian young people together and put on a play called *Savitri* at the London Theatre in Georgetown, in 1937. After this play we called together a group of Indians to meet at Dr Singh's home and form an organization. Mr Francis Kawall acted as chairman, and we drafted rules for what come to be the "British Guiana Dramatic Society." Mrs Singh was elected as first President, and I was the Secretary. The Society existed from 1937 until about the 1950s. During 1937 to 1947, when I was an active member, we put on one play every years in May. On 5 May 1938, East Indians had a big celebration on the One-hundredth Anniversary of the arrival of Indians to Guyana. We put on a play in the Assembly Rooms which were part of a club for sugar planters. In later years we put on works by Tagore and Kalidasa, for example, *Sakuntala*. One problem was whether to call ourselves the "British Guiana Dramatic Society" or the "British Guiana East Indian Dramatic Society." We chose the former.

Q: But was there not a national dramatic society to which that name was better suited?

A: That happened later. We were the first organized dramatic society in Guyana. The later group called theirs the "Georgetown Dramatic Club." They were racially mixed, although the head of it was an Indian named Ranny Morgan. Their group originally consisted mainly of "high coloured" people. But later they took on others.

Q: Did the British Guiana Dramatic Society have Hindus, Christians, and Moslems? Did that matter at all?

A: No. That wasn't a factor. We deliberately embraced both Eastern and Western cultures. We invited people to play the sitar or piano, to sing Indian or Western songs, and to address us on topics of general cultural interest.

Q: What was your personal impression of Dr Singh or Mrs Singh?

A: I think they really loved the Indian race and wanted to dedicate their lives to the service of Indian people. I would say they succeeded in doing that. Mrs Singh later formed a group called the "Balak Sahaita Mandalee"[12].

Q: It was largely a women's organization?

A: Purely women. They had men only as auxiliary members.

Q: What role did the Presbyterian Church play in your life at this stage?

A: Around 1944, I was elected as an Elder in Burns Presbyterian Church, Georgetown. Of course, I used to teach Sunday School before that. I would say the church made a great difference in my life. My father was an Elder. He was one of the first ordained Elders in the Canadian Mission Church in Guyana. I say "Canadian Mission," because there was an evolution from the Canadian Mission, when Canada managed everything, to the Canadian Presbyterian Church which encouraged local people to be trained as catechists and ministers then to the Guyana Presbyterian Church which is run entirely by Guyanese. The Guyana Presbyterian Church is not dependent on Canada for grants. Today, Canada is not giving funds for salaries and wages, but for special projects only.

Q: Were you very active in Burns Church?

A: For many years, I was Elder for Burns' Church representing them in Presbytery.

Q: Wasn't Burns regarded as the main Presbyterian church in Guyana?

A: We used to say that Burns was the "Cathedral Church" of the Canadian Presbyterianism in Guyana. It was named after Mrs R.F. Burns of the Women's Missionary Society in Canada. She left a bequest that provided funds for building the church in 1939. The site of Burns Church was chosen by Dr Cropper between 1910 and 1915. The first building on the site was called St Cuthbert's Church, but it was set aside for a new building that became Burns.

Q: Was Dr Cropper the moving spirit behind both St Cuthbert's and the building of Burns Church?

A: Dr Cropper was the pioneer Field Missionary for Demerara, Dr James Scrimgeour for Berbice, and Rev. Gibson Fisher for Essequibo. Dr Cropper served in Guyana from 1895 to the 1930s. Although he chose the site for St Cuthbert's, Burns Church was built when Dr David Marshall was the minister.

Q: Cropper's contribution is immense, if he did all this work setting up churches and schools in Demerara.

A: Yes. But Scrimgeour did the same thing in Berbice and so did Fisher in Essequibo. In fact, the credit for Berbice High School[13] goes pretty well to Scrimgeour. He was the first principal. If I may say this, looking back, Scrimgeour was more an educationist than an evangelist. At that time too, each district had its catechists, because Dr Cropper and the other missionaries couldn't manage everything. The most he did was go once every three months and take Communion, so as to be in touch with each of the congregations.

Q: It seems that many of the early Indian leaders and professionals had some connection with Berbice High School.

A: I would say that many of the Berbice professionals who came to Georgetown to practice had their basic secondary education at Berbice High School. They also had the influence of the Canadian Mission Church—that must be said.

Q: How were the Canadian Mission Churches governed in Guyana?

A: We had two bodies: the Guyana Council of Churches and the Christian Social Council. The Guyana Council of Churches was made up of representatives from all the denominations, but the Christian Social council was a little higher, and their chairman was anglican, Archbishop Allan John Knight. I represented our church on both bodies at one time. I was chairman of the governing body for schools, and

I chaired the Canadian Mission Council, during a period just before the incorporation of the Guyana Presbyterian Church. The Canadian Mission Council received grants from Canada and decided how they were to be spent. With the impending transfer to the Guyana Presbytery, comprising mainly local Indian ministers and elders, there was no further need for the Canadian Mission Council.

Q: What was the job of the Canadian mission Council when it flourished?

A: It was incorporated within the laws of Guyana. So, until Presbytery became an incorporated body, the Canadian Mission Council had to remain to give the church its authority.

Q: In addition to your activities in the church and on the cultural scene, did you have any political awareness? Did you for instance feel that Indians were being poorly represented?

A: I don't know when it started exactly, but we had the British Guiana East Indian Association[14] which was active since the 1920s. In it were people like Arnold Emmanuel Seeram who became President of the Association at one time. He was from Mahaica, and was one of my father's students who went to London and studied law. He was very articulate and fluent. He went into politics and won the seat for Mahaica where he was born. He told the voters he was a son of the soil. Then there were members like C R Jacob, and H B Gajraj who helped to make the East Indian Association a body to be reckoned with.

Q: Was it largely cultural?

A: No. Its aim was to look after the welfare of the East Indians, particularly those who were still living on the sugar estates. When C R Jacob was in it, he was a thorn in the flesh of the sugar planters. Jacob knew the inside workings of the sugar estate, and used to put fire to the tails of sugar planters to secure better living and working conditions for the sugar workers. As a matter of fact, I believe his agitation led the British Government to set up the Moyne Commission;[15] and about 75% of the recommendations that the Commission later made involved matters that Jacob had previously discussed with the sugar planters. I remember being present on the first occasion when the East Indian Association met with Lord Moyne. Lord Moyne looked at the submission Jacob had made and asked him; "Mr Jacob, we have received this submission by the East Indian Association. Do you wish to remain as Guyanese, or do you wish to become a separate entity of East Indians?" And Jacob said: "No, my Lord, we do not wish to become a separate entity, but we wish to preserve our racial and national identity." I thought that was hitting Lord Moyne for a six.

Q: What was Jacob's background? Was he a professional man?

A: He was a businessman. He eventually had a store in Water Street after he left the sugar estate business. He also ran for a seat in the North West District and was elected to the Legislative Council.

Q: Were there many Indian legislators in the old Legislative Council?

A: There was Seeram, Dr Singh and Jacob. E A Luckhoo was a nominated member of the Executive Council at one time. So was J A Luckhoo. But the Luckhoos were safe.

Q: You mean that they were not expected to give trouble to the colonial government?

A: Some people felt that they did not represent either East Indians or East Indian causes.

Q: Was that one of the problems facing Dr Cheddi Jagan[16] when he began political agitation in 1947: that he came into conflict with those who should have been his natural allies, for example, this group of influential Indians in the East Indian Association? Did Dr Jagan believe that they were reactionary and did not really represent the cause of the working people?

A: The advent of Cheddi Jagan gave an impetus which was not there before—a remarkable impetus. The Indian leaders before him agitated in what may be called the conventional way. They kept meetings in school buildings and other similar places. But Cheddi Jagan and his wife went on the street corners carrying their message. It was a great pity, I think that they returned from the United States with a communist smear. If they had been just nationalists, without the communist smear, they would have fared much better as leaders. Still, they brought significant change. Dr Jagan couldn't help but put these old fellows in the shade, and I think that they realized it too. That is why the East Indian Association went by the board. The time was ripe for that sort of thing, because in the words of Jock Campbell, the chief executive of Bookers, a "wind of change" was blowing over the colonies. Remember that by 1947 India was independent, and soon afterwards Africans were calling for Independence. By the 1950s the British realized that they could no longer maintain the system of colonialism.

Q: Do you remember Indian Independence, when it came in 1947?

A: They had a big celebration at the East Indian Cricket Club grounds, and there were congratulatory speeches and messages. Indo-Guyanese did get a lift out of the Independence of India. I remember seeing Jai Narine Singh who was in the old Legislative Council, and later became a minister in Dr Jagan's government: he was shouting "Jai Hind! Jai Hind!" and another fellow on the outside was shouting "Pakistan, Zindabad! Pakistan, Zindabad!"

Q: If the British Guiana East Indian Association helped to raise the cultural awareness of Indo-Guyanese, and Cheddi Jagan awakened their political consciousness, where did the Afro-Guyanese come in? I believe, in the 1950s, they had the League of Coloured Peoples. What was the relationship between Africans and Indians?

A: Prior to about 1950, Indians and Africans lived together well. As I told you, Mr Richmond who taught me, was African, but he was like a father to me. He showed no distinction between me and Lucille Campbell, who was African. Mrs Richmond used to tell people that I was her first son, because when I used to go to their home for lessons, her oldest son Makepeace was just a toddler. And later, when Mrs Richmond saw me, as a grown man, she would kiss me, even on the street. My friends included Francis Vaughan-Cooke who later became Principal of the Teachers' Training College. He sometimes slept in the same bed as I did. I visited him, and he was always in our home. Racial relations were courteous, at least on the surface. But perhaps the seeds of rivalry were already planted by the divisive structure itself of a colonial society. For, around the 1930s, when the Indians began to educate their children and send their sons abroad to become professionals, the rising proportion of Indian against African professionals became noticeable, and the latter began to react. One incident from the late 1940s will illustrate this. The Government decided to give two medical scholarships—one of which went to Captain Nobbs's son, who was white, and the other to Balwant Singh. But the African community, through the League of Coloured People, raised strong objections, and a third scholarship had to be created for Frank Williams who was African. Other things happened too. The main businesses were traditionally white owned—Bookers, Fogarty, Geddes-Grant, Sandbach Parker. But now, by the 1950s, from the top of Water Street coming right down to Lombard Street, those white signs began to change, as Indian-owned shops sprang up. I remember attending a meeting at Bourda Green and I heard a group of African men talking among themselves. One turned to the other and said: "Man, the whole of Water Street is coolie." I think that helped to create envy between the races—the Indian advance into the professions and business. More Indian teachers also were entering the education system. Indians began buying up houses in Georgetown—prestigious homes. I think all that fanned the flames of racial rivalry, and the politicians took advantage of it and put one group of people against the other.

Q: So the evolution of social and cultural relationships between the two races was exploited for political purposes?

A: In most British colonies, I believe, Independence came as a result of a straight fight between the people and the British. But in Guyana the people were divided almost equally into two racial groups. Many Africans saw themselves as fighting the Indians more so than the British, and it suited the British to continue their traditional role of playing off one group against the other. In the process it was the Indians who suffered most because they had more to lose in terms of property and possessions.

Q: Since you remained in Guyana until 1978 when you came to Canada, you were able to observe, at first hand, that crucial period of political change in the 1950s and 60s.

A: After Dr Jagan returned to Guyana in the mid 1940s, he and Burnham[17] were best of friends, and as you know, they together won the 1953 elections. But the British government was scared that communism was going to take over. They sent troops, and suspended the constitution. There was then an interim period of political stalemate from 1953 to 1957 before the British Governor decided to call fresh elections. Dr Jagan won again. The British had to do something, because that was not what they expected. They had spent a lot of money during the period of interim government to try and win people away from Cheddi Jagan. Then, to crown it all, he won once more in 1961. By that time, of course, Burnham had split, and formed a separate party, and Dr Jagan defeated him.

Q: How do you see Dr Jagan's administration between '61 and '64? That was when all the violence erupted.

A: You must remember that we were still a colony, and the government most likely had to take instructions from Britain. I guess there were other pressures from the Americans, not to let communism take over. It was really difficult for him to govern. He was elected, but he didn't have the power.

Q: What's your impression of Burnham? Was he a man of good

instincts who went wrong?

A: I think Burnham might be called an opportunist. He saw the possibilities and took them. Seeing that the British and the Americans wanted an alternative to Cheddi Jagan, he seized the opportunity of playing the role they wanted. But I think he gave them a hard time over the years. I think he made demands on them which he normally might not have made, if he had been fairly elected. Because he was their "blue-eyed boy," so to speak, he knew that they had to give him everything he wanted. It was later on, when he realized that he couldn't really win a majority in fair elections, that he created the one-party state. Of course, he had Ptolemy Reid[18] who carried the racial message. Burnham did not advocate race openly: Reid did. He once claimed that the revolution is not over. What he meant was the revolution by Africans to displace the Indians.

Q: Burnham was preeminently concerned with his own selfish interests?

A: Yes. Burnham wanted to get as much for Burnham as possible. He liked power. He liked the limelight. I think somewhere he did claim to be an admirer of Machiavelli.

Q: What about other political leaders, for example Peter D'Aguiar?

A: There again, Peter D'Aguiar[19] was a businessman who made his way up from the bottom. He had a typical Portuguese rum shop business mentality. He acquired wealth but not recognition. He had style but not class. D'Aguiar always wanted to make out that he had class; but I don't think he ever succeeded. He was very ambitious. I would say he was as ambitious as Burnham, and by 1960, the time was ripe for anyone who opposed Cheddi Jagan to throw his hat into the ring. He was disillusioned when Burnham made Reid Deputy Prime Minister. But D'Aguiar knew, like everybody else, that Burnham was going to use him to get funds to borrow from abroad; then, as soon as he got more entrenched in power, he'd let him go. That is what happened. But I don't know whether D'Aguiar was so blinded by ambition for power that he didn't see it coming.

Q: Perhaps D'Aguiar hated Jagan and what he saw as Jagan's communism so much that he didn't really care about the alternative?

A: I think that D'Aguiar expected that more Indians would have voted for him in the 1964 election. I believe he was very disappointed in that. They were carrying the line abroad that Indians did not want communism, and that Indians would not vote for Cheddi Jagan.

Q: That may have been true for the city Indians, but not for the rural Indians. In any case, the 1964 election which introduced proportional representation was decisive in allowing Burnham and D'Aguiar to pool their votes and initiate a political process that not only destroyed Cheddi Jagan but Guyana as well. Guyana has been ruled by a one-party government for many years, and this has caused thousands of people like yourself to leave and come abroad. I'm sure you never envisaged you were going to end up in an apartment in Toronto. How do you feel about that?

A: I feel very, very frustrated. Even when I came over in 1978, I was still hoping that somehow or other we would get a change and be able to go back. I had rebuilt my house in Guyana, in preparation for retirement. But things got worse. My pension in Guyana now would probably just buy a loaf of bread. It is frustrating for people of my age to think of the potential we had, of what we enjoyed, and could have enjoyed, had it not been for this political morass that enveloped Guyana after 1964.

Q: There are many people like you for whom life over here is not one of choice, but second best. I believe that most of these people would want to go back to Guyana if they had the chance.

A: I'd go back and ride my bike tomorrow.

Q: What specifically do you think is responsible for Guyana's decline? They say that Guyana is the second poorest nation in the Western Hemisphere, after Haiti.

A: I would say that the blight started in 1964. I think if we had elections, and things could have been changed, then we might not have been in this situation. It was that frustration of not being able to bring about a change in the government, (from 1964 until now), that is responsible, I think, for Guyanese being at the bottom today.

Q: In a way it's ironic that those of us who were brought up in the Canadian Presbyterian church, should come to Canada. I remember as a boy in Guyana, hearing about Knox College and other places like that, and meeting Canadian Presbyterian ministers who seemed to represent wealth, modernization and spirituality all at once. What do you think the future holds for us in this country, especially for the younger ones?

A: I don't see that they have any option other than to integrate into this community, especially those who were born here. My daughter is 42 and my son is 35. Neither has any nostalgia for Guyana. Even if they went to Guyana for a holiday, it would be more or less for sightseeing. First of all, there are few people there whom they would know. Secondly, they wouldn't have any special concern for the remaining Indians there, because they are not related. That is a different generation there now.

Q: Does this mean that our Indo-Caribbean culture will become integrated here in Canada and gradually, as far as we can see, become erased perhaps in a few generations?

A: I would imagine that that is inevitable. In Guyana, the Hindu man taught his children Hinduism. Whether they liked it or not, the children sat there while the pandit went on with the ceremony. They still remember something about it. On Sunday morning, my wife would say to the children: "It's eight o'clock, get ready and go to Sunday School," and they would go. The Muslim man would do the same thing. he'd say: "Boy, it's time to go to the Mosque. It's Friday, you have to be there at one o'clock." But what do you tell them here! Here they say they're taking away the Lord's Prayer in schools because it violates other peoples' human rights. In all schools in Guyana, we had Christian religious instruction, and you tell me one Hindu or Muslim child in the whole history of Guyana who went astray because he heard the headmaster or teacher giving religious instruction!

Q: It is quite a journey for our people, from India, to the Caribbean, and now to Canada.

A: But I must ask you this, you and all the others. Please do not let what those people did die. Please let it be recorded, so that they'll be remembered. They were pioneers. They suffered in the mud. They worked day and night. Rain came and wet them; the sun came and dried them. They would get up at four o'clock in the morning, and walk miles to the backdam without any transportation to take them. They carried their saucepan with a little rice and pieces of bora or a piece of squash, and they sat down about half past eleven to eat by the trench corner, after which they would wash their saucepan and use it to drink trench water. It was they who built Guyana prior to 1964. Future Guyanese of all races and groups should know this.

SIMON RAMESAR

Simon Ramesar was born in Port of Spain, Trinidad on 8 February, 1924. He now lives in Kingston, Ontario, where he teaches at Queen's University and practises as a psychiatrist. The interview was recorded on 6 March, 1992 in Kingston, Ontario.[1]

Q: Was it your father or father's father who came directly from India?

A: My father's grandfather and my mother's grandparents came from India.

Q: Do you have any information about the circumstances under which your great-grandparents came to Trinidad?

A: No.

Q: What did your father do?

A: He was a jeweller in Chaguanas, a primarily Indian community.

Q: Was he Hindu?

A: No. He was Christian, but of Hindu background. We went to Sunday School and church. A lot of the people in Chaguanas were still Hindus, but my family had converted.

Q: What happened after primary school?

A: I went to secondary school in Port of Spain. I first went to St Mary's College which was run by the Roman Catholics, and then to Queen's Royal College. I did not like St Mary's because it was too authoritarian. I also thought that the discipline was unfair. The atmosphere discriminated against non-Catholics, and especially against those who weren't white.

Q: Were you happy at QRC?

A: Yes. I went on to my School Certificate there. I remember one teacher Gordon Pilgrim, who taught mathematics. He instructed us on being good people. He was a strict disciplinarian, eminently fair, and a good model of a man. He was a Barbadian who had won a scholarship and had gone to Oxford where he did an MA.

Q: Was snobbery a problem at QRC?

A: There was an hierarchy with the sons of British colonial administrators at the top. The local whites came after them, and then the rest of us. This was how it was in the population at large, and it simply translated itself into the school. Most boys were black. There were very few Indians. The Whites were few too, but they had prestige. Still, there was no real discrimination.

Q: Did you go on to the Higher School Certificate?

A: No. I wanted to get into university, and as soon as I had the entrance requirements, the School Certificate, I went on to have a good time.

Q: Did you know what you wanted to study?

A: It was understood in the family that I'd be a doctor. I don't know why.

Q: Where were you going to study?

A: I was to go to England, but the Second World War intervened, so I came to Canada instead.

Q: Where in Canada did you come to?

A: To McGill University, in Montreal, in 1942.

Q: How did you get on at McGill?

A: It was a novel experience. I was free from parental constraints and I learnt to do things that I never dreamt of doing before, like playing billiards and poker, and going to nightclubs. Studying was secondary, although I did the minimum amount of work in order not to get kicked out. But I didn't stay at McGill. I won a Colonial Development and Welfare Scholarship to study Medicine at Sheffield University in England.

Q: How did you win this scholarship as a Trinidad student in Canada?

A: The British colonial government asked McGill to advertise the scholarships, and then appointed someone at McGill to interview students and make the selections.

Q: When did you go to Sheffield?

A: I went in 1944 and entered the second year of the medical course.

Q: How did you find Sheffield?

Q: England was a sad place in 1944. I arrived in Sheffield on an October evening about 4 o'clock: it was dark, and Sheffield was very dirty at that time, with a lot of smog and coal dust in the air. I practically cried. I felt I had come to the worst place I could have imagined. And it remained like that for quite some time. There were a few colonials in Sheffield at that time, and they provided some company; but there was a distinct sense in which we were not English, which meant that we were not really *personae grata*.

Q: There was no discrimination as such?

A: Not overtly.

Q: Did things change from 1944 to 1949? It was the end of the Second World War and you had moved from a colony to the imperial centre. Did your colonial world become enlarged?

A: I became interested in politics and music. I was active in the Socialist Society, and took part in occasionally sports like boxing and cricket.

Q: Did you get married in Sheffield?

A: Yes. I got married in September, 1945; and my daughter was born in December, 1946. I had met my wife while I was at McGill. She joined me one year after I went to Sheffield.

Q: Did your scholarship funds entirely support you and your family?

A: I got some additional support from my family in Trinidad.

Q: What happened after graduation?

A: I went back to Trinidad to work for the Government, because that was required by the scholarship: after becoming qualified, one had to go back and work for five years in the Government service.

Q: Going back to Trinidad gave your family in Trinidad an opportunity to meet your wife and daughter?

A: Not really. My wife had met my mother earlier in Baltimore where my father had gone for medical treatment. My father died in January 1945 while he was in Baltimore.

Q: Did you establish a career in the Government service?

A: No. I worked in a Government hospital in Port of Spain, for one year and then I quit. Of course I had to pay back the Government a certain amount of money.

Q: Did you become politically active?

A: In a marginal way only. I took a great interest in politics, without being a politician.

Q: What was the political situation like in Trinidad at that time?

A: It was in a state of transition. The British were leaving the colonies and setting up some sort of self-government, so there was a growing sense of becoming free to govern ourselves. But there was no organized party with an outstanding, recognizable leader.

Q: I suppose you were more interested in your professional career?

A: Yes. I was busy establishing a career. I tried to make money and be as comfortable as I could.

Q: Were there other children?

A: Yes. My son was born in 1950.

Q: What about the rest of your family?

Q: After my father died, my mother continued to run the family business, which was a jewellery and pawn shop. I have one brother, and when I returned, he went off to England to study law. He came back in 1955.

Q: Did you have a hand in paying for your brother's studies?

A: No.

Q: I wonder if you felt obliged to help with other family members.

A: My mother claimed my first pay check, because she bought me a big, American car, a Studebaker, when I returned from England. There were times when she was broke and I gave her money, but I was never made to feel obligated or indebted.

Q: It seems that you adapted remarkably well to the power structure in colonial Trinidad. Isn't there a slight contradiction in having socialist principles and not practising them by taking a stand against colonial rule? Or had you given up your socialist principles by then?

A: I was not willing to sacrifice either my welfare, or my family's, in order to aid the poor. I had a friend who was an ardent communist, and I remember writing to tell him that I didn't believe that communism or socialism was from me. I was going to look after myself first, and if poor people benefited in the process, then that was a bonus. But I wasn't going to go out and look after them at my expense. A year after I started to practise, I got into a serious car accident, and was laid up for about three months. After that, I went back to practising, and within five years, I had made so much money that I started to feel I could retire. But I kept on working and having a good time. That was a very great part of my whole orientation in life—to have a good time.

Q: It was the mid 1950s, the beginning of the agitation by Eric Williams. Are you saying you were detached from all that?

A: No. I went to listen to Eric Williams in Woodford Square, and when he said that he had disciplined the Hindu Maha Sabha[2], which he described as a "refractory minority," I recognized that I had to get out of Trinidad. I didn't like Eric Williams; I didn't like the PNM; and I didn't like anything they stood for because they were a Negro racist party.

Q: When did this awareness come about? Was it after they won in 1956?

A: No. It came the night I hear Eric Williams say, in so many words, that the Hindu Maha Sabha, as a group of people—that meant all Indo-Trinidadians—were *personae non grata*: he was making the point that Negro nationalism was going to take over in Trinidad. And I decided that I had to get out.

Q: There is a perception that Eric Williams and the early PNM were well-intentioned, and nonracial.

A: Absolute nonsense!

Q: So those Indians who joined the PNM in the beginning were fooled by Eric Williams?

A: Deluded. They were interested in being part of a power structure. That's all. I know for a fact that some had no principles at all.

Q: Isn't it a little defeatist for someone like you to come back as a professional person to Trinidad, and perceive the bleak future for the country as you saw it, then jump ship as it were?

A: You're asking about loyalties now. I do not own my first loyalty to any race: I am not a racist. Eric Williams was a racist, but that did not mean that I had to become a racist in order to oppose him. I got out of a situation in which I was going to be involved in racism.

Q: But you were leaving behind people who were going to be the victims of racism.

A: I am not a rescuer. They can look after themselves. I am not on any mission. I was not out to save the world. People who do that usually get crucified.

Q: For someone living in the confused situation of a British Caribbean colony in the 1950s, you appear to have had remarkable clear-sighted values, even if they were dominated by self-interest What role did religion play in your thinking?

A: I had to go to Sunday School until I was fourteen. But internally, I abandoned the Church by the time I was eight. I recognized the hypocrisy in the whole structure, and had no respect for it.

Q: When did you leave Trinidad this time?

A: I left in 1960 to study psychiatry at McGill University. We had four children by then.

Q: Since your wife was Canadian and you had already studied at McGill, it must have been like coming home.

A: Yes. I qualified as a psychiatrist in four years, and then worked at McGill. I got an appointment as a junior academic. In 1965 I came to Kingston to join the University's medical staff and have been here ever since.

Q: Did you maintain a connection with Trinidad at all?

A: I used to visit my brother there, but I have been doing that less and less often. My mother died two years after I came to Canada, and I knew then that I wasn't going back to Trinidad to live. I was going to be resident in Canada.

Q: Since you left Trinidad, the PNM remained in power for about thirty years causing large-scale emigration from Trinidad of all sorts of people, but particularly Indians. Indo-Trinidadians are now doubly exiled, firstly from India, and secondly from the Caribbean. They have suffered cultural loss twice.

A: I don't believe they lost anything, because I don't believe they brought much with them to Trinidad. I learnt more about Indian culture from reading than I ever learnt by living in Trinidad. Indians in Trinidad were uncultured. They brought with them a smattering of knowledge about their holy books. They came to Trinidad as the lowest of the low, and remained like that, just struggling to keep body and soul together. They didn't bring any culture!

Q: That's culture—the struggle to stay alive. But you're right, by and large, these were people who got the wrong end of the stick in India and met a similar fate in Trinidad.

A: I don't feel I got the wrong end of the stick, not my family anyway. I was well off ever since I can remember. I did not feel economic deprivation, but I was aware of the fact that I was a second class citizen in my country.

Q: You do not feel you are a second class citizen in Canada?

A: No. I do not feel like that.

Q: You speak of yourself very much as an individual, detached from any cultural group.

A: That's quite right. I am what is known as a "marginal man" with no identity. I have multiple identities, but I do not have a primary identity.

Q: But people belong to communities, or groups or cultures.

A: Some people belong, while other people are mysteries. I am a mystery. I do not fit in anywhere.

Q: Marginalization usually entails intense agonizing and even self-torture.

A: I had to do a lot of work in straightening myself out to accept the fact that I am a marginal man, and a mystery. And I look after a lot of people every day who are mysteries. I understand them very well because I know what they go though.

Q: It is important understanding and coming to terms with yourself, but understanding a situation of loss or marginalization, does not seem enough. Shouldn't one try to rectify the situation? Is there not a basic human instinct to reintegrate our lost or marginalized selves into something that is more whole?

A: Suppose I suggest that I have been reintegrated in the process of becoming acculturated into Canadian society? In this process I have adopted many Canadian attributes, ideologies, and attitudes.

Q: These attitudes are fairly loose. On the whole Canada seems to have a flexible nationality that is accommodating to marginal people, for example. But Canada may be suffering from the national delusion of offering a home to all the world's unwanted people. The openness of the Canadian identity has still not produced agreement on bilingualism and Québec. Canadian nationality is based on "two founding races" which was a false concept from the beginning, since the first founding Canadian race was people of the First Nations, not the British or French. Yet, you and I and many others like us have come here to lead a new life while the community from which we came is still there in the Caribbean, suffering great political injustice and insecurity. Some of us grieve over what we left behind.

A: I don't have any sense of grief. I see the Caribbean, and I only know Trinidad, as a cesspool of iniquity. All the races are involved in it. I have no sympathy for [Basdeo] Panday and others who are agitating for change. What is important is that there is no law and order in Trinidad. The country is corrupt from the top right down. It needs to clean up its values, and its ideologies. That's all I see there, and I don't want to be part of it.

Q: *The Middle Passage* was written in 1962, saying virtually what you have said, and Naipaul was roundly abused. Albert Gomes's *Caught in a Maze of Colour* also recalls the "farmyard ethos" of his early years in Trinidad in the 1920s and 1930s. He notes how people delighted in cruelty and laughed at the pain of others.

A: This is not peculiar to Trinidad. Fifty million Americans look at Tyson beating Spinks and are hurt because the bout only lasted about seventy seconds and they did not get their money's worth. Football on a Sunday afternoon is also part of the business of inflicting pain. It's a very human quality.

Q: But surely Canada is not the same as Trinidad or we would not be living here. There would be nothing to gain by remaining here.

A: The more economically well-developed you get, the more necessary it is to have law and order in order to retain your wealth. If there was chaos, everybody's wealth would be in danger. We have an organized society in Canada because we are rich. The poorer you get, the less law and order you need. When you get down to the really poor, you find no law and order; usually it's dog eat dog. If you believe it's idealism that runs the world, you're making a sad mistake.

Q: I suppose you would point to the kind of idealism which fired the Socialist Revolution in the Soviet Union. It cherished the ideal "from each according to his ability; to each according to his need." I agree that Marx, Engels and Lenin might have been too idealistic and that socialism became totalitarian. But I come from a part of the world which was colonized, and colonized people constitute a majority in the world. I believe that the peace of the world depends on a stable relationship between this majority of "colonized" people—the Third World—and the others who possess economic wealth and technology. To me, it approaches something close to irresponsibility to assert that human welfare is determined entirely by economic and technological factors.

A: I believe that our highest virtue is to seek our own self-interest. That means we should endeavour to develop ourselves to the fullest potential, socially, economically, physically, mentally, morally, and spiritually. When we have reached our full potential, we must recognize that our self-interest will be best served if we take care of those on whom we depend. Therefore, if I develop myself to my fullest potential in every way possible, and I give my best to those who depend on me, then I can expect that they will give their best in return to me when I am in need. Then we'll all benefit.

Q: What if they don't give you their best after you have taken care of them?

A: I have to have enough others on whom I depend in order to get the benefits that I give as a quid pro quo.

Q: Have you visited India? Naipaul's *Area of Darkness* is a bitter account of his first visit there.

A: That was not my experience. I went to India twice. I got depressed the first time, and the second time I was able to seek out the background from which Indians come—their temples and mythology.

127

It was fascinating. I had already seen the poverty, dirt and disease, and regarded them as the price I have to pay for the other things.

Q: Did you know V S Naipaul?

A: His grandmother and my grandmother were neighbours. They had the Lion House which was about a hundred yards away from us. I knew him vaguely at school but I was ahead of him.

Q: After he immigrated to England, Naipaul said that Trinidad didn't have the social complexity and psychological intricacies that a serious literary imagination could feed on: therefore he had to live in England. Yet when I look at his more recent books written about England, they do not compare in literary merit with the earlier ones based on Trinidad or the Caribbean. The filth, disorganization and chaos that you see in Trinidad were also reported by him in his early books. They were his most deeply felt experiences, and he has made solid art out of them. It is for this early work that he has been lionized by critics, and knighted by the Queen. His recent work is different. The technical efficiency is still there, and may be even better. But there is apparently less for his imagination to feed on, less substance. I suspect Naipaul was mistaken in believing that Trinidad society could not support his art.

A: What you're claiming is that Naipaul has lost touch with his soul. There is now an artificial soul that has been erected over time, and it is made up of intellect. He has adopted a new identity.

Q: I think there is a danger in adopting the hard headed, realistic outlook that you espouse, although it tempts those of us who have also adopted a life of exile.

A: I look after people, who come to me with sick souls. I have to improve my soul in order to attend to their soul, and that keeps my soul in good repair. My soul is not Indian or Negro or English; it is just a soul. It has become just a poor soul looking after other poor souls, who are trying to do the best we can in a world where there is a lot of misery and suffering. I am very much aware that what makes us all equal as human beings is the fact that we are weak, helpless and suffering, and that these qualities form a common denominator which exists in all people. But I am aware of equality with my fellow man, not with my fellow Trinidadians or Africans or Indians.

Q: Are there not cultural components to these abstractions? Love for one's fellows needs cultural or social expression to be translated into concrete action.

A: I have forms of cultural expression. I would prefer to eat curry rather than anything else. Other people might have a preference for something else. But these are not things that have to do with a real sense of belonging.

Q: Surely people do feel a need to identify with such clearly marked habits and customs as food, tastes, language expression and so on.

A: It is all illusion. The fact that they feel it or do it does not mean that it is real. They have to be able to separate the real from what is the illusion.

Q: What you describe sounds like the Hindu concept of "maya."

A: Very much so. If there is any culture inside me, that is it. Not only is it Hindu: it has been refined by Buddhism, and then refined again by Zen Buddhism. That is what can get us down to the real Indian culture which is based on the wisdom of the mythology which came out of India; not superficial forms of culture or linguistic expression.

DR IBBIT MOSAHEB

Dr Ibbit Mosaheb was born in Trinidad on 28 October 1919 in the village of San Francique. His mother died when he was two years old. The interview was recorded in Kingston, Ontario on 21 February, 1992.

Q: What is your family background?

A: My father was a businessman who ran the village grocery store. He was a Muslim but became first a Catholic, and then a Presbyterian. Since the village was mixed racially, my father's customers consisted of all races and included many people from the smaller islands—Grenadians, Barbadians, Vincentians. We had a large cistern in our yard and all the villagers used to come there to obtain their drinking water. At one stage the Muslim community took objection to my father selling pork and alcohol, and this caused some friction. But my father had by that time become a Catholic and the friction died out.

Q: What schooling did you have?

A: At first, the nearest government school was about four miles from our village, but when the Canadian Presbyterian missionaries came, they built a school nearer to us. That's where I received my elementary education.

Q: What about secondary schooling?

A: I left San Francique in 1931 when my father moved to San Fernando. I spent one year at San Fernando Presbyterian School to complete my elementary education. Then, I went to Naparima College in San Fernando.

Q: How did Canadian Presbyterian missionaries become established in Trinidad?

A: The first Canadian minister who went to Trinidad was Rev John Morton.[1] He had health problems and decided to take a holiday in Barbados. He sailed on one of the Lady boats[2] out of Halifax. The captain was taking a cargo of staves (metal to wrap around wooden casks of rum), but he discovered that he could get a better price for the staves in Trinidad. There, Rev. Morton started a church with the help of some plantation owners. He took over a church from the Baptists in the village, and his first congregation was black.

Q: How did you get on at Naparima College?

A: I passed the Senior Cambridge Exam in 1938.

Q: Did you go on to the Higher School Certificate?

A: No. My father was prepared to send me away to study. So I left Trinidad in 1939 to go to Howard University. The night before I left, my father had a big reception for me, inviting almost everybody in the village. We had moved back to Penal where my father had resumed business in order to earn money to support me in university. I travelled on a Dutch boat and met two other young Trinidadians who were also going to study dentistry in the US. I also met Elsie, Eric Williams's[3] first wife, on board the ship. She, Eric and I later became friends.

Q: Did the war have any impact on your studies at Howard?

A: War was declared four days before we arrived in New York, and when I got to Washington, where Howard is, I discovered that the university was predominantly black: all of its students were of African origin whether they came from the United States, the West Indian islands, or from Africa itself. Those were the days of apartheid, and Jim Crowism, when every American city had its white section and black section.

Q: If you didn't know that Howard was a black university, you could not have known very much about it. Why did you pick it?

A: I picked Howard because the dentist who advised me in Trinidad had gone to study there. In those days most Trinidadian students went either to Howard or to England.

Q: What was life like at Howard?

A: I found Howard to be a very good school. Most of the heads of department had graduated from Oxford, Yale, Harvard or Princeton. I met Eric Williams there. He had just graduated from Oxford and started teaching at Howard. He was in charge of the Social Sciences, and I was taught by him. If I developed a West Indian consciousness at Howard University rather than in Trinidad, it was because of Eric Williams's influence. His subject was Caribbean history. He was writing *Capitalism and Slavery*[4] at the time. The subject—the economic reasons for the abolition of the British slave trade—was also the subject of his dissertation at Oxford. It had been suggested to Eric by CLR James.[5]

Q: Did you experience racial prejudice at Howard?

A: I was surprised to find that Americans distinguished between Blacks and myself. I discovered this when I wanted a job, and had gone to the black employment bureau. The place was filthy and the seating accommodation consisted of hard benches. I don't think I was there longer than two minutes when a white American came up and said that if I had come to look for employment I was in the wrong place. He sent me to another employment bureau for Whites which was beautiful, with lovely chairs and carpet. So I had an interview there. White Americans regarded all Indians as Hindus. Even though I was Muslim, they classified me as a Hindu. But there was strict segregation between Blacks and Whites, and since I associated throughout with Blacks I was able to observe prejudice at first hand. At the time, Canada was in the war, but the United States had not entered yet. So my exit from Washington was very peaceful when I left for Montreal to study dentistry. At first, I stayed in the men's residence of McGill University—Strathcona Hall—but the residence changed hands and we had to leave. Afterwards, I lived mostly with French families in Montreal. There was less discrimination among the French. I can't say the same for the English in Montreal.

Q: How long did you stay at McGill?

A: About five years. I made many friends, and married a girl from Montreal. Her father was from Barbados and her mother from Scotland. We're still together.

Q: How did your wife's parents meet?

A: Her father left Barbados in the 1920s and met his wife in Montreal. They had four children—two girls and two boys—who inherited both a West Indian and a Scottish heritage. So when we returned to Trinidad after my studies my wife had no problem fitting in to Trinidadian society.

Q: After graduation you went straight to Trinidad?

A: No. I first went to Eastman Dental Dispensary in Rochester, New York and did a postgraduate course in Children's Dentistry. This took four months. But I should mention one important thing that happened in Montreal. There was a strong West Indian Society at McGill, and I played a very active role in it. I found myself more at home with my fellow Caribbeans than I did with Indians from India, who seemed to shun us Indo-Caribbeans because our ancestors came as indentured labourers from India. I always called myself a West Indian to distinguish myself from Indians from India. But I noticed that my Indo-Caribbean colleagues were not active in the West Indian Society. I felt that it was more important for Indo-Caribbeans living in places like Montreal to have a good relationship with students of other ethnic groups coming from their own country. I couldn't support the idea of thinking that it was better to associate with the Whites rather than with our own West Indians. Anyhow I graduated from McGill on 28 May 1947, in dentistry, and got married on 31 May. Then, after my brief stay in Rochester, I went back to Trinidad to set up practice in 1948.

Q: Were your studies supported by your father?

A: Yes. Throughout my years away.

Q: Did he also help you to buy your practice?

A: He bought a practice and a car for me, and I got established in San Fernando.

Q: You left Trinidad as a young man in 1939, and returned nine years later with a profession. What changes did you notice?

A: The war had made an impact on Trinidad, as a result of the American Military Base. A lot of money was being circulated. Trinidadians were working for the Americans and getting higher wages than from local employers. In 1948 the island economy was sluggish just after the post-War boom. The former Leader of the Opposition, Bhadase Maraj[6] used to be a scrap dealer, and made money by buying supplies from the Americans, and reselling them. Everything was available at the Base, including cars, washing machines, and dishwashers. Some of my patients were prostitutes who were not only paid by American soldiers with American cigarettes, but would pay my bill with the same cigarettes.

At the same time I was toying with the idea of coming back to

Canada, but deep down I knew that I could not leave Trinidad while my father was alive. I owed him a debt of gratitude for financing my studies, and I knew that my being in Trinidad as a professional made him happy. Still, after a year or so, I visited the Canadian High Commission in Port of Spain in order to get my papers ready, in case I wanted to come back to Canada. At first, the Canadian High Commissioner said it would be almost impossible for me to get into Canada because I was classified as an Asiatic, and Canada did not want any more Asiatics; but when I told him that my wife was a Canadian citizen by birth, he offered me a Canadian cigarette, and brought forms for me to fill out. Within three weeks I had my permanent residence acceptance to come to Canada.

Q: Why did so-called Asiatics have a problem getting into Canada at that time?

A: A black West Indian would not have had the same problem. I think it was because the Canadians felt Blacks would not give them the same economic competition. They were afraid of the Asiatic skill in business.

Q: How did your political career start?

A: In 1948 Eric Williams was on the Anglo-American Caribbean Commission[7] which involved only the English and the American. Later, it was changed to the Caribbean Commission involving governments that had an interest in Caribbean, for example, the French and the Dutch. The Commission was set up in Port of Spain—in Kent House—and Eric at the time was Secretary of its Agricultural section. The post of Secretary General of the Commission rotated between the British, French and Dutch, and when the time came for the British to appoint someone as Secretary-General, Eric felt they would appoint him instead of an Englishman. During this time, Eric was lecturing all over the island and helping to develop a West Indian consciousness. But when the time came, instead of appointing Eric to the Caribbean Commission, the British fired him.

Q: On what grounds?

A: No grounds. This happened in 1955 and Eric asked me to bring Winston Mahabir to his house. We met him there with Dr. Elvin Richardson, and the four of us decided that Eric should go into politics in Trinidad. We looked at existing political organizations like the Democratic Labour Party (DLP), headed by Bhadase Maraj, with its base in the East Indian population, and decided to form a new political party. We were going to start from scratch. We left it to Eric to pick more people to enlarge our base from four to twelve. We didn't want anybody with a political past. We wanted new blood, and an interracial or multiracial party. I was elected chairman of the group, and we set up committees to draft a constitution and a charter. Eventually we enlarged the group to fifty, and called ourselves "foundation members." Then we grew to one hundred and fifty.

Q: All this must have been done very quickly if you were to win the election in 1956.

A: It was really fast! Soon we were five hundred strong, and had a People's Charter and Constitution ready. During this time, Eric still delivered his lectures. Albert Gomes[8] was influential in getting Eric to lecture. Gomes also got other intellectuals to lecture. We named the party the "People's National Movement." For the party colour we picked the balisay, a flower, on account of its fertility. I still have my balisay tie. We had the shirts printed with the balisay colours, and everyone wore a balisay shirt. It was like Ghana where Nkrumah fought his first election wearing the prison cap.

Q: That was the same time too—1956.

A: We launched the party with five hundred people at Gray Friars Hall (the Presbyterian Church in Frederick Street). Eric wanted me to be Chairman because he thought it would help the party to have an Indian as Chairman. But I suggested Learie Constantine[9] who was working with Texaco Limited, the oil company, at their refinery in Port of Spain. Learie had a legal background, and was highly respected all over the world. So Learie Constantine became Chairman of the party, I became First Vice-Chairman. The party was launched again in Woodford Square on 22 February 1956. We fought the first election later that year. I myself ran in a constituency where, in hindsight, I should not have run. I ran against Ashford Sinanan, who was Speaker in the previous House. I lost, but we won eleven seats altogether out of a total of twenty-four. The Opposition was loud in their disapproval of the PNM forming the Government. The Governor sided with the Opposition. Then he found himself in a fix, because Eric refused to form a Government. Eventually, the Governor had to make sure that the nominated members supported the party, and after that was done, we formed the Government.

Q: The appointed members gave the PNM a majority?

A: That's right.

Q: Was the Opposition united at that time?

A: The DLP under Bhadase Maraj had some organization, and showed their strength later in the Federal Election of 1958 when, as the Opposition Federal Party in Trinidad, they actually won six of the ten seats allocated to Trinidad. I think we lost because the PNM had increased taxation. Besides, Indians were sticking together politically to vote for the Opposition. So there was a racial element there too.

Q: After the 1956 election, how did the PNM government perform under Eric Williams?

A: After five years we introduced another House. We decided that the Upper House or Senate would consist of twenty-one members of whom the party in power would nominate twelve, the Opposition four, and the other five would come from other pressure groups—churches, the labour movement, oil companies, insurance companies, and the Chamber of Commerce. We had one representative for all churches, religions and denominations—Rev Roy Neehall. He was a very good orator, and a decent person. We also decided that the life of the Senate appointment would be five years, or the life of the Legislature.

Q: How did the PNM treat the issue of Federation?

A: One of the things we felt strongly about was the formation of the University of the West Indies. We felt it should be situated in Jamaica, since Jamaica was the English-speaking territory, with the largest population. We wanted a university of our own because we were having problems getting admitted to universities abroad, especially in medical schools.

Q: The University was a product of the Federal idea?

A: Yes. We were talking about it since the 1940s. But the West Indies Federation was formed in 1958 with ten islands and two parties. One party was formed by Norman Manley[10] in Jamaica (the West Indian Federal Party), and there was the West Indian Labour Party with Bustamante also from Jamaica. The structure of the Federation was weak from the beginning: its budget was only nine million dollars. Another thing was the location of the Federal capital in Trinidad. With hindsight, it might have been better if it had been situated in one of the smaller islands; but Trinidad was chosen on account of its communication system: regular airline service, and telephone service. So we had a Federal structure that was weak, located in a unit—Trinidad—that was strong. We had a Prime Minister of the

Federation—Sir Grantley Adams[11]—who was getting on in years, and a young, vibrant, very active Prime Minister in Trinidad which was only one unit in the Federation. Hence inevitable conflict. The fact that the Federal opposition party in Trinidad was led by Bhadase Maraj also introduced a racial element into Federal politics.

Q: I remember Guyanese Indians fearing that if Guyana joined the Federation, the majority status which Indians held in Guyana would be neutralized by an overwhelming majority of Africans within the new Federal structure.

A: That was also the feeling in Trinidad. We tried everything to force Cheddi Jagan[12] to come into the Federation. We even offered Guyana more seats than they themselves expected, but Cheddi made the excuse that Guyana had a "continental destiny." Williams felt that Guyana was essential to the success of the Federation, because it had space, and untouched resources, such as the scope for hydroelectricity, and the development of waterways, minerals, forestry, and dairy farming. Guyana had probably more to contribute to the Federation than all the other territories, including Trinidad. Thus there are many reasons why the Federation failed. It had a top-heavy administration with a Secretary-General, Governor, and Prime Minister. Administrative costs alone took up more than half of the Federal Budget. The leaders, too, were not willing to give up some of the powers that they had, and that caused personality clashes. So when Busta[13] challenged Manley to a referendum and won, the Federation broke up. Williams then announced in Woodford Square: "One from ten leaves nought," meaning that the Federation was dead. He then spoke vaguely of forming a unitary state, but nothing came of it.

Q: You obviously admired Williams in those early days—his ideas about a West Indian Federation and national consciousness, his scholarship, and leadership. I think Williams's books show that he was a scholar of some originality, and a politician of vision, at least in his early days. But after he had been Prime Minister of Trinidad and Tobago for many years, he introduced a law which the British had used in the 19th century to restrain dissidents, and subdue dissent. As someone with a specialist's knowledge of British colonial history, it is surprising that Williams would resort to the very mechanism employed by colonial authorities he had opposed all his life. Did power corrupt him?

A: Williams' personality was complex. There was Williams the professor at Howard, and Williams the student. He went into politics because he wanted power. To show his power, he used to say, "When I say, 'come,' you cometh. When I say, 'Go' you goeth." He was power-hungry, like most politicians.

Q: But did he become corrupt? How did he win so many elections and stay in power for such a long time?

A: He was able to win election because over 50% of Trinidad's population is situated in what is known as the "Eastern Corridor," which runs from Port of Spain on the West Coast going all the way back to Arima. The population there is mostly black.

Q: Both Guyana and Trinidad have large Indian populations, and in Guyana Indians have had no political power for twenty-eight years.

A: It is not much different in Trinidad. Williams made a terrific contribution to Trinidad politics. He educated the people. There was no race in that. He wasn't a racial person himself, although I believe there were black racists within the PNM.

Q: What sort of political leader was Capildeo?[14]

A: Capildeo was an academician. He also wanted power. The Indian population replaced Bhadase Maraj with Capildeo as leader of the Opposition because Capildeo had a PhD. But Capildeo was no match for Williams. His PhD was in Mathematics whereas Williams had a PhD in political science and history, and knew the history of the Caribbean. Also, Capildeo continued teaching in London while he was Leader of the Opposition in Trinidad. That was not good for the DLP either.

Q: How could you estimate Bhadase as a political leader?

A: He was regarded as a leader of the East Indians. He was involved in the introduction of schools which were to be partly administered by the Hindu Maha Sabha just as schools were administered by Christian denominations. Later, Muslims were also able to secure Muslim schools.

Q: There have been Indo-Trinidadian leaders like Adrian Cola Rienzi,[15] Bhadase Maraj, Capildeo, Ashford Sinanan, and now Basdeo Panday.[16] An Indo-Trinidadian writer like V S Naipaul is probably the best writer that the West Indies has ever produced. The first great Trinidad bowler also happened to be an Indian—Ramadhin. It seems therefore that the Indian community in Trinidad, which is now close to a majority of the population, is not getting the political representation it deserves. What has gone wrong with the political process to produce such imbalance?

A: Indians have been divided; everybody in the West Indies has been divided. But Trinidad is not as polarized as Guyana along racial lines.

Q: You may be right because it looks as if the political process in Trinidad is being restored and Indians are now getting some representation.

A: Panday and A N R Robinson defeated the PNM when the party was very corrupt and several of its members were stealing money. Panday only had twelve seats, and A N R Robinson had two from Tobago. Panday come into leadership with A N R and created a united front between Indians and Blacks. Indians had a good political representation then, but Indians in Panday's party told me that they didn't want him to be Prime Minister because they were scared we would have riots. They also had personal reasons for believing that Panday was not appropriate as Prime Minister. In any case, A N R Robinson became Prime Minister and had an opportunity of cementing the races together. But he did just the opposite. He got rid of Panday, and some other Indians, although he kept a few. It was the divide and rule game all over again.

Q: It sounds depressing. Although Trinidadians of all races have emigrated, I think that Indians have felt particularly insecure because they thrive in shopkeeping and business, and are more vulnerable than other groups because they own more. If they can't emigrate, what is there to sustain them apart, perhaps, from religion?

A: I'm not a practising Muslim, I'm not a practising Christian either. What the minister is going to tell me, I already know. I follow the ethics that I learnt in Christianity as a young man. As far as I am concerned, the ethics of the various religions are important for me to get on with my fellow men. I follow just one rule "Do unto others as you want them to do unto you." I believe that if you just follow that one rule, you can't go wrong.

ISMITH KHAN

Ismith Khan was born in 1925 in Port of Spain, Trinidad.[1] His father first came from India to Guyana, and then to Princes Town, Trinidad. The interview was recorded in Toronto on 22 July 1992.

Q: Why did your grandfather leave India in the first place?

A: Because of the Indian "Mutiny"[2] when Indian soldiers were called upon to shoot fellow Indians. Some soldiers rebelled and turned their guns on the British instead. My grandfather was one of these rebellious soldiers. Consequently, he was on the run from the British authorities. I know that my family left from Kanpur Railway Station, but I don't know how they made it to Guyana.

Q: Your father and grandfather were probably recruited by one of the "arkhatis" who were sent around scouting for anyone feeling discontent in India; they were probably told fantastic stories about the Caribbean, and induced to emigrate.[3]

A: As I understand it, my grandfather did not come as an indentured immigrant; he came as a man with some means and skills.

Q: He paid his way to come?

A: Yes. I do not know the details, but he paid his own way and brought his family. He never worked on a sugar cane plantation; he worked as a jeweller as soon as he got to Guyana. As a matter of fact, I think that he had contempt for those Indians who, he felt, were browbeaten by the Raj: he was very rebellious. He felt that indentured immigrants were cowering, and unable to stand up for their rights.

Q: I can see the parallels in Kale Khan in *The Jumbie Bird*.

A: Yes, that novel is semiautobiographical, and some of its details are what I heard growing up. My grandfather, for instance, took part in the Hosay riots of 1884, in San Fernando.[4] He was shot in the leg, and was supposed to have shot people too.

Q: Did you and your family, including your grandfather, all live in the same house in Port of Spain?

A: My grandfather came to live with us when he was quite old. He lived downstairs in the back room of my father's jewellery establishment. There were five children. I was the only boy. I came in the middle.

Q: You were educated at Queens Royal College[5] (QRC)?

A: Yes. My father was a very forward looking person. He wanted to send my eldest sister abroad to become an optometrist; but she got married instead. My second sister did not display any interest in going abroad to study; so as the next in line, I was sent to QRC. If I am not very familiar with Islamic tradition today, it is because, to some extent, it was felt that girls should take religious instruction and study the Indian classics, whereas boys should go to western schools.

Q: How was your time at QRC?

A: This was during the late 1930s and early 40s when the school had largely English boys, and only a few East Indians and Blacks. The teachers were also English, although, perhaps due to the Second World War, there were some local ones. I passed the Cambridge School Certificate exam, then went to the US to study engineering, but after about a year I saw that I was never going to be an engineer. I went back to Trinidad and joined the *Trinidad Guardian*[6]—as a reporter, while Sam [Selvon] was there. I then came back to the US in 1948.

Q: Where did you come to in the US?

A: I had a scholarship at Michigan State University.

Q: How did you get the scholarship?

A: My first wife was the daughter of one of India's early revolutionaries, and she had come to Trinidad as an anthropologist to study Indians and the indenture system for her Master's dissertation. We met when I went to interview her for *The Guardian*. She was able to arrange for me to come to Michigan State University.

Q: Was your wife Muslim?

A: No. Her father's name was Saliendranath Ghose. He was a good friend of Subhas Chandra Bose,[7] and he had fled India in the 1920s because he was caught making bombs in the basement of the University of Calcutta. He came to the US, and married his secretary who was American. Later, the British felt he could come back to India, and they made him President of the University of Dacca. So his daughters went back to India when they were teenagers and then returned to the United States when they were ready to go to college.

Q: After Michigan State, what happened?

A: I was at Michigan State from 1948 to 1952. Then I went to New York. I had a scholarship at the New School for Social Research.

Q: Had you got a degree by then?

A: No. I was short by two courses. But I had what was called a

Divisional Major in the Social Sciences: Sociology, anthropology, psychology and economics. When I went to the New School for Social Research in New York, they said I had to choose one social science, so I chose sociology. I thought it would help me to become a writer, not of fiction, but of journalism, seeing that I already had some practical experience in journalism at the *Guardian*. But while I was at the school, I took some fiction workshops and became so fascinated with that kind of writing, that I decided that was what I wanted to do.

Q: It was partly accidental that you took up fiction?

A: Yes. It was pure chance that the New School for Social Research had those writing workshops. When I went there, Norman Mailer[8] had just graduated, and used to come back to visit, as I did myself after I became published. As a matter of fact my professor encouraged me to teach Creative Writing there, which I did on a part-time basis. But I was still on a student visa, and would have gone on to get a Master's degree, except that my wife got a job with the Department of Far Eastern Studies at Cornell University and we moved there instead. By that time, I had already started writing *The Jumbie Bird*. Then my wife's program at Cornell closed down, and in 1956 we went back to New York, where I worked for the New York Public Library for a number of years, while doing part-time teaching at the New School for Social Research. I also completed *The Jumbie Bird*.

Q: How was the novel published?

A: Through my professor, I got the names of publishing houses in New York city and approached them myself. There was always interest, but there were problems. Dodd Mead were willing to publish it if I toned down the dialect, but they felt that they could not give me a contract. Then I met a literary agent, who happened to have good connections in England and the book was first published in England by MacGibbon and Kee. It was also published in New York a little later by McDowel Obelensky.

Q: It is curious that you should live in the US and have your first major work published in England. As you know, many West Indian writers—Sam Selvon, George Lamming, V S Naipaul and others[9]—had gone to England and were getting published in the 1950s. There was a British historical connection, and cultural appreciation of the creole language to which Americans were perhaps less sympathetic.

A: They still are.

Q: Did you ever think about moving to England at that time?

A: I seriously thought of going to England but dreaded it because I felt that people like Sam [Selvon] and George [Lamming] were really living in squalor. I saw Sam frequently when he came to the US on fellowships. He would tell me about the circumstances under which he lived and I thought that although I lived in a tenement in New York, at least I had heat and hot water.

Q: From your novels I get the feeling that you are culturally dispossessed in the sense of not belonging to one settled culture. You also married someone who is culturally dispossessed through the ambivalence of having an Indian father and a non-Indian mother. Did that create problems between you and your wife?

A: We did not have any problems; but there was a great deal of discussion about identity. I think we both realized that we were outside the mainstream of any traditional culture or religion. I think that we clung to each other for as long as we did because we were outsiders, while everybody else seemed to have a sense of belonging. I wondered whether there might not be something wrong with me as an individual in a psychological sense. Perhaps I still feel that way; but at this stage of my life, I think that I will simply have to learn to live with isolation and alienation, loneliness and boredom. They have always plagued me. All I can say is I do not think that there is anything wrong with me. If, through my study of the social sciences, I used to think these problems could be overcome, I can now see that they will never be overcome.

Q: These problems have less to do with you as an individual than with either a universal human condition, or a specific cultural one in Trinidad—a colonial situation.

A: I often use one term to describe my situation,"my historical past"—which encompasses all that I have lived through historically, socially, geographically.

Q: Was the second novel *The Obeah Man* easier to write or get published?

A: It was both easier to write and get published.

Q: As you have already mentioned, *The Jumbie Bird* is semi-autobiographical. It is a novel about identity, which was a fashionable literary theme in the 1950s when Selvon, Lamming and others were writing similar novels. The 1950s was a time when the British Caribbean colonies were trying to assert their separateness both from Britain, as well as from their African and Asian origins in order to claim their own identity. From that point of view, *The Jumbie Bird* deals with a normal preoccupation. But there is something special about the novel which I don't see, for instance, in Selvon's work or in V S Naipaul's: the strong feeling for India. The characters of Selvon and Naipaul talk about identity too, but Kale Khan asserts the power of his Indianness and the value of connectedness with India in a way that is unique in Caribbean literature. This strong feeling for India pervades the novel.

A: My entire family were very Indian. We frowned upon anything and anyone who attempted to assimilate Western traditions whether in food, dress or social terms. I was brought up to feel, and I still feel this way today: that I am from India, no matter where I may be or go.

Q: You see the contradiction: that you are Indian and yet you are not fully Indian. You are Westernized. You do not even speak any Indian language.

A: I do not speak any Indian language, and I was not sent anywhere to learn. But I love Indian music, and my younger relatives listen to Indian film songs although they do not understand the words. I prefer Indian classical music. My father played several Indian instruments. He used to import harmoniums to Trinidad from India.

Q: We are caught in this ambivalence of having Indian origins, perhaps even of feeling Indian, and yet living in a situation where Indianness was dominated by creole or western manners. In *The Jumbie Bird* you mention rootlessness when Rahim tells his wife Meena: "We ain't belong to Hindustan, we ain't belong to England, we ain't belong to Trinidad" (p. 54). Whether we call Rahim's sense of not belonging, cultural rootlessness, or lack of identity, it implies awareness of a new identity emerging out of the mixture of several cultural traditions in the Caribbean. This was increasingly recognized after the 1950s. Your first two novels accurately describe the situation in Trinidad, in the 1950s, by illustrating rootlessness or a sense of not belonging to any of the three places that Rahim mentions—India, England or Trinidad. You also show three generations of attitudes in Kale Khan, Rahim and Jamini. *The Obeah Man* is similar too. In these two novels, you reveal the darker reality under the bright, tropical liveliness and gaiety of Caribbean society. Now, you have lived abroad since the 1950s and observed the darker reality, for example, of materialism affecting Caribbean immigrant communities in North America. But in your fiction, in *The Crucifixion*, which comes twenty-three years after *The*

Obeah Man—I do not see you engaging with the immigrant community as Sam Selvon does. As you know, Sam has been writing about Caribbean immigrants in England for a long time.

A: I am not familiar with the Caribbean immigrant community in New York largely because they would all be black. I live in Brooklyn on the edge of the (black) West Indian community and I do not know any East Indian community.

Q: I believe there is a large Indo-Caribbean community in New York.

A: To tell you the truth, it probably has to do with me. I have little in common with recent immigrants to the US. Most of my friends are artists, painters, sculptors, or writers, with whom I can feel a sense of community. They are, like myself, people who stand outside of their own cultures, and I find a kinship with them that I do not find with my fellow West Indians.

Q: The fact that you do not interact with this contemporary Caribbean community in the US means that your literary subject goes back to the Trinidad that you knew four decades ago, as in *The Crucifixion*. The world of *The Crucifixion* is not all that different from the world of *The Jumbie Bird* and *The Obeah Man*. There are some differences, for instance, Independence has happened in *The Crucifixion*. Doesn't it create a publishing problem to write now about Caribbean subjects of forty or fifty years ago? Would publishers be interested?

A: When I came back from Trinidad to New York in 1962, I was so angry that I decided I would never write about the Caribbean again. The reception of my first two novels was not positive enough. It is as though I said to myself, I am going to punish them by not writing about the Caribbean, without knowing who they are. I have written a novel set in New York in the 1960s. I have not shown it to more than one or two publishers, and they tell me quite frankly that I write much better about the Caribbean. I still have the manuscript: it is two-thirds done and I would like to go back to it. I also have some short stories that are set in the US. But I was really devastated by the reception of my books, and by the failure of my continued efforts to get *The Jumbie Bird* republished.

Q: That is a great pity; for your powers as a novelist have not diminished at all. *The Crucifixion* proves this, it has the zest and vigour of the creole language, as well as the humour and energy of characters like Miss Violet. The jokes are wonderful, and leave me helpless with laughter, for instance, the one about the one-legged man whose unerring aim with his crutch makes him the most feared chicken thief who could out run any chicken and spear it with his crutch. It is amazing that you can remember the humour so well after forty years. It is as fresh as anything written by Selvon, Lamming or Naipaul in the 1950s.

A: I was talking to Austin Clarke in Guyana, at Carifesta in 1972, and he asked me how Sam [Selvon] and I captured the music of the creole language so well. I do not know the explanation. If I were married to a West Indian who spoke creole, or if I mixed with West Indians socially, that might explain it. But I hear the music of the language to this day. I like to think of myself as bilingual, speaking both standard and creole English. *The Crucifixion* exists in two versions, an unpublished one completely in standard English, and the published one in which the chapters alternate between standard and creole English. The publisher preferred the second version because, he said, he had to consider his readers.

Q: You now appear to be reconciled to the unfair way in which your first two books were received. What do you think about younger writers like Neil Bissoondath[10] and Caryl Phillips[11] who were writing about Caribbean immigrants in North America and England.

A: I wonder how they can write about places like Canada, England and the US to which they may not have a strong sense of belonging.

Q: That is a problem. They consider themes of racial discrimination, discontinuity, exile, alienation which may appear similar to those of the fifties' novelists, but are really quite different. Their sense of disillusionment is much stronger because they have to face the fact that emigration from the Caribbean has not justified the promise that it held for characters in the fifties' novels. Your first two books, for instance, might express a lack of identity or form a sense of belonging, but they are still rich and full blooded. Kale Khan has such a striking, personality. There is no other character like him in West Indian literature, not even Mohun Biswas an Indian of such cantankerous strength, rousing flamboyance and fearless drive.

A: Another thing that I am hearing more and more, usually from women, is how well I have represented my female characters, compared with other West Indian writers.

Q: Yes. There is Miss Violet in *The Crucifixion*, and earlier characters such as Binti whose independence and resilience are quite unusual for a woman protagonist, especially an Indian one, in West Indian literature. There is Meena also, who is strong in her own quiet, more conventional way. Yet Kale Khan is sexist. Not that you advocate sexism, but you report the sexism that would have been part and parcel of Kale Khan's character alongside his more admirable traits.

A: That is true. I have tried to represent the society as accurately as I possibly can. If my readers see sexism, that does not mean I am advocating it. Incidentally, when I was at Berkeley, I had a student who specialized in gerontology, and she was very interested in Kale Khan and how the society treated him as an older person. In Trinidad we had many people like Kale Khan; they might have been colourful or nasty; but they were not going to be beaten down or locked away in any old people's home. They had spunk and spirit.

Q: You've expressed that very well in *The Jumbie Bird*, and I think it will gain more recognition as time goes on.

A: I am glad that *The Jumbie Bird* was recognized in the Caribbean educational system, by being selected as one of the texts on the Caribbean Schools Exam list. Some writers probably don't live long enough to see that kind of recognition and appreciation.

JANICE SHINEBOURNE

Jan Shinebourne (née Lowe) was born in Canje, Berbice, Guyana, but now lives in England. Her father is Chinese and her mother part Indian and Chinese. The interview was recorded in Toronto on 13 July 1992.

Q: Was it not unusual for Chinese to be living in a predominantly Indian village?

A: No. Not at all. Immigration General reports show that Chinese immigrants came to Guyana in the 1880s and 90s and settled all over the country, in villages such as Rose Hall.[1] My father told me that his parents came from China straight to Rose Hall. In the Immigration records, I looked in particular for my family name—"Lowe," or its more common form—"Lo," but found neither. All I found was "Lau"; so I believe my original family name was "Lau."

Q: The names of indentured immigrants who crossed the Atlantic from India and China suffered the same fate of anglicization, simplification, or arbitrary change that African names had suffered earlier on the middle passage.[2]

A: My husband's family suffered a similar fate: they were Polish Jews fleeing Nazi Germany. When they arrived in London, the immigration officers could not spell their name and gave them the name "Shinebourne" which sounded similar.

Q: But the Chinese did not remain on the sugar estates for long?

A: No. They drifted into the towns. When I was growing up, in the 1950s, I had a sense of belonging to the only Chinese family in Canje. Each village had one Chinese family.

Q: And they owned a grocery store?

A: Yes. We owned a grocery store. I think when the Chinese were found to be unsuitable workers on the plantations, they were given pieces of land and allowed to build shops.

Q: How did your father—a Chinese—come to marry your mother who was only partly Chinese?

A: We were all creolized. My father spoke "Bhojpuri"; all his friends were Indian. He was not Chinese culturally. I think I spoke a bit of Hindi and "Bhojupuri" as a child, but when I went to school I was threatened with a whipping if I spoke anything but English; so Hindi and "Bhojpuri" were erased from my tongue.

Q: After primary school in Rose Hall you went on to Berbice High school?[3]

A: Yes. Then I started teaching in primary school during the middle 1960s, before going to the University of Guyana in 1968. Those were very interesting years. Edward Braithwaite had returned to Jamaica with new ideas about Caribbean history. Students questioned the British syllabus at the university and wanted to study more Caribbean history and literature. There was the Brathwaite/Walcott controversy[4] and the racial politics of Guyana were also involved, along with questions about the nature of our culture, history and identity. The university, established by the previous government, was a forum for questioning our history. I also met my English husband at the University of Guyana: he worked in the university library. We got married and went to England in 1970.

Q: How did you become a writer?

A: My mother considered education as a way out of the oppressive condition on the sugar estates. I read all the books in the sugar estate library and took extra lessons. My school essays were thought to be very good. My parents, grandmother, and my father's friends gave me a kind of education which was also important. All the village came to our shop, and as they talked, I listened. My father's friends were Indian estate workers and African sugar cane cutters who came between shifts and talked about working conditions on the estates, problems in maintaining the villages, the medical service and so on. The women spoke to my mother about their problems, and it all made our shop into a kind of community centre. Later I went to Berbice High School and discovered Dickens, George Eliot and Shakespeare. I was especially interested in George Eliot. I was fascinated by the scope of the novel in being able to portray not only characters but a whole society. I remember loving Dickens for that.

Q: I can see Dickensian characters and social vignettes having an impact on you, and perhaps an early Eliot novel like *Adam Bede* — with its portrait of Wesleyan religiosity and English Midlands rural society. Can you remember your first attempt at writing?

A: After my GCE Ordinary Level exam, my grandmother died, and I was given her room. The first thing I did was ask my mother to buy me a desk, and I wrote a story, "Water and Trees," which was about the rain forest. "Water and Trees" was published later when I went to Georgetown and met people from Queens College and St Stanislaus College.[5] I had previously been too shy of thinking of myself as a writer, but I think I always wanted to write, and when my grandmother died I tried to immortalize her in a second story called, "The Room" which was also published in "Expression."

Q: "Expression" was started in Georgetown by your circle of literary-minded friends?[6]

A: Yes. We were encouraged by Martin Carter.[7] I found this urban, Georgetown literary culture so stimulating that I came out of my sugar estate shell. I met not only Martin Carter but A J Seymour,[8] and I discovered local novels in the Georgetown library. Mittelholzer's *Corentyne Thunder*[9] hit me for six. I felt so thrilled when I opened it and found that somebody had described the same landscape, climate, rivers, trees, people, speech—everything that I wanted to do. In addition to Mittelhozer, I found V S Naipaul's *Miguel Street* and *A House for Mr Biswas*.[10] Cheddi Jagan[11] was also very important. He gave us a different sense of reality by saying that the country was dominated by the sugar barons. No one, before him, had challenged the political authority in the country by saying this in public, loudly and clearly, and offering an alternative. He gave me the capacity to question things. He also gave me a sense of pride by saying that we were not just indentured immigrants or oppressed people: we had contributed labour for which we should be rewarded. All these things created a certain outlook in me.

Q: I can see evidence of this outlook in your novels. I like particularly your descriptions and dichotomies, for example, the town/country dichotomy. In *Timepiece* though, how can Sandra Yansen whose father is Chinese, have a family name that is Dutch.

A: Because of what I just told you about names being anglicized or modernized. If you broke "Yansen" in two, it could sound like two Chinese names "Yan" and "Sen." These parts were brought together and made to sound English, or at least creole.

Q: The social portrait in *Timepiece* is of post-Independence, or at least post-1964 Guyana. 1964 was a watershed year marking the change from Cheddi Jagan to Forbes Burnham.[12] Your portrait in *Timepiece* is one of virtual dictatorship, of a ruler who insinuates his tentacles into the whole society. People live in an atmosphere of fear, suspicion, intrigue, and shady loyalty.

A: That was what it was like in the 1960s and it got worse in the 1970s and 80s, when Burnham's terror machinery was completely in place, and people were being openly persecuted.

Q: *Timepiece* gives us the beginning of the process of Burnham's terror?

A: Yes.

Q: The character, Clinton Persaud, the journalist who gets fired, rings a bell.

A: That character was based on Ricky Singh with whom I worked on the *Guyana Graphic*.[13] I was there when he was sacked.

Q: But in this novel Persaud simply disappears.

A: I think Ricky Singh went to Barbados.

Q: That is in real life, but it does not happen in the novel?

A: I do not make it clear. I tend to leave loose ends like that.

Q: What I saw in *Timepiece* was an enthusiasm for making the point about a cruel dictator and the situation of fear and oppression which he created, but not going beyond making that point.

A: The story I read at Harbourfront[14] provoked a similar reaction. The audience liked the story, but wanted to know how the woman [Mrs. Vincent] died. I told them that was not important. The important point was the contrast between the people reacting to her death—those who had become westernized and lost their roots because they lived in a newer, urban world, and someone like the maid [Vera] who came from an older, more rural world (in Plaisance). Details about the dead person were secondary, and I therefore neglected to discuss how she died. If she had decided to die, that was all that mattered.

Q: I agree that the point of the story is the contrasting reactions to death between the black maid and her black middle class employers, who were living in houses which used to be occupied mainly by rich, expatriate Whites working for Bookers.[15] The story illustrated a social transformation in which some Blacks replaced Whites in post-Independence Guyana. The same social and class structure remained; but a different (black) group was now occupying the upper levels of the structure. The contrast between the maid from Plaisance and her employers is effectively made, and the reader does not miss the details about the woman who died. In a novel, however, where an author has more room to develop characters, the reader may miss a character of some importance who simply disappears from the action without further comment, unless the disappearance itself has special significance.

A: I think I have a short story approach to character.

Q: That may well be. In a short story one expects the glimpse, the vignette, the character sketched out rather than filled in. It seems to me that your technical gifts for social vignettes and character sketches suit the short story form particularly well.

A: There may be something in that.

Q: The social descriptions and glimpses of characters are very well done. The journalists at the *Daily Mail* are wonderful portraits of young, ambitious, vocal, articulate, bright people struggling vainly against frustration. They are touching. At the same time, their talk about the need for racial cooperation and unity sounds clichéd, banal.

A: They were different from the generation who came before them—those who graduated from Queens College and Bishops High School.[16] The older generation knew they were going to be the leaders of the country: there was a secure place for them at the top. These young men [in *Timepiece*] also came from those schools; but the society they are in is breaking up, and there is no secure place for them. Cheddi Jagan is calling for a change. There is all this talk about communism, and the break up of colonial society. So all these young people are floating around in a kind of existential haze. They have a sense of not going anywhere, and in the end, frustrated they talk about leaving the country. I suppose I am mourning this tragic situation of fragmentation, frustration, uncertainty and fear.

Q: You capture the mixed atmosphere of confusion, despair and inertia very well. Perhaps it was the sense of powerlessness inherited from colonialism that inhibited them from analyzing their situation, or confronting it more directly. In any case, Burnham ran a dictatorship that did not permit dissent. In the *Last English Plantation* you recreate the 1953 period in Guyana just after the suspension of the constitution. Lucille, the mother in this novel, is fascinating because she embodies both the mixed quality of West Indian culture, and its powerlessness. We grew up under the shadow of a dominant British culture which was the passport to social and economic success. Lucille's rather excessive adulation of British culture, speech and manners embodies an important problem in Caribbean social history. Perhaps, you treated Lucille's problem somewhat negatively in the novel.

A: I think my generation sees her problem differently. We are more unsympathetic to colonial influences. Of the men in *The Last English Plantation*, Cyrus is Indian and Chinese, and Boysie is an Indian who is also a political activist. The cultural interaction between these men fascinates me more than Lucille's dilemma. Lucille's daughter, June, instinctively feels that she can relate more to her father's world than to her mother's. Her mother is pushing her out of the village, like a duck, saying you must go out and learn to swim because that is the real world, not your father's escapist cuckoo land of mixed cultures and democracy.

Q: But her mother does it out of love.

A: That is why, when June finally has the great outburst against her mother, she feels a kind of psychic disintegration, and she goes to "nani" to be healed. I think June represents my generation. Cheddi Jagan made us look deeper into ourselves, and I think I am beginning to explore myself in this novel. The politics of race in Guyana presented me with a crisis. African friends were giving up Indian friends; Indians were giving up Africans. I had to deal with these issues caused by a negative sense of racial difference. I needed to know about why we were in Guyana, and what we really had in common. In my books I am trying to formulate answers to these questions.

Q: June is a "seeking" character with a growing consciousness.

A: June is getting an education, but before she can do so, she encounters Guyanese class and race differences in the classroom. It is not her mother who has prepared her to deal with that, but her father, through the model he presents of his relations with other people. Her mother, meanwhile, has cut herself off from people, and does not want to know about her Indian roots. This is not helpful. It is very sad, because Lucille is such a pillar of strength in her family.

Q: Lucille's portrait is very good, as is the conflict with June, and June's growing awareness, especially of class difference in her association with the families of white overseers. The school scenes are brilliant. These scenes and the mother/daughter relationship savour of lived life. I also think you have a good eye, and an exceptional ear for Guyanese speech which is reproduced in perfection—rhythm, vocabulary, accent and intonation. But again I react slightly negatively to June's preference for her father's cultural mixing as the way to the future in Guyana. It is not that cultural mixing and racial cooperation are not desirable goals in Guyana, but their achievement by June's father has a synthetic ring similar to the plea for racial cooperation by the young journalists in *Timepiece*, who feel a supposedly existentialist despair over the failed possibilities in Guyana, the impasse of dictatorship, and consequent need for fleeing abroad.

A: I think your comments are partly inspired by the present situation in Guyana. What you are saying is that the kind of community that I am portraying didn't have what it took to stand up against the terror and destruction brought on Guyana by Burnham. As a child I had so many surrogate mothers, both African and Indian. I remember going to Indian weddings in which African people would take part. Mothers looked after each other's children. I am not saying that everything was rosy. We were very poor and lived in terrible conditions. There was no running water or electricity. I am not looking back and idealizing the past. But the whole village came to my mother's funeral. Indian women dressed in saris and African women dressed differently. When my father died too, Africans and Indians all came to our house. I am portraying an extraordinary society in which the races in Guyana, especially the African and Indian races, experience more unity between them than they have ever done. That unity has vanished because of the traumas we have been through, and I am trying to immortalize it in these novels. When I go back to Guyana now and tell people about this unity, they look at me blankly, because today the races are more separate than they have ever been in Guyana.

Q: It now seems a figment of your imagination—an idyllic age of lost innocence and beauty.

A: It looks as if I invented it. But I know it from experience. I moved very easily among European, Indian, Chinese and African friends and family who were all equally important to me. Although I don't suppose, for one minute, that I am similar to Wilson Harris,[17] I think this is what Wilson is getting at himself: a vision of humanity that comes from the positive influences which shaped our childhood.

Q: Wilson's fiction is enveloped in a surrealistic aura that gives his philosophical speculations a certain intellectual validity, although I find them difficult to understand and apply to real life. You work in a more realistic mode.

A: Yes. Before me, only two people had written about Canje—Wilson Harris (*The Secret Ladder*)[18] Mittelholzer. *My Bones and My Flute* and all the Kaywana[19] books were set along the Canje river where the Dutch plantations were. I think that *The Secret Ladder* catches the Canje atmosphere of smells, water and the whole feeling of being there. On the other hand, I could not quite relate to Mittelholzer's *Corentyne Thunder* which looked like a glamorized picture of rural Berbice, full of stereotypes, although some descriptions of the landscape were good. There was also Peter Kempadoo—(*Guiana Boy*) and (*Old Thom's Harvest*).[20] But I could not relate to Peter's old fashioned style because I was influenced by modern writers like Faulkner, Hemingway and Sartre. I wanted to write like Hemingway and Faulkner.

Q: But if your subject remains a vision of interracial harmony deriving from childhood influences, isn't there a problem of chronology in writing about it after it had virtually disappeared under Burnham's dictatorship?

A: I had a sense that it had disappeared, but when I went back to my village in 1987, after about sixteen years, I was amazed to find that nothing had changed. Georgetown had decayed and changed completely. But Africans and Indians were still living in that village as if the '60s had not happened. The tree with the board on which men would pin the times of their shifts was still there. They were living as they did in the period described in *Timepiece*. I was greeted as if I had never gone away. Timelessness! In Georgetown, people and things change: you prepare for the future. In Berbice, the past is ever present.

153

Q: Is that why the novel is called *Timepiece*? The word "timepiece" is not used in the text.

A: I think that coming from Berbice, as I did, with a sense of timelessness, I was trying to tell myself that what was happening in Georgetown was a little piece of time that would be a temporary lapse.

Q: Your characters, by the way, seem remarkably well informed and knowledgeable.

A: I think my father knew a lot more about Guyana than I know now. He had no illusions about the British. He didn't like me going to Berbice High School. He said the kind of education I was getting would not take me very far. What he was saying was that it was more important to understand that we were living in a sugar estate world. He was more involved with his friends and their difficulties as men bringing up families in a sugar estate setting. They were having to cope constantly with the humiliation of overseers telling them where they could go and what they could do. They could not get proper water supply for their families. They were angry about these things and talked about Guyanese sociopolitical history without realizing they were doing so.

Q: I got the feeling that you were drawing on insights from the post-Independence period and transferring them backward, and there was a slight chronological conflict in my mind. For instance, I felt that June could not know so much, partly because of her youth, but also because those insights didn't become clear to us until after the 1960s. She seemed precocious. Then there was Boysie, and talk of revolution, opposing the powers that be, whisperings of clandestine action and strikes. All that seems premature in the 1950s.

A: We were politically educated by Cheddi Jagan. I learned that my education was subsidized by the sugar plantation. The church and everything that I went to were dependent on the sugar estate which had the money to run them. The education I had was circumscribed by these conditions. Cheddi Jagan was saying, in a more articulate and educated way, exactly what my parents were saying in their own way. These people did have political awareness. Village councillors, for instance, were very active in Guyana, constantly trying to negotiate with the estate managers to run their villages with some form of economic independence from the estate.

Q: You risk a sense of disappointment by extolling these resources and the great political awakening inspired by Cheddi Jagan without saying why they failed.

A: I do not think it was so much that they failed: they were defeated by greater forces.

Q: The CIA, British Intelligence and their local collaborators?

A: Yes. That reveals the vulnerability of the sugar estate society.

Q: This is the point: I do not get a sense of vulnerability from your novels. It is the revolutionary forces in them that are emphasized, and then apparently neglected.

A: They are defeated.

Q: At the end of *The Last English Plantation* what we are worried about is whether this boy will come out of jail or not; and then he comes out. The strife and political revolution recede into the background. Our concern is directed instead to the question of whether Ralph threw something at an overseer's daughter. This seems a much milder form of political protest than promised. The title "The Last English Plantation" has a revolutionary ring to it, referring to remnants probably of an oppressive system; but we are deflected from that at the end. Maybe that is your message: that there are the makings of revolution to redress historic injustices, but that the wherewithal to marshall them is not forthcoming. I do not think you are trivializing important issues; yet I am left with a feeling approaching bathos at the end of *The Last English Plantation*.

A: I think the resources of the community are very important in generating change whether through revolution or not. I don't think we value these resources. Lucille does not value them. I didn't value them, and Guyana does not value them. These are the resources that Wilson Harris is talking about. I am getting at the same thing, but I am taking a different route. I am trying to be more concrete about it.

Q: Will your future writing continue in this vein?

A: Now, I am writing in a different way. I think I am finished writing about Guyana. I am still interested in what is happening in Britain where I see our young people growing up in a dominant host culture which defined them as ethnic minorities and gives them a negative sense of racial difference. I think that my children are going to have the same difficulties that I had in Guyana. They go to school with English, Indian, Greek, Iranian, and Ethiopian children, and get along with them at school just as we did in Guyana, but those who govern the country and give people jobs exercise discrimination, so that when these children leave school, some of them are going to be better off on the basis of their skin colour. What are my children going to do about it?

Q: This is a contemporary topic which publishers might find more interesting than Guyanese subjects. Am I right in thinking that your novels would probably not have been published had you not left Guyana?

A: Yes. I wrote *Timepiece* for myself. I didn't think it would be possible to publish it while living in Guyana. After I came to London, I sent the manuscript to Longman in 1976. My husband forced me to send it because I did not think anybody would be interested in a little village in Guyana. I got back a glowing report of the novel saying it was worth publishing, and that I was a promising young writer. But Longman said that their [English] readers would not be able to understand the speech of my characters, and I would have to change the dialogue into standard English. I was horrified by this. I thought long and hard: but said I could not change the dialogue. After all, that was how Guyanese spoke. If I was faced with the prospect of writing novels which English publishers would then rewrite so that English people could read them, I would have to stop writing. I would be killing the source of my inspiration. I sat on the novel for the next ten years. Meanwhile, I was trying to write a novel called "Victory" about the late '70s in Guyana when terror was institutionalized. I sent an abstract of this novel to Ken Ramchand[21] who had liked little pieces that I previously wrote for *Expression*. The abstract I sent him was called "Victory" and it was published in *The Trinidad and Tobago Review*, where Jeremy Poynting[22] saw it. He had also read a short story of mine called "Chuni" which was published in *Race Today*[23] London. He liked both pieces and wrote to me asking if I had a longer work. So I pulled out *Timepiece* again and sent it to him. Within two weeks, he replied saying he would send me a contract without any conditions. I did rewrite sections of the novel knowing it was going to be published without editorial interference. Then I was interviewed, and I began to look at my writing more critically. I thought I had to go back in history and get more background about the trouble in Georgetown; so I did a lot of research, and because of Jeremy's encouragement, felt a tremendous growth of confidence in myself. It was in this frame of mind that I wrote *The Last English Plantation*. I completed it in about six weeks, and sent it to Jeremy who did not hesitate saying he would publish it.

Q: With two novels behind you, your writing career is fully launched. Do you think your mixed racial background has been an asset to your writing?

A: I think it gave me an advantage because of the race politics in Guyana, especially the African/Indian problem. There was a tendency to nationalism that came to the fore in the '70s in the Caribbean, and race and nationalism always lead to disaster. I think it is dangerous to shape a political, social and economic culture purely on the basis of race. Look at Hitler!

Q: What comes out of your novels is a national culture in the sense of different ethnic groups willingly cooperating in it.

A: I do not know if any government has ever succeeded in managing such a culture. I do not think it is a political issue; it is a human problem.

KAMALA-JEAN GOPIE

Kamala-Jean Gopie was born in Kingston, Jamaica on 7 November 1941. In 1949 she was sent to live in rural Jamaica where she attended a Quaker school. This interview was recorded in Toronto on 27 January 1996.

Q: How is it that you attended a boarding school run by Quakers for Indian girls?

A: When the Quakers—the American Society of Friends—came to Jamaica around the 1920s, they felt a need to work with Indians, and they set up missions in Portland and St Mary. I was at Lindale, a school primarily for Indian girls. When I got there (1951) a fair number of students were still Indians, but by the time I left (1957), the home was used for all girls who perhaps were orphaned or needed help. But certainly in the 1930s and 1940s, I would say maybe ninety per cent of the students were Indians.

Q: Did you take any exams?

A: I took the first, second and third Jamaica local exams. When I was eleven I was supposed to take the Jamaica scholarship, or common entrance exam to go to St Hilda's [Secondary School in Kingston] but for some reason or other I wasn't allowed to take it. I'm not sure if they recognized that I was bright and wanted to keep me; but I remained there and did the three Jamaican local exams. In the third one, I ranked third in the island and I decided to move to Kingston and Queen's, an Anglican girls secondary school, where I did the School Certificate exam.

Q: Was your family from Kingston?

A: No. My father was born in St Mary. His father was a jeweller and when he died, my grandmother moved to Spanish Town and worked in the market selling produce. My grandmother's brothers were jewellers as well.

Q: Did you hear about India from your family?

A: I heard things, but I was not interested. Essentially, I grew up in Jamaica being ashamed that I was Indian. Because we were a minority, we were constantly teased and called "coolie." We were never expected to amount to anything. We knew we had connectedness to India, but I was not interested, and secondly most of my family lived in the country anyway, including those who might know about India. It is only after I became an adult that I wanted to know, and then the relatives were no longer there for me to ask them questions.

Q: In Guyana and Trinidad, we grew up in larger Indian communities. Indians held positions in the professions, business, and the civil service. When I went to Jamaica in 1957, as a university student, the only Indian I saw on the campus apart from my fellow students from Guyana and Trinidad, was a Jamaican Indian gardener. In downtown Kingston Indians (from India) had a few shops. There is a clear difference between your upbringing and mine: I came from a large Indian community and didn't feel insecure because I was Indian.

A: There was what was called the India Club in Kingston. It was not for Indo-Jamaicans but for Indians who had freshly arrived from India as business people. I would look in and feel that I was an outsider. I also remember friends of my family who went to Trinidad and came back and told us of all the Indians they had seen. I felt envious that I wasn't in Trinidad. It felt good to know that there were successful Indians somewhere in the West Indies.

Q: When you talk about a sense of insecurity in Jamaica, you do not mean you were a victim of racial discrimination?

A: No. Things were said. I remember someone saying to me: "You could never get to the States [the US]," and I said: "why not," and they said: "because your people came from India and they don't take people from India in the States." This was when there was a quota on Indians who were admitted to the US. Meanwhile, a lot of Jamaicans were migrating to the US. Things like that set me apart. Then I remember being told that all I was good for was to sell calalloo [spinach] in Spanish Town market. So the notion was there: that as an Indo-Jamaican, I could only be a higgler, or work on a sugar estate. Dr Harry in Port Maria was the only Indian professional that I knew in Jamaica.

Q: While you were at school in the 1950s there was no significant Indian community in terms of a mosque, a temple or anything like that.

A: No.

Q: What did that mean in terms of religion for instance?

A: We all grew up Christian. I grew up in the Quaker School. Then, when I went back to Kingston I was in an Anglican girl's school. My grandmother used to sing in Hindi. I would hear her songs and sing too, but I didn't know what they meant. She'd talk about the "pani" and the "dal" and other things which, outside of my grandmother's life, I didn't hear at all. The cooking that my grandmother did was clearly not what I ate at boarding school. She'd make curry, dal and "dal baht," chutney etc.

Q: While Indians were socially inferior in Jamaica certainly in the 1950s when I lived there, I noticed some ambivalence because of the prevailing race and class hierarchy in which white was regarded as superior and black as inferior. Many Afro-Jamaicans admired Indians for what they called Indian, that is to say, white or European features, for instance, straight hair and nose and other physical features. So, although they despised Indians socially, they wished they could have Indian physical features.

A: This is why marrying an Indian girl was attractive: people felt that Indian girls were pretty.

Q: It would help the offspring to become more European because Indians were regarded as half way between African and European. It was a brutal system of values. When did you migrate and why? Couldn't you have studied at the University of the West Indies in Mona?

A: I migrated in 1962 right after Independence. After I did the school certificate, my parents had been separated for a while, and my mom, who worked as a maid, could not afford my school fees. I told the head mistress that I couldn't come back, but she said I had to come back, which I did since the Anglican church paid my school fees to take the Higher Schools Certificate exam. I felt proud and won prizes for biology, English and geography. But my mom could not afford to send me to university and my dad was in the country where he had started another family, with five children. So I decided to leave Jamaica. My mom had a brother in the US and I went to New York to go to University there. I stayed with my uncle in New York and did a secretarial course. Then, I decided that I did not want to be a secretary, and applied to come to Canada.

Q: You came as a Landed Immigrant to Toronto?

A: Yes. I had a Jamaican friend who lived here. I came on the 30th of November, 1963, and within ten days I had a job as assistant librarian at the Bank of Commerce. I liked the job but I wanted to be librarian in a school, so I went to teacher's college. Then I started to teach and take the librarian courses. I taught for three years in the classroom and then went into the library. I also got married. My husband was English.

Q: What was Toronto like in the early 1960s?

A: When I went to New York, my sense of being Indian became more heightened than it was in Jamaica. I guess in Jamaica I was either Jamaican or Indian and it didn't matter, except that I was at the bottom of the social scale. In New York, American Blacks noticed me because of my accent which they found interesting. They would also touch me because I used to have very long hair. All of a sudden my sense of being Indian became heightened. I knew that I was not American, not even American black. I was Jamaican but I was Indian. One day I was on the subway and an Indian man looked at me and smiled, and I looked at him and smiled. I just felt there was a connection. It was a kind of affirmation of who I was. Then when I came here I saw a few Indians, but not very many. People would ask me if I was from India, and I would say either I'm Indian or Jamaican, depending on where I was and how the question was posed.

Q: Did you know many black West Indians at that time?

A: No. I began to know Jamaicans in 1976 when there was a discussion at my school about students who had come up from Jamaica. What was said made me wonder what was happening to black or West Indian kids in the school system. This led me to find out about the Jamaican/Canadian Association. I did some volunteer work for them and they asked if I would sit on their Executive. I later became Secretary, then President for two years. I became very involved, and began to meet more Jamaicans, but never any Indians. By the mid-80s I was getting tired of the focus of everything being black, because there were other issues and other groups that were not involved. I'd say these things at some of the meetings, and people would tell me that that all groups were included. But it was not convincing. Therefore when I met you and OSSICC I was ready to move beyond what I had done. I was ready for something where there was a sense of connectedness.

Q: What about other minorities, like the Chinese, for instance? Did the Jamaican/Canadian Association have Chinese members?

A: I don't think so, because there is also a Caribbean/Chinese Association that includes all Chinese from the Caribbean. They are mostly Jamaicans and quite vibrant.

Q: So we should make it clear that this attitude of ignoring or neglecting Indians in Jamaica is not due to anti-Indian feeling specifically.

A: It's what happens in a society when the majority are not aware of, or don't consider what minorities are feeling. Because the majority are dominant, they think that the way things happen for them is the way things happen for everybody. The only thing is that in Jamaica the Chinese had some economic power. They had their own schools. And in a society that values skin colour, Chinese were white in terms of the gradation of skin colour. If you have some economic power and you have a skin colour that's valued, you are likely to be more valuable. But if, like Indo-Jamaicans, you have neither population nor economic power on your side you are at the bottom of the pile.

Q: How did you get involved in special teaching for immigrant children?

A: In March 1975 a conference was held on the special needs of black children in Canadian schools. This led me to volunteer my help in a school with immigrant children, and the headmaster asked me to take over from the ESL teacher who was leaving.

Q: In addition to teaching you became active in social organizations?

A: I had met Wilson Head through folk dancing and in the late 1970s I worked with him and Howard McCurdy in trying to revitalize the National Black Coalition. I was also in the Jamaica/Canadian Association like other people who belonged to both organizations. I became Ontario Representative of the National Black Coalition and stayed with the group until 1982. I also stood as Liberal candidate for the constituency of Oakwood in the provincial elections of 1981. I was one of three racial minority candidates in the Liberal Party out of a total of about 125, and I was one of about four or five women candidates. The constituency was mainly Jewish, Italian and black, and most candidates were Jewish and Italian. But despite the incredible apathy of the black voters I still got 22% of the votes. I then became involved with the United Way and later the Advisory Council of Multiculturalism and Citizenship, the Ontario Housing Corporation. Harbourfront, the governing council of the University of Toronto, the Task Force on Race Relations and Policing, the Board of the National Ballet, International Social Service Canada and OSSICC.

Q: Your volunteer activities in child care, immigration, the arts, housing, social work, and so on cover an extraordinarily wide spectrum. You certainly lead a full life, and one of great social activism. Do you act as a Canadian, an Indo-Caribbean-Canadian, a Jamaican, a black woman?

A: Canada is home. If there was another place I'd like to live it would be Kerala in India. When I went to Kerala in 1991 it reminded me of Jamaica. It wasn't just the palm trees, I felt I was part of the setting. I felt I had come home. There were things that appalled and other things that enthralled me.

Q: What were some things that enthralled you?

A: I was impressed by the richness of heritage that we in the West have not acknowledged, for instance the architecture in various parts of India. Then, despite the poverty and devastation, I could see joy in the eyes of a child. Intangible things like that touched me.

RAMABAI ESPINET

Ramabai Espinet was born in Trinidad and educated both in Trinidad and Canada. She is a writer and academic and lives in Toronto.[1] The interview was recorded in Toronto on the 15 February 1996.

Q: What impact did the Canadian Presbyterian church have on Indians in Trinidad?

A: By the time I started going to school in the 1960s, the missionary impact had largely faded, although there were still many Canadian missionaries around. In my parents' generation, the missionary impact was much more significant. Members of my extended family, not only my immediate family were brought up in the Presbyterian church for generations. My grandfather was a catechist and head master. My maternal great-grandfather, John Kunjah, was one of the first three Presbyterian converts in Trinidad. These relatives saw themselves as people who belonged to a particular social class, for the Presbyterian church and school system were in the process of creating a middle class that was quite different in values, lifestyle and attitudes from other upwardly mobile Indians who had risen socially because of capital acquired through means other than education. I'm referring to the small business élite, which grew up over the years. There was overlap between these groups, but there were distinct ideas of class differences as well.

Q: Can we imagine what would have happened to Indians in Trinidad if this Presbyterian middle class had not been created?

A: There is a critical discourse raging right now about the impact of the Presbyterian missionaries and about whether they acted out of self-interest or humanitarian motives. I don't think this is a very useful discourse. The fact is that the Presbyterians did come and their impact was much larger than the number of their converts might lead one to believe. The majority of Indians chose not to send their children to the government schools but to Presbyterian schools which were understood to be Indian although they were not called Indian schools.

Q: In this way, even Indians who were Muslim and Hindu were influenced by a Presbyterian style education?

A: Yes, and they were socialized into Western norms, ethics and values that they adapted to their context in order to create an Indo-Caribbean world view. There were no Hindu or Muslim schools at the time. Muslim and Hindu schools began in the 1950s, so there was almost a century of Indo-Trinidadian education managed largely by the Presbyterian church. And this was delivered at both the primary and secondary levels. There were also teachers' training colleges and a theological college.

Q: You don't think it is useful to reassess the motives of Canadian missionaries?

A: Their motives are less important than how they impacted upon the entire Indian population. "Impact" is something that we should begin to evaluate critically so that we can begin to understand how certain distinct characteristics that we share were perhaps socially constructed.

Q: A lot of Indo-Trinidadians, especially those in their sixties or older, are very grateful for the influence of Canadian missionaries in Trinidad. A previous interview with Margaret Jagesar illustrates this.

A: That is understandable because of the opportunities that such people were given through their Presbyterian education. They tend to view their educational and other other avenues for growth as an "only chance." For them this is true and valid, perhaps. But I'm more interested in the influence of a Canadian world view of neutrality or non-interference on Indo-Trinidadian thinking; it created a buffer class between the creole population and illiterate Indians. The Presbyterian Indians, by and large, did not see themselves as spokespersons for those Indians still labouring on the estate, especially in the immediate pre- and post-Independence period. They saw themselves as people who had left that behind. Education caused the Presbyterian class to distance themselves from their kind. Someone has described it as "Indo-Saxon" behaviour, but I prefer the term "Indo-Creole" because by the time Indians came to the Caribbean, Western and African customs had mixed to the point where there was an identifiable creole culture. Indians became Indo-Creole rather than Indo-Saxon, but Presbyterian Indians became Indo-Creole-Canadian. This represents a double colonization, because the Canadian "way" was largely made up of a colonized world view, and we became another colony within an existing British Caribbean colony.

Q: Because of its relationship with England, Canada itself suffered from dependency and attitudes of inferiority, certainly in the nineteenth century. But how did that influence Trinidad where colonial attitudes already had their own creole forms?

A: It might even be triple colonialism, because these colonial attitudes had their own creole forms which influenced the national culture. As White Canadian missionaries were not critical of the existing hierarchical structure of creole social values.

Q: They worked within the feudal, colonial structure of white, brown, black. In his book Origins and Development of Racial Ideology in Trinidad Dennison Moore confirms that John Morton[2] secured the patronage of the white plantation administration before he started the work of the Canadian Presbyterian church in Trinidad.

A: "White, brown, black" is a problematic description of this structure. If "brown" refers to the educated Indian person, then this may have some currency, but the rural peasant Indian would still be at the very bottom of this ladder. But the educational system that Morton and his fellow missionaries brought with them already had the stamp of colonialism on it. The curriculum in schools was influenced by Canadian (colonial) ways of teaching and Canadian ways of situating oneself in the world, that is to say not as *managers* but as *the managed*.

Q: It is hard to define Canadian ways at that time.

A: It is hard even now. But I am getting at something that I feel deeply. Why is it that Presbyterian Indians are so uncreative as a group? After all, they were educated for such a long time—over 100 years—and they had such opportunities; they had ways of inventing a new world but didn't do so. Meanwhile, look at the parallel achievement of J J Thomas and C L R James[3] in Trinidad.

Q: They were creolized Africans. What was different about their process of development that made them so productive?

A: I don't know. I'm asking that question. Here you have creolized Indians; here you have creolized Africans; but original and independent thinking occurred much more fully in the African than in the Indian sector. I think one reason is that Presbyterian-educated Indians were taught to think by colonials who had not invented themselves yet. These Presbyterian Indians formed a significant middle class in the South of the island. Yet they were not *known* by the larger island population as late as the 1970s and 1980s. I don't think I'm overemphasizing it: there was a solid block of Presbyterian Indians who made no real impact until the late 1980s and the formation of the National Alliance for Reconstruction (NAR) government. They were taught to be an invisible buffer class and to keep the peace. I say this in spite of the fact that I know opportunities for Indians to participate at a national level were limited since the 1950s and the rise of the PNM. The Presbyterian Indians never threw in their lot with the opposition Indian party—they remained an apolitical group. This needs further investigation. Religion (Hinduism) was an important factor in Democratic Labour Party (DLP) politics in Trinidad and, as Christians, the Presbyterian Indians had already left the fold of Hinduism or Islam. Besides, some Canadian missionaries and their offspring accumulated significant wealth in Trinidad. That's the kind of economic investigation that needs to be done. Were the missionaries accumulating wealth in invisibility, while Indians accumulated capital (educational and otherwise) in invisibility as well? If this movement had come to the attention of the creole population at an early stage, there might have been some kind of confrontation.

Q: Naipaul attacks West Indians generally for being uncreative mimics, consumers rather than creators. It seems that the impact of colonialism on African West Indians has been similar to its impact on this Presbyterian educated class of Indians. In that case, Indian sterility or lack of creativity should not be attributed to a Canadian brand of Presbyterian indoctrination. But, no doubt, Naipaul overlooks the creativity of creoles like Thomas and James.

A: From the 1860s on, there was interesting debate and self-examination going on throughout the Caribbean and in Trinidad, perhaps among an élite group of creoles, but this did not involve the Presbyterian Indians. They were content with received opinions. They looked outwards—maybe towards Canada. They didn't want to disturb their universe at all. They wanted everything to stay as it was and maintain a nice mediocrity.

Q: Is your claim that the Presbyterian Indians were more uncreative than other Indians as well—the Hindus and Muslims?

A: Yes—because these other groups had a voice and were active in party politics. I'm also saddling them with more responsibility because they had more mobility at an earlier period. They have had a longer history of having access to education which might have led them to thinking through things and speaking out and being a part of a nationalist discourse.

Q: I agree that they did not break out of their restricted colonial mold. But I wonder if that is a result of their Presbyterian indoctrination specifically rather than of their status as Indo-Caribbean people, what you call Indo-Creoles. I think we should debate the term "Indo-Caribbean." I believe there is good reason for seeing ourselves as Indo-Caribbeans rather than Indians or West Indians.

A: "Indo-" and "Afro-" and all those terms are coming under a different kind of scrutiny now when people feel compromised by such abbreviated forms. Why can't we say Caribbean-Indian or Indian-Caribbean? No one says "Afro-Caribbean" anymore: they say "African-Caribbean" or "African-American." It is important for both strands of our heritage—the Indian and the Caribbean—to have a name. For that reason I resist being subsumed into the category "South Asian" in Canada although we are also part of that grouping. We are people who emerged out of the South Asian diaspora and are forming another diaspora here, but we are also Caribbean people. In a definition of our identity I don't think that we can homogenize the multiple subject identities that we bring to that definition. "Indo-Caribbean" is not a homogenous group because Indo-Caribbean people are Muslim, Hindu, Christian, atheist, etc. The process that we are engaged in now is describing our multiple subject identities. "Indo-Caribbean" is now a hot site of contestation. It should remain so, or else we'll have somebody from on top saying we have to be this or that; and I would resist that. I don't know if "Indo-Caribbean" is the best term for us. We ought to be prepared for it to shift and change as we come up with other categorizations. At the moment it is the most useful term to describe who we are: people who come out of India and the Caribbean.

Q: There is also perhaps another rationale for "Indo-Caribbean": just after Independence there was a an idealistic nationalist impulse to name everybody West Indian or Caribbean, as if we shared an all-embracing regional nationality. In the process though, the Indian-ness of Indo-Caribbean people was ignored or played down. It was important to re-assess our Indian-ness. It may be that in the future the Indian-ness of Indo-Caribbean people will either disappear completely or become so diluted that there is no rationale for it. For example, if a collective West Indian-ness or Caribbean-ness does evolve to take proper account of its Chinese, Indian, African or other parts, then we might be able to dispense with these cumbersome, double-barrelled distinctions.

A: The world is not going in that direction. The world is going in the direction of ethnic identities. I merely observe this, and I don't think this will change in the next little while. What is happening in Trinidad is that when Indo-Caribbeans call themselves "Trinidadian" or "Caribbean" people, what they are doing is practically asserting their Indian-ness, at a national level, so that the national culture can no longer ignore the Indian presence in Trinidad. By sheer force of numbers they are saying to the rest of the Caribbean "we are here" and the rest of the Caribbean has to sit up and take notice.

Q: That is very recent.

A: It is very recent, but there is no sign that it will go away. Yet in the diaspora in Toronto, Caribbean spokespersons who have been here for twenty years or more, do not reflect what is happening now in the Caribbean. Among these spokespersons you still hear the Caribbean being described as a black or African place: they have forgotten us. It is contradictory because they are lagging behind what is happening in the Caribbean. "Caribbean discourse" as articulated by its scholars also ignores the Indian presence: a change in this has begun only recently.

Q: If different Caribbean groups can express their national consciousness as Trinidadian or Guyanese, without defining themselves as Indian, Chinese or African, we will have arrived, and there will be no need for concocted descriptions, but in the post-Independence period, during the 1960s, 70s, and 80s, under Williams and Burnham, that did not happen.

A: I don't think we have arrived now either. I think that what has happened is that through increased numbers and economic clout, Indians have claimed a different kind of place in the landscape. In my view we will have arrived when we have ironed out the kind of racial tensions and nastiness that still occurs. At the moment we don't talk about it: it is swept under the carpet and people live in separate ethnic groups. The Trinidadian case has undergone tremendous change in the last ten years at the level of the national culture, although I'm not saying that this is harmony.

Q: I thought you meant that there is an appreciation of Trinidadian activity performed by Indo-Trinidadians and accepted by African-Trinidadians as Trinidadian pure and simple. Maybe what is happening now is a preliminary stage to fuller acceptance that will come later on, in which case it is still in the right direction.

A: It is a stage and it may go in a right or wrong direction. I can't see a fundamentalist, revisionary assertion of Indian identity as being a positive step.

Q: Caribbean territories are too small to think in terms of an Indian-Trinidadian state or an Indian-Guyanese state. Some form of collective unity has to evolve. Trying to work out descriptions for different groups is part of the process of evolution and some terms might have a certain currency now and disappear later on. African-Americans have gone through this process. They debated what they should call themselves for centuries and only settled on "African American" a few years ago.

A: Yes, and it is still changing. That's what I'm saying. Nothing should be seen as monolithic. I accept the term "Indo-Caribbean," but many people are resistant to it. Women who were at school with me, for instance, ask me: "What do you think about this Indo-Caribbean thing?" as if it was not automatically part of them, but something they could choose to be part of or not. I think we should debate it some more and look at how we name ourselves. We don't have avenues for doing that. We don't have places where people can come together to do that. We haven't created that kind of space.

Q: That is one reason why OSSICC [The Ontario Society for Services to Indo-Caribbean Canadians] was formed. And that, ironically, may be why OSSICC will ultimately fail: it is simply not getting support from enough Indo-Caribbean people. Some Indo-Caribbeans who have not joined OSSICC resist doing so on grounds that they are Caribbean, not Indo-Caribbean. Some of these are young people who feel they are West Indian and regard the description "Indo-Caribbean" as racist. These are inexperienced people who have not understood the racial antagonisms that corrupted politics in Trinidad and Guyana in the post-Independence period. Other Indo-Trinidadians and Indo-Guyanese who are professionals in many cases resist the description "Indo-Caribbean" although their lives are to all intents and purposes exclusively Indian: they marry Indian partners, mix socially only with Indian company, eat Indian food, and generally practise customs that are noncreolized. Yet they emphasize the creoleness of their position. This is sheer hypocrisy.

A: I would hesitate to call it hypocrisy because that gives it too much consciousness. I think it is the importation of an old fear from the Caribbean, one of being obliterated through asserting Indian-ness in any public or obviously identifiable way. It is spineless rather than hypocritical. It is a kind of attitude that cynically sides with whatever power is going. They haven't noticed that the power that is going here in Toronto is not black and that the negotiations needed are not the same. What we need to do is build a different kind of allegiance here. These people do not take a stand for reasons that they feel are strategic.

Q: But, in fact, their strategy is mistaken because they are not dealing with a creole government with whom they have to curry favour to prove their credentials as genuine Caribbean (not Indo-Caribbean) people.

A: Partly that, but also the majority of Caribbean people here who take the risk of speaking out against racism and winning rights for their people, not simply now, but over the last twenty-five years or so, have not been Indo-Caribbean people: they have been black, Afro-Caribbean people. It is reprehensible that for the sake of getting benefits, some people should pretend to be part of that black group, at least nominally while they do nothing themselves to speak out. On the other hand, if they could also stand up as another consolidated front of Indo-Caribbean people, in solidarity with African and other peoples: that would be taking a political principled stand, unlike their current apolitical curry-favouring stand. You can't live in a place without being political. Whether you're passive or not the politics acts upon you and you're part of it. If you choose that sort of slinking invisibility what will it mean for future generations, unless we all aspire to change colour gradually? I worry about the fact that Indo-Caribbeans are not leaving a political legacy for their children: they are not giving them a leg to stand on. This place is going to get much more racist in the next little while; we are seeing it already; and we are not providing the kind of foundation that our children will need. Afro-Caribbeans have taken significant risks to create political awareness among their people. Their efforts have established Black Heritage programs in schools, for example. What is happening in North America right now is the evolution of a discourse that is unabashedly Afro-centric, in scholarship and in popular political movements. This means that people who say they are not Indo-Caribbean but West Indian would be left totally in the cold unless they begin to build allegiances actively. But this is not happening.

Q: Afro-centricity will exclude us regardless.

A: It has already begun to exclude other people of colour in favour of an Afro-centric discourse. What is happening is that people are consolidating their gains. They have fought for them and feel that the fruits of their labour should be theirs.

Q: The survival techniques employed by Indo-Caribbeans included attitudes such as hypocrisy, duplicity, cunning, deviousness and obsequiousness in relations with plantation managers and administrators. But these vices became stereotypes that followed Indians long after they left the plantation. It is possible that these vices are the real cause of the fractiousness and opportunism which are such a regrettable feature of Indo-Caribbean social and political conduct. Is the plantation the real source of communally self-destructive behaviour that has disfigured the coherence of Indian political activity, in Guyana and Trinidad, since Independence? And is this behaviour now rearing its ugly head in Indo-Caribbean diaspora communities like ours in Canada?

A: I don't know if it can be ascribed to the condition of the plantation particularly. Opportunism exists everywhere. In East Africa, there was a similar pattern where Indians felt no commitment to the national or common good; there was no sense of building a community. There was no need to build a community if everyone was part of India. Inventing a new society was viewed almost as a betrayal of India. Perhaps "overseas Indians" are caught in a pattern of "struggle, survival and return," as the *Ramayana* teaches, even if it is mainly metaphorical, so the sense of building a community never occurs. In Trinidad, there were many Indian political opportunists, but there were also Indians who joined the People's National Movement (PNM) out of a genuine sense that they were creating a new nation. They really believed in decolonization and in creating something new. But these Indians did not expect that they would be obliterating themselves in the process. Williams spoke a lot about creating a "new nation". I've heard different versions of his speeches on this subject and know how his view was popularly experienced among Indians in Trinidad: people felt that he had an agenda to breed a new nation off the backs of Indian women despite any consequences to the manhood and self-respect of Indian men. This was perceived as sexual or genetic warfare, and certainly offended Indians, many of them Presbyterian Indians, some of whom became alienated from the PNM. But they did not necessarily join the DLP whose following was largely Hindu and peasant. These Indians had been enamoured of early PNM rhetoric but quickly grew disenchanted. Some were cynical enough to stay with the PNM and carry party cards, but many left. In addition, educated Indians who worked in the civil service and in teaching felt that they were being passed over for promotion constantly, and I remember conversations among people when I was growing up, talking about migration because of similar dissatisfaction. This is one of the reasons for the large wave of Indian middle class migration to Canada in the 1960s. They felt they had hit a ceiling and couldn't go further.

Q: That was the case in Guyana too: a sense of alienation felt by Indians as a result of discrimination or marginalization. At the same time, Indians were very fractious: rivalry and infighting were endemic among them. To some extent, they came to the Caribbean bringing an Indian baggage of social, caste and religious divisions. But the plantation had a levelling effect that strongly reduced caste loyalty, although it didn't remove it by any means. You made the point that they didn't come to the Caribbean to build a new nation, like the pilgrim fathers who went to the US. They came to stay for a time and go back. I would have thought that that particular attitude had long disappeared, but you seem to think it still persists in a psychic way.

A: I think so. The return might even be fulfilled in the form of a pilgrimage.

Q: One visit might take care of it, you mean?

A: Indo-Trinidadians seem to have a great longing to go to India once enough wealth has been accumulated. I remember in the late 1960s and 1970s, tours to India were advertised, and became popular— four or five tours a month. It might be that a pilgrimage takes care of this return phase.

Q: I went to India at the same time as Naipaul (around 1962) when he was writing *Area of Darkness*, and my impressions are identical to his. What he says about the squalor and breakdown is quite true, although I don't think Indo-Caribbean tourists who stay in posh tourist hotels and visit ancient monuments will see squalor and breakdown. I wonder if this is another example of Indian economic enterprise: there is the enterprise of the tourists earning enough money for the trip, and the enterprise of the tour operator in arranging the trip. It raises a question about the role of money in Indo-Caribbean society. Anthony de Verteuil in *Eight Indians* makes a plausible case for greed as a beset-ting sin in Indo-Caribbean culture. I know that he speaks from the lofty position of a well-heeled creole priest who, unlike early indentured labourers from India, has no worries about sheer physical survival. Yet the uses to which Indo-Caribbean wealth is put seem to me utterly stale, flat and unprofitable.

A: It is clear that the creation of wealth is a duty in the Hindu world view. What interests me is that that is where it stops in the Caribbean: it does not go to further stages of political responsibility, then renuncia-tion, reflection and meditation. There has been a truncation of the next two stages. We don't have traditional philanthropy or a tradition of valuing what is not materially tangible. Is this a phase that will change with more education and more exposure to what is happening else-where in other postcolonial areas such as India and China? I think it must. With more access to education and awareness, people will begin to learn more about India. There is a lot going on in India. There are these other two steps to be made. This is perhaps in the future, but what I see happening now is a blaze of consumption of wealth, and the most vulgar, empty display of wealth.

Q: I believe de Verteuil has put his finger on an important aspect of Indo-Caribbean experience. When Cheddi Jagan came back from America to Guyana in the 1940s, one of the biggest obstacles was the opaque intransigence of the rich Indians. The role played by these Indians in the defeat of Jagan's PPP in 1964 is still not fully appreciated.

A: Their interest was to continue being rich, not to build anything. I think this fits in very well with what I see happening in Trinidad and Guyana right now. There is a dearth of nationalist discourse. You are not getting the kind of critical discourse that would force people to think through what they are doing with their wealth, or how they are living their lives, or relating to the larger community.

Q: When Cheddi Jagan spoke to such people about a different approach by which they could use their wealth more creatively, they thought he had betrayed them as their political representative. Instead, many of these Indians preferred to throw in their lot with Burnham or D'Aguiar. It may have to do with their original role in the Caribbean as mere transients; it may have to do with the fact that their Hindu philosophical continuity was broken; or it may have to do with plantation ethics as well.

A: One also has to ask if philosophical continuity was not broken in India too.

Q: That is a good question. Also, I don't know if this is shared with other groups, but the Indo-Caribbean attitude to religion seems to encourage people to buy their way into heaven. You talked about charity and philanthropy; they do some of that; but it is done in a commercial way as if they are bribing God to get surreptitious favours from Him.

A: I know that large amounts of money are given to places of worship. I also know that in the Caribbean, they do things like feeding the poor. Once that is done they have no more obligation.

Q: Exactly; it frees them to go on making more money.

A: Another question arises out of that: who is their community? Their community is really very narrow: it is their immediate family. Canadians have been described as having a "garrison mentality"; but in the case of Indo-Caribbean people the garrison is infinitely smaller. It is not a mentality that allows you to go out and interact with the whole environment: it makes you live fearfully in a sort of cloister. Your community is defined as very small and narrow, and so long as it remains intact, everything else can go to hell.

Q: But these negative features of Indo-Caribbean experience, have a positive side, for example, intense loyalty to family which, ironically, often ends in conflict, especially when the loyalty is broken or betrayed. Indian family murders are well known in Trinidad and Guyana, and they do not exist with anything like the same frequency in other ethnic groups. Yet family conflict is often a direct result of one family member's generosity or sacrifice being ignored or abused. Indian families are famous for joining together to support one member in going abroad to study.

A: Yes it is true that family wars are a part of this Indian garrison mentality, but I'm interested in the gender politics within that. The boundaries for gender rules are very strict.

Q: Indo-Caribbean women have always taken second place to men in the family structure and in public life. Maybe I should ask how you see female Indo-Caribbean experience in light of the discussion we have had. How have Indo-Caribbean women suffered more than men?

A: There is an emerging discourse, claiming that the Indo-Caribbean woman held the family together, and served as a silent but strong presence at the core of everything. This discourse suggests that we do not pay enough homage to such a woman or venerate her enough. Instead, we simply see her as victim. I agree that in a lot of families the woman really held things together. Part of her holding things together was due to her almost complete self abnegation: she endured many things which contemporary women would find quite horrible, and would refuse to endure. Perhaps some of the violence against Indo-Caribbean women occurring today is due to the fact that contemporary women are refusing to endure abuses as they used to. They are asserting different choices and the gender role structures in which they function do not allow them these choices, so they have to seize them against opposition. When I was growing up, socialization took fairly distinct forms. The majority of girls were not pushed towards education. At an early stage they went into an arranged marriage. In homes where girls were put through an educational process, many still expected a good marriage or a better marriage at the end of high school. In my own case I can say that I was blessedly free of this. My family expected me to achieve academically; marriage was never part of the expectations imposed upon me. The other thing was that I went to an all girls school. While I was at high school many coeducational government schools were built, and we thought it was an attractive idea that boys and girls would learn in the same environment; it was less artificial and more modern. We thought we were deprived in an all girls' school, but current educational theory suggests that single sex schools provide a more stimulating academic environment for teenaged girls.

Q: What about any special roles that Indo-Caribbean women may have played in the family structure?

A: In the early days of indenture, stories abound of individual women's independence and the way that they would move from place to place, many of them with children, having left relationships that were not working out. One of the ways that Indians saved money was through the acquisition of jewellery which women wore. It was like a bank. Not only did early indentured women assert their freedom to leave, but they often took the family jewellery (savings) with them, and this was a factor which led to many wife murders. At the beginning of indenture, I would say up to the early 1900s, this loose family structure existed although it became less the norm as society reorganized itself, and other norms were introduced for instance, through the socializing effect of the Presbyterian church. At first the Presbyterian missionaries were scandalized by the ease with which Indian women moved households, and they certainly tried to reinscribe ideas of fidelity which many women had already abandoned. The general independence of Indian women, coupled with the need to reestablish a workable family unit, produced a structure in which Indian women were policed rigorously by the men in their family. I remember hearing stories at school about girls who travelled by bus from a country district to school in the city and back: there would be times when they would be accused of talking to boys and punished if they came home even a half an hour late.

Q: Then they could be beaten by their fathers or brothers.

A: I remember one case where this bright girl got into secondary school and her brothers did not, and when she got home from school her brothers would curse her on a daily basis, accusing her of "looking for man." This was not uncommon. Such a girl would be policed by all the male members of her family who exercised an unquestionable patriarchal authority over her, and instinctively suspected her of sexual crimes.

Q: The atmosphere you describe fits in with my experience of gender relations in Indian families in Guyana in the 1940s and 50s. It was the duty of males to protect the virtue of females in their family and this could often lead to violence.

A: The protection was not benign: it was rife with suspicion, accusation and feelings that the woman had betrayed the family. Don't you think that is unusual? Why should men have taken affront in these ways? It was as if they felt that being a woman was like having original sin. A woman did not have to err or transgress to be suspected.

Q: Women were vulnerable, powerless. In medieval Europe there was the literary convention of courtly love which influences Chaucer's poetry, for instance, in *Troilus and Criseyde*. A woman was an object of sexual purity and her conduct was governed by a convention of chastity which entailed strict supervision (policing).

A: Almost every patriarchal society has that, but it doesn't explain the rage, almost the malevolence of Indian men towards women before any "fault" is found. From the time the Indian woman reached puberty and shows signs of sexuality, she is under suspicion. The way in which this operates should be investigated. I don't know if it comes from the fact that in the early days of indenture Indian women were so free and asserted such independence, that the family structure now needs more rigorous protection. This phenomenon does not exist among African-Caribbeans or mixed race people like Chinese or Syrians, according to what I know of these groups. Men also feel the need to protect their women folk, but not in the same manner of accusation and rage without any apparent cause.

Q: The intensity was much stronger with Indians, I think, including the sense of honour.

A: It is sheer misogyny.

Q: Do you think it comes from India? Is there something in the Hindu scriptures, for instance, the story of Ram and Leela that predisposes Indians to misogynistic attitudes.

A: If it comes from India, it's probably through the laws of Manu. I know that it is evident in all the kinds of abusive attitudes towards Indian women. But there is something else in the Caribbean. I don't know if these attitudes have been reinscribed in a more intense way in the Caribbean.

Q: That certainly needs to be investigated. But let me ask about your coming to Canada and your role as an Indo-Caribbean woman writer.

A: When I first thought of writing I didn't see myself as an "Indo-Caribbean woman writer" because I was extremely young: I just saw myself as writing. Through a series of steps I began to see myself as being more and more particularized and began to describe myself as an Indo-Caribbean writer. The particularization or specificity of that position has become quite important to me. One of its key features is the scarcity of other people like myself on the landscape. There isn't a community of people that I can talk to, even through writing: I don't experience a shared investigation of my community. I experience alienation and isolation and a sense of people hardly understanding what I am trying to do. I also do not experience support from the community for my endeavour. And here I'm not talking particularly about myself as an individual. I don't think "writing" is something that the Indo-Caribbean community wants, is interested in, or has any engagement with. Therefore when I position myself as an Indo-Caribbean female writer, I dislike the terminology, and to some extent it's meaningless, but it can't be helped.

There is much more nourishment for me as a writer participating in the larger Caribbean community, and finding people (Caribbean and other) interested in what I'm doing because they know so little about the Indian community in the Caribbean. I am very conscious of the fact that I am not speaking on behalf of the Indo-Caribbean community; I'm neither trying to shore it up, nor explain it to anyone. I am engaged in a creative process which I describe simply as making art.

Q: Wouldn't the lack of support or awareness of the Indo-Caribbean community for your efforts be part of the same sort of sterility and philistinism that we've talked about? You're quite right. The reaction of the Indo-Caribbean community to OSSICC is similar. OSSICC has little appeal except to a small group of enlightened and faithful supporters. In ten years it has made almost no inroads into the Indo-Caribbean community. But if we had opened a business selling fish from the Caribbean at a low price, or offering advice about immigration or refugees, we would probably flourish.

A: I don't know why we lack any readiness to investigate the self honestly, and to look at our shortcomings and strengths in order to build from them. This is what all thinking people engage in, I don't know why it is so absent from the community that we come from, and why instead there is an overlay of received philosophy and sterile pieties.

Q: That is very Indian: the overlay of tradition upon tradition without knowing the reason for each tradition, or the meaning behind ritual observance of received practice.

A: A friend of mine, a scholar of linguistics, is researching the way in which *Ramayana* stories were narrated by women in Trinidad. What I didn't know was that the *Ramayana* was not sung verbatim. The stories were interpreted and adapted to the contemporary setting. Many stories had a subversive feminist slant that problematized Sita's fidelity and did not simply offer it as a model for all women to aspire to. The stories register the autonomy and independence of these early women. Why that has gone out of the window and been replaced by expectations and codes not connected to our daily lives, I don't know. I think that literature can potentially serve the purpose of interpreting and documenting ordinary lives, and histories that may be lost to us in a few years. What I just described was the literary effort of women engaged in an oral tradition. I think it is interesting that women engaged in it in this way because there were so few women, and they had to deal with troubling questions of fidelity and choice. They must have had to resist the suspicion of the male gaze as well—some of the stories speak to this. All of this has been thrown out and replaced by a consolidated joint family structure.

Q: Wasn't this joint family structure another survival mechanism that Indians evolved in their alien creole environment.

A: Yes, but having survived and reached a position of consolidation, we can now look at these things for what they are, and not continue to perpetuate their repressive elements. It is not a question of ascribing blame. These repressive elements are so deep in people's psyche now that many don't even realize how they are continuing them and limiting future generations in the process.

Q: Can you suggest some future directions for Indo-Caribbean people in Canada, especially our young people?

A: I think that there is a pressing need for us to move into the arena of self-investigation with rigour and honesty. Nostalgia may be nice and comforting but our needs have now gone beyond that. And even though we are in the process of adapting and integrating ourselves into our adopted country, Canada, it is vital to remember that we are travellers moving with a lot of "cultural baggage." We have not properly assessed this baggage; not yet, and we need to continue the efforts made by pioneers such as V S Naipaul and Sam Selvon—to make sense of our experience. The Caribbean experience is still fresh and we are still implicated in it and will be for decades to come—the time for honest appraisal is now. I don't mean only by writers or academics or people committed to this kind of enterprise by virtue of their daily work. I mean also the cultivation of a critical self-awareness that is lacking in our community; the development of a readiness to engage in ideas of who we are and where we are going, what baggage is negative and should be jettisoned, and where we should begin to reinvent ourselves. Do I see this happening? Only in very isolated instances and not at all as a community. We have a long hard road ahead, but I don't feel hopeless about it. I suppose you could say that we have experienced "exile" and are now at the stage of survival and struggle, as narrated in the *Ramayana*.

ALVIN KALLICHARAN

Alvin Kallicharan was born in Guyana in 1949. He made his Test cricket début for West Indies against New Zealand in 1972. He played in 66 Test matches and scored ten Test centuries. The interview was recorded in Toronto on 15 April 1992.

Q: I believe you were greatly influenced by Rohan Kanhai?[1]

A: Rohan had a great impact on my career. I had heard of him when I was a little boy growing up in Port Mourant. Then I met him when I made my début in Shell Shield[2] cricket in 1966. Joe Solomon[3] created an even greater impact on me because he was a very good coach. The whole idea of playing Test cricket for my country first came to me when I saw Rohan Kanhai, Joe Solomon and Basil Butcher[4] playing Test cricket. It was then that I felt I wanted to do it too.

Q: How did you actually get into the West Indian Test team?

A: I did a lot of work from 1966 to 1971, and produced results in Guyana cricket. It took hard work. This is something I try to impress upon kids at home who may want to do the same thing but are not prepared to put the hours in.

Q: Your Test début against New Zealand in April 1972 was fantastic. You began with two successive centuries.[5] You also made some high scores in the next series that West Indies played against Australia. Then your career went progressively up. You were scoring regularly until the hitch came with Packer.[6] What about the captains you played under?

A: If you recall, the West Indies were not doing too well in the early

1970s. Things improved when Kanhai took over the captaincy on the Australian tour of 1972–73. Then he took the team to England in 1973 and we won handsomely.

Q: What was it like on that 1973 tour to England?

A: It was an eye opener—going back to the mother country. But I did my job, I made 600 runs. It was a tremendous feeling. I also made a lot of friends.

Q: What about later tours?

A: We got beaten 5–1 in Australia in 1975–76.

Q: What was responsible for that? By then Lloyd[7] had replaced Kanhai as captain?

A: We weren't a team. We were a good side, but there was no control. Everybody wanted to be captain. In sport it is when you're losing that you need team spirit the most. We didn't have team spirit.

Q: What is the Packer story?

A: I didn't go to Packer. Warwickshire[8] said if I went to Packer they were not going to renew my contract. I was married, with a young family and because of the politics in Guyana,[9] there was no way I was going to take the chance of bringing up my family in Australia. I preferred to stay with Warwickshire. Simple as that.

Q: In April, 1978, you became captain of West Indies in three matches of a home series against Australia. Then you were captain again on the tour that followed to India.

A: When we came back from India I learnt that the senior West Indian players who had signed with Packer were reinstated in the West Indian team. I had gone to India with a very young side and scored well. Soon after returning, I had a call from the Secretary of the West Indies Cricket Board of Control (WICBC). He asked if I was available to play in the World Cup. There I was, sitting at home in England, without even having finished my captain's report for the tour to India, and I was told that Clive Lloyd had been appointed as West Indies captain for the World Cup. It took me weeks to reply. As a matter of fact, I never replied to the actual telephone call, but they picked me, and I played in the World Cup. I also went to Australia afterwards. That's when things started getting a bit distant between myself and Clive. I had a successful tour though. But I started to think, while I continued playing for the West Indies: I thought that if I didn't look after myself, I was not going to enjoy playing, and my cricket would suffer. So I felt I must look after myself professionally first, and when the offer came to go to South Africa,[10] I was ready, although it still took me a whole season to accept it.

Q: You were aware of the consequences?

A: Yes. I weighed the circumstances. I knew what was going to happen. And I did it. It prolonged my career. If I had continued to play for West Indies, I would not have enjoyed it because of the bickering. And my cricket would have suffered. There's a lot more to what I did than appears on the surface.

Q: The fact is though, Alvin, that it put an end to your Test career.

A: Yes, I missed international cricket. I missed it badly. But we all make certain critical decisions in life and I made one that cut my international career short. I am not disappointed.

Q: You still play for Warwickshire?

A: No, I had to retire last year. When I say retire, I was told not to play because of a back problem, so I did not play last season. But I hope to play for a couple more seasons. Then I'll try to do something for our kids in West Indian cricket. I believe they deserve it.

Q: What you say reflects on the administration of the game in the Caribbean. Since you left Test cricket, the West Indian team has been spectacularly successful under Lloyd using a battery of fast bowlers. Do you have any feelings about this relentless use of fast bowling?

A: Only that I feel sorry that captains like Sobers and Kanhai did not have the same battery of fast bowlers.

Q: Lloyd was succeeded by Richards as captain, and during the last ten years there have been no Indian players on the West Indian cricket team. Why?

A: Usually one Indian player should appear in ten years. Look at Kanhai and myself! We did not come at the same time. There must be a reason. After all, Indians play in the same domestic cricket competitions like Red Stripe and Shell Shield. You would expect those competitions to produce some Indian Test players.

Q: I believe that the Guyana team is about half black, and half Indian. Yet this proportion does not seem to affect the West Indian team selection. Clyde Walcott, President of the West Indian Cricket Board was in Toronto last year and was asked about this. He said that Indian players were usually spinners, and spinners were not needed when West Indies had a winning combination of fast bowlers.

A: But Indians can bat too. His explanation doesn't appear adequate.

CLEM SEECHARAN

Clem Seecharan was born at Palmyra, Berbice, Guyana in 1950. He studied at McMaster University in Canada and the University of Warwick in England. He now teaches Caribbean history at the University of North London in England. The interview was recorded in Fillongley, England on 29 June 1996.

Q: Would you say that when elections were held in Guyana in 1961 racial polarization had already taken place?

A: Very much so, yes.

Q: How did this sharp division between African and Indian, in terms of politics, take place between 1953 and 1961?

A: In the 1961 election, the People's Progressive Party (PPP) did not even bother to field a candidate for New Amsterdam because they saw it as a lost cause—a People's National Congress (PNC) or black [African] people's constituency. So although we [Indians] went to New Amsterdam[1] for education or business, and were very much a part of the town, we understood it as enemy territory. Racial polarization was taking shape since the 1920s. In the 1920s, soon after indentureship ended, some Indo-Guyanese such as Dr W Hewley Wharton and J A Luckhoo[2] were thinking of bringing more Indians into Guyana. They talked about British Guiana becoming an Indian colony, which invoked fear and foreboding among Afro-Guyanese. The Indian independence struggle also had a negative impact on Guyanese race relations because it galvanized Indians in Guyana and gave them a clearer sense of themselves that tended to distance them further from Afro-Guyanese. On the other hand, by the 1920s, Afro-Guyanese were already aware of Marcus Garvey,[3] and by the 1930s, the invasion of Ethiopia by Italy[4] was also a very powerful issue in Afro-Guyanese society. Both tended to create within the African community in British Guiana a sense of their own antecedents, in the same way that Indo-Guyanese were lifted by the rise of the Gandhian movement and the emergence of Indian nationalism. There was already the sense of a bifurcated or two-dimensional nationalism in Guyana, long before the emergence of the party politics of Jagan and Burnham, in the 1950s. Racial instincts are deeply rooted in Guyanese culture.

Q: This is a crucial issue for the Southern Caribbean, Guyana and Trinidad and Tobago, where there is still a feeling that during colonial times, until about 1960 or 61, animosities between Indians and Africans, were more or less superficial or mild, and that these animosities only flared up after Independence, with the removal of British rule, when Guyanese and Trinidadians had to work out their own destiny. It is interesting that you perceive seeds of racial division well before Independence.

A: I agree that racial division assumed a more pernicious form in the 1960s, and that it would be wrong to say that the character of this division in the 1920s and 30s was equally serious. During the 1920s and 30s, supervision by the British colonial authority limited the expression of internal divisions; but this doesn't mean that divisive issues were not already reverberating within the society, and when the movement for decolonization accelerated after the second World War, it simply exacerbated these issues: who was to inherit the kingdom?

Q: Indians were first brought to Caribbean territories in 1838, about two hundred and fifty years after Africans were already there. This encourages a perception of these territories as being African, and this may be acceptable in most territories where the population is mainly African. But in two territories—Guyana and Trinidad—Indians are numerically the majority, certainly in Guyana, if not quite so in Trinidad. Does this not raise a question about nationality and democracy? You have already confirmed the existence of ethnic division in Guyana well before 1960. What is the implication of this division in terms of a national future for Guyana and, by extension, Trinidad and Tobago?

A: When we speak of Guyanese nationality we are not speaking of something concrete. It is more of a construct—something we should like to see, or to form and develop; that is a long way off yet. Until a few years ago there was very little historical writing about the polity. What existed was primarily a political construction or perception that attempted to engineer a sense of being. That is why the idea of national unity itself was a tenuous thing, and when virtual civil war broke out in the 1960s, there was nothing in our educational experience that equipped us to understand why. The Marxist-inspired national dream was alluring because it papered over severe cracks, and compensated for our absence of history by creating a Utopia that we could all aspire to. When we speak of a Guyanese identity we are really speaking of an artificial creation because we are still framed by ethnic perceptions of ourselves, which can be activated very quickly.

Q: I agree that our frustrations as British colonials might have bred somewhat romantic notions about nationality, based on a Marxist philosophy; but surely we have to have a nation which consists of a unified grouping of disparate races and cultures?

A: Yes I agree. But the efforts to engineer a national perspective are not based on an understanding of our history. It is vital to understand that our society contains seeds of disintegration fed by primordial loyalties to each major ethnic group. We must acknowledge the contribution of different ethnic groups in our historiography. If we try to deny their existence, we are not going to be able to evolve a concrete Guyanese nationality. In the past, the Marxists and nationalists have tried to conceal the resilient fact of ethnic particularism and the result has been disillusionment and racial insecurity that sustain a sense of exclusion and political chaos.

Q: In colonial times Marxism was seen as perhaps too easy a remedy for the evils of colonialism. But we must remember that colonialism itself was very divisive. British colonial rulers brought Africans, Indians, Portuguese, Chinese and others into the Caribbean in their pursuit of economic benefit. They were not interested in the divisions created by bringing these different groups together; and when the anticolonial movement emerged in the 1940s and 50s, not only was Marxism seen as a liberating creed, but as a means of achieving anticolonial solidarity by papering over actual divisions in our society. In view of the racial polarization that has already taken place in Guyana, what hope is there now for understanding these divisions?

A: The construction of a Guyanese nationality took place between the formation of the Political Affairs Committee (PAC) in 1946 and the founding of the PPP in January 1950, and this hurried nationalist agenda, which was based on class rather than cultural autonomy, ignored the very distinct experiences of the 1930s and 1940s when Indians were moving fast. Many Indians had done well in business, in rice production and cattle rearing. Both Indians and Blacks were building a consciousness, but it was a consciousness that was reinforced along ethnic lines. I don't think that was necessarily a bad thing. But the politics that emerged, by speaking almost exclusively in class terms, denied what could have been an asset, something that might have been worked into a broader, richer national perspective. Instead, by denying this cultural autonomy, we ensured its recrudescence, its breaking out from time to time.

Q: Cultural autonomy did become the cause of ethnic or racial antagonism. But I wonder if the antagonism does not have even deeper roots. When Indians first came to Guyana in 1838, they were used as strike breakers by plantation owners to undercut the bargaining power of the newly freed Africans.

A: In 1842, for instance, on various plantations, Blacks working in task gangs withheld their labour and were beginning to bargain as if they were a rural working class, or a kind of rural proletariat, so that when the planters reduced wages unilaterally, Africans were able to strike and push up the price of labour again. By 1848, however, the planters had started to bring in Portuguese from Madeira and Indian indentured labourers—bound coolies—who could not bargain, but had to accept the statutory one-shilling-a-day wage, and work with their prescribed employers. This time, when the Africans went on strike, they could not hold out because of this bound labour. From the beginning the perception of the "coolie" was of someone who was a scab, a strike breaker, and to compound the problem, Africans realized that the fiscal policies of the colonial administration were designed to levy inordinate taxes on the commodities that they were consuming, for example, salt fish and lard. Excise taxes were being used to fund the importation of Indian indentured labourers. Blacks were, indeed, contributing to the subsidizing of people who were coming in as scab labour.

Q: They were undercutting their own strategy of resistance.

A: That's right. When writing his great book *A History of the Guyanese Working People*,[5] Walter Rodney did some interviews with Blacks in poor Guyanese villages, many of whom were growing up in the 1920s. They spoke often of what had become a part of their lore: that "de collie tek way de bread out ah we mout." That enduring perception sustained a black sense of grievance against the Indian as a perennial threat to his well-being, and indeed as the cause of his deprivation.

Q: In a previous interview, Robert Janki said that Indian economic activity—their propensity for commerce—and their movement from rural areas into the cities, reinforced this impression of the Indian as a threat. By building big houses in Georgetown, and sending their children to train as professionals abroad, Indo-Guyanese posed a visible threat to Afro-Guyanese.

A: Long before that, in the 1850s, land policies were drafted to reduce access to land and make it increasingly difficult for people to become independent farmers as the freed Africans had begun to do by establishing village settlements. It was a deliberate policy to try to inhibit the emergence of an independent peasantry, and to stall the advance of anything other than the sugar industry. This is where Indians had a comparatively better environment for development than Africans. From the 1890s they were able to acquire land at a much cheaper rate.

Q: Why were Indians able to acquire land and not the Africans who were there long before them?

A: Because the 1880s and 1890s marked a period of prolonged depression in the sugar industry, when there was such a catastrophic fall in prices that some people were predicting the end of sugar which had been Moloch, to which everything had previously been sacrificed. By the 1890s, although so much had been given to sugar, there was still no significant development of the colony. The Norman Commission which visited British Guiana in early 1897 categorically said that the colony could not continue to depend on sugar monoculture. The Commission[6] recommended the encouragement of alternative industries and the creation of an independent peasantry with a stake in the future of their own environment. In this context, many Indians were able to acquire land, Crown land, for instance, which fell in price from something like one dollar per acre to fifteen cents per acre.

Q: I can see the fact of Indians acquiring land more rapidly than Africans, and their commercial acumen generally acting as factors that fuelled animosity among Africans. Are there other historical factors which aided the development of the Indians vis à vis Africans?

A: Indians were not slaves. People try to see indentureship as a new kind of slavery, but however slavelike the conditions of Indian indentureship might have been, Indians were not things—the mere property of planters; nor did they have to adopt the life of the planters; they always retained some cultural autonomy. Besides, indentureship went on for over seventy years; new immigrants were constantly coming from India, bringing aspects of their culture, and renewing the cultural pool. There was no terminal break with the homeland. Another factor was that a high percentage of Indians came from the so-called Hindu heartland of Eastern Uttar Pradesh and Western Bihar where the great Hindu classic *The Ramayana*[7]—is set. Whether Indians in Trinidad or Guyana knew anything at all about Indian history, or whether they had any sense of ancient Indian civilization, is immaterial: they carried with them a notion of their own scriptures and of the story of—*The Ramayana* which was an integral part of their own sense of history. Their notion of self was rooted in a mystical/mythical past intertwined with the story of Ram and Sita which was located in places that they knew. This story of the enforced exile of Ram and Sita was part of their history; it had special resonance, and it gave them a sustaining vision which they took to Trinidad, Guyana and elsewhere.

Q: So we should see *The Ramayana* as a document of exile that was as sustaining to indentured Indians as *The Odyssey* was to ancient Greeks or *The Iliad* to ancient Romans? It provided psychic or psychological ballast which helped Indians to survive in a situation of exile?

A: Of course. Without the deeper meanings of the story, just at the level of the narrative, of Ram being exiled from his kingdom, of his wife Sita being taken away by people of a lower state of development, *The Ramayana* reinforced a notion of exile, of being torn from one's umbilical connection with one's own ancestral place. This struck a very powerful chord. But it also spoke of displacement, loss, oppression and the inevitability of triumphal return.

Q: If our discussion is leading to the fact that Indo-Guyanese and Afro-Guyanese are mutually opposed by racial or cultural inheritance, and that migration is their only option, we must realize that the majority of Guyanese cannot migrate. I think we have to face the fact that a Guyanese nation has to be formed or there will be continuous conflict.

A: It is also a fact that we have lost the core of our society to migration—the best intellectuals, technical people, fishermen, canecutters, everyone.

Q: Are we to see migration as a solution to a universal problem. In places like Nigeria and India, for instance, the British encountered societies with historic differences of culture, religion and language, and they imposed a supranational form of government on all of them, creating immense postcolonial problems, including civil war. In our case in the Caribbean, there was no pre-British history since the indigenous population was eliminated. So the answer was to form a new nationality out of freshly arrived groups. Is it the case that the groups coming in are incapable of forming a collective nationality and therefore have to settle for forms of break-up, migration or dispersal?

A: No, I don't think so. But we have to try and understand both the African and Indian contribution to our environment, the things that have divided us, if we are to avoid another explosion.

Q: What do you mean by explosion?

A: I mean a racial war. In the 1970s and 80s Indians fled because they felt totally excluded from the political process in Guyana. In recent years, with what is now seen as an Indian government, although it is democratically elected, Blacks feel terribly alienated. A new approach has to be found to avoid such deadlock. First of all, local government should be depoliticized so that people are elected irrespective of their ethnic background or political affiliation. Secondly, I think that people who are likely to win general elections because of the built-in majority of Indian votes in the country, must be willing to go beyond the winner taking all. A new constitution must ensure a broader plurality of representation; there should be no losers.

Q: Who will make those changes? The country seems to lack the personnel capable of implementing such changes.

A: Most of the bright, imaginative people have migrated, and for a small place like that to be stripped of its most capable people is to produce acute intellectual poverty. In the present government, many people in the cabinet are essentially party hacks, who fear bright Guyanese overseas. I don't think they are capable of running a modern state in a delicate multiracial environment like Guyana. But in spite of what I've been saying, I believe that the level of ethnic intolerance in places like Trinidad and Guyana is much less than in many older societies. As Guyanese, we can create a nation out of our disparate groups. I think we've gone about it the wrong way because we tried to latch on to a foreign ideology which could just wish away our problems. I still meet Guyanese intellectuals who tell me that race is kind of a mirage. This is misleading. It is better to see how deep-seated our racial problem is. If we start from this position we will realize the futility of much of what passes for national politics, and accept the inevitability of compromises. We've got to start from the position that we have a very tenuous grip on any kind of a self-sustaining state, and that therefore compromises—giving and taking—are indispensable for our survival.

Q: Race, class, and colour have been crucial in creating the problems that we have, and perhaps wishy-washy political theorizing may have been a factor in our understanding of Marxism.

A: It was strongest in Guyana, not in places like Jamaica or Barbados. It was in the territory that seemed to have the greatest racial problem that every political group virtually tried to outdo each other with a Marxist agenda.

Q: Why do you think that was?

A: There were specific reasons. Absentee landlordism played a major role in the Guyanese sugar industry. In Barbados, for instance, there were white people who owned plantations and remained on the island. However élitist their role might have been, they were an integral part of Barbadian society. That had a long term beneficial effect on the evolution of Barbadian political democratic culture. In the Guyanese case, however—and Cheddi Jagan was influenced by this—the sugar industry was so heavily concentrated in the hands of two or three major British multinational corporations, that it was seen as an implacable enemy, infinitely less responsive to the needs of the local people. That was very deep-seated, and it prompted a strong Marxist reaction. Marxism was not only a question of trying to wish away endemic racial problems.

Q: It is also true that Dr Jagan, who introduced Marxism into Guyanese politics, had an American education. If Burnham was presumably Marxist since the 1940s and 50s, what would have happened if Burnham alone had come back to Guyana as a political leader in the 1950s? I suspect he could have implemented similar Marxist policies without the catastrophic effects that we have seen with Dr Jagan. In other words, Marxism itself probably was not the problem: it was more a kind of Republican/American/ radical Marxism combined with the fact that Dr Jagan happened to be Indian.

A: Dr Jagan's style of politics might seem more radical or left wing than the politics of someone from the British Guiana East Indian Association who would have been more limited by loyalty to India. In actual fact, neither was terribly democratic. Marxism was an élitist concept that did not translate into broadening of a democratic outlook within Indian village branches of Jagan's People's Progressive Party, for instance. It was a kind of brahmanism in which everything was handed down and clearly defined. That is what made it so attractive. Not only was it going to create a Utopia that would deliver the workers from Bookers, the plantation and oppression, but in a kind of brahminic fashion, it would deliver this new world ready-made, already recreated for them. The sugar workers, mainly Indian, had virtually no political experience, not even the kind of village political experience that the African people had in Guyana through their involvement in local government, trade unionism, the church, and the burial and friendly societies. That embryonic leadership had deep roots among the African people in both urban and rural communities. That was less so the experience of the Indians. What they had was the diktat of the brahmins who defined the world for them and offered solutions in and out of season. The Marxism that came from a man like Dr Jagan gave you basically the same kind of prescription: it defined the world for you and told you that there was Rama (socialism) who was going to deliver you from oppression of Bookers, and Rawana (capitalism) who was going to keep hitting you over the head. It simplified the world. That is why it could coexist with the brahminism that was so much a part of the Indian community.

Q: I would like to ask a little more about Indo-Caribbean culture and the role of brahminism in it.

A: I think brahminism is an important component of Indo-Caribbean culture. Hinduism cannot be separated from brahminism in the Caribbean, and this has had a largely negative effect. Brahminism didn't allow Hinduism to develop and adapt itself as a creative force within the Caribbean environment. Although Hinduism was self-sustaining, and contributed a sense of self-esteem and well-being to Indians, it was rooted in a brahminic way of seeing that prevented it from adapting and modernizing itself and building bridges with other religious and racial groups. The inspired leadership that a Hindu teacher might have provided did not materialize because of brahminism, which excluded people on the basis of birth without recognizing their ability or achievement. There were Hindu religious leaders, and by extension political leaders who were chosen not necessarily because of their ability, but because they were seen to be born into a particular group. Jagan's Marxism undermined this old Indian ascriptive basis of power somewhat, but it did not democratize Indian politics: the pressure to conform was not diminished; to challenge Jagan was like challenging Lord Rama.

Q: Of course the Arya Samajists[8] were opposed to brahminism, but they were only a small sect of Hindus. How does brahminism influence politics or race relations?

A: Through the character of leadership. I got into trouble for challenging the brahmins in my temple when I was about sixteen years old. The women especially condemned me for challinging their learned pandit. One thing about the "learned" pandit was that he didn't want the rest of us to become too learned at all. The nature of the leadership that we got from the Hindu priest or pandit was one where everything was dictated to us, and the more I think of the way politics percolated down to our village level through the PPP and Jaganist Marxism, the more I discern the very powerful authoritarian tendencies in it.

Q: Was Jagan himself authoritarian?

A: Jagan was always authoritarian. He didn't have room, and still doesn't, for bright, intellectual people around him. Intellectuals don't last long with Dr Jagan. If you question anything you are immediately seen as some kind of enemy. We in the villages had to be satisfied with virtual diktats that came from Freedom House.

Q: You would say that the root of that authoritarianism is in the Hindu religion?

A: Yes. I see a parallel between Dr Jagan's politics and Hindu temple politics where the powerful hand of brahminic doctrinal dictates held complete sway. Priestly authority was utterly intolerant of any attempt to question or challenge it.

Q: Nobody could have been as authoritarian as Burnham, and he was not Hindu. The Caribbean, after all, is well-known for its slavery/indenture culture and plantation authoritarianism. Frankly, I would have thought Dr Jagan the least authoritarian of Guyanese leaders, certainly compared with a man like Burnham whose unbridled lust for political power was unaccompanied by any moral compunctions.

A: It was a different kind of authoritarianism. Burnham's bordered more on totalitarianism. Burnham had basic vulgarity, arrogance and intolerance which thrived in the sterile soil of Guyanese Marxism and Anglo-American hatred of Jagan. Dr Jagan's authoritarianism stemmed more from his intellectual deficiencies, and these deficiencies fitted into a community where, even in the home, there were strong patriarchal tendencies. This was a community that gave a tremendous amount of authority to the patriarch: conformity was prized, debate discouraged, and when it surfaced, it did so as rage.

Q: It is true that paternalism, patriarchism and hierarchy are standard features in Caribbean society with a history of the plantation system and values based on race, colour and class. Indo-Caribbean culture is influenced both by a Caribbean environment and an Indian cultural inheritance. Is it possible to determine which aspects of Indo-Caribbean conduct and behaviour come from one side or the other?

A: The plantation environment has not precluded the emergence of a healthy democratic tradition in Barbados and Jamaica with their largely African populations. This is evident in their range of organizations and associations which help to articulate public opinion, and their press, with its tradition of investigative journalism. Such freedom of opinion comes less easily among Indo-Caribbean people, and that, I believe, is due to the negative influence of this brahminic tradition. I would argue that while this tradition helped Indians to adapt to a very hierarchical Caribbean plantation environment, the long-term consequences of that adaptation have been more severe among Indians than among people of African descent. Afro-Caribbeans have inbibed aspects of the liberal democratic British tradition in a more unmeditated and forthright way than Indo-Caribbeans, who were already buttressed by their own essentially patriarchal and hierarchical tradition.

Q: Does that make the gulf between them more unbridgeable?

A: No. The long term security of Indians cannot be divorced from the long term security of Africans in Guyana or Trinidad and Tobago where both communities must share the same space. Now that Indian people seem to have political power in Guyana and Trinidad and Tobago, they must be seen to take the initiative of walking that extra mile to win African confidence. We must remember that during the 1960s, 70s and 80s, political domination by the Williams régime in Trinidad and Tobago, and by the Burnham régime in Guyana led to the same situation—a sense of exclusion, alienation, and marginalization—which forced tens of thousands of Indo-Caribbean people to migrate. Now that Indo-Caribbeans seem to have some political say in a democratic environment, they must take the initiative and ensure that the African people don't feel equally marginalized.

ARNOLD THOMAS

Arnold Thomas was born in St Vincent in 1942. He studied in England and the US. He also worked in Guyana during the 1970s. He now lives in England and teaches at the University of London.

Q: Can you tell me about your family's arrival in St Vincent?

A: My maternal grandparents came from India in 1886, and one of my paternal grandparents came from India in 1880. They came directly to St Vincent. The story of my mother's family is that on 20 January

1866, a ship called Countess of Ripon was wrecked off the coast of Barbados on the way from India. There was an Indian woman on it who had just given birth to a son. The mother was very ill and as she was brought ashore in Barbados, a black woman, seeing the plight of mother and child, came forward from the crowd, took the child, and breast-fed him. The police magistrate concluded that that act saved the child's life. The child who was rescued on the ship in Barbados was none other than my mother's grandfather who was born on the 4th January, 1866, somewhere in the south Atlantic, on board ship. His name was Gangaram; his father's name was Kowlessur, and his mother's name was Bachia. They came from India with two sisters and another brother. My father's grandparents came on the last ship bringing Indians to St Vincent in 1880. His grandfather's name was Ramphal and his grandmother was Anopia.

Q: Do you know the circumstances under which your relatives left India?

A: We don't know much about why they left India. In the ships' lists which I consulted, the section that deals with their villages or districts of origin was left blank. They spoke of the Rajputs, and I suspect they came from a warrior caste. They also had a tradition of stick fighting.

Q: How did you get the family name "Thomas?"

A: My paternal grandfather was christened Thomas; his father's name was Gowkool. Early in the indenture experience, the churches in St Vincent, and I suppose elsewhere in the Caribbean, tried hard to convert Indian immigrants, contrary to what was agreed, namely that Indian immigrants would be allowed to practise their religion in the Caribbean. Perhaps because of the small size of St Vincent, there was less supervision and less structure to ensure keeping to the letter of the agreement. At any rate, the rigorous attempt at christianization meant that Indian children born in St Vincent were given Christian or Anglo-saxon family names.

Q: That was not the practice in Guyana, where the Canadian Presbyterian church would baptize Indians and give them Christian first names, but retain the Indian family names. I assume that the church that you mention in St Vincent was Anglican?

A: Anglican, Methodist, and Roman Catholic. The Methodists were most popular among Indians in St Vincent.

Q: By 1868, about six years after indenture started in St Vincent, the churches began to compete very aggressively among themselves to convert the Indians. The Anglican church, which had a monopoly on churches and schools on the island, took exception to missionary activities by the Methodists in particular, and whenever the Methodists baptized Indian children, the Anglicans would rebaptize them. It took the Archbishop of Canterbury to end the religious in-fighting.

Q: How did your own family fare in these circumstances?

A: At the end of indenture in 1890, most of the Indians remained on one estate called Argyle; they had no opportunity to purchase land. It was not until the 1920s that Indians made their way from the estate, bought up lands and created villages. My father's family acquired a fair bit of land in three estates called Akers, Calder, and Richland Park, which are the main Indian villages. If you go to St Vincent, you will find that descendants of both my grandparents dominate Calder, Akers and Richland Park. My father was a tailor and spent most of his working life between St Vincent and Trinidad, where he had a shop in Port of Spain.

Q: What about your own education?

A: I went to Mesopotamia Primary School, about two miles from the village, and then to high school in Kingstown. After finishing my "O" levels, I came to England in 1962. At first I worked in a factory, then as a clerk before going back to college in 1964 for my "A" levels. After finishing my first degree from London University, I went to America in 1969. I got my PhD from City University, New York.

Q: What impression did you form of Indo-Caribbean culture in St Vincent?

A: We were creolized very early and didn't have a very strong commitment to Indianness in terms of food, dress or religion (I use the term "creolized" to mean the process of adapting to the local way of life, while maintaining racial/ethnic identity). Our people had gone with the mainstream of society and became Christians, largely as a means of survival. For example, we had no special school for Indians as in Trinidad and Guyana; we had to adapt to public schools.

Q: Were Indian activities in any way recognizable as different from African activities? For instance, were they as good at business as Indians have a reputation of being in Trinidad and Guyana?

A: Noticeably so. My father was in business and his parents—my grandparents—were also shopkeepers. In the Indian village, all the shops were owned by my family. I also remember weddings which had many of the Indian traditions. When I later went to Guyana, I saw similarities between their Indian weddings and ours. Even the funerals of the older people were conducted with some ritual. When my grand-father died, the eldest son had to shave his head. We did not know the significance and only found out later when we met Trinidadians and Guyanese.

Q: Did the fact of Indians in St Vincent being so thoroughly creolized and forming such a small community create any psychologi-cal problems, for example, of inferiority?

A: No. But there was always a semblance of animosity between Indians and Blacks, and we were not unfamiliar with being called "coolies". I grew up in a village of six hundred people of whom less than a dozen were black families at the time. Culturally, we might have been creolized, but we saw ourselves as Indians by race. We went to the same church, for instance, first as Methodists and Catholics, then as Seventh Day Adventists. A majority of Indians from St Vincent living in England belong to the Seventh Day Adventist Church. Following in-denture, there were about 1500 Indians in St Vincent. This number was reduced by the hurricane of 1898. Then the volcanic eruption of 1982 reduced the number even further, but the few remaining Indians still married among themselves and kept the Indian presence alive.

Q: Did Indians in St Vincent generally know much about Indians in Trinidad or Guyana?

A: Yes, they were always travelling back and forth. In the early 1950s, we had radio, so we knew what was going on. Not only my father, but a number of people from my village travelled up and down the Caribbean selling goods, produce and live animals. Several Indians became wealthy, after which they stopped trading and set up busi-nesses in St Vincent.

Q: Did they, like in Guyana and Trinidad, start up in business and then acquire money to send their children to be educated abroad so that they could come back as professionals?

A: Many did that, except that opportunities were so limited in St Vincent that the ones who went abroad to be educated seldom re-turned.

Q: What about political activity? Did Indians take part in it, and how did it affect their lives, if at all?

A: We got the full franchise in 1950 or 1953 when two Indians con-tested seats under the new franchise and one won. Unfortunately, not long after winning the seat, our duly elected representative emigrated from the island. This created enormous problems for other Indians who later wanted to get into politics; people never forgot that they had elected an Indian who left the island as soon as he got into power. During the 1950s everyone thought about England as a place with fantastic opportunities, and this Indian MP simply joined the queue.

Q: Did he pursue a professional career in England?

A: I believe he did continue studies in England, but I don't know what his personal motivation might have been. What I do know is that, even now, whenever any Indian suggests getting into politics, Vincentians always remind him or her of the 1950s and the former Indian MP. Since then Indians have been shying away from politics.

Q: In Trinidad and Guyana, the political history is different: Indians have been very active in politics even though they haven't been very successful. Perhaps Indo-Trinidadians and Indo-Guyanese were politically active because their larger numbers gave them a real prospect of political power.

A: In the 1950s Indians in St Vincent were not interested in political power: they were interested in survival.

Q: This seems reasonable, since their numbers did not allow them any real possibility of political power.

A: I don't think we had that sense of needing our own "Indian" representative: we did not see ourselves as separate from the mainstream in a political sense, although we were aware of cultural and racial differences.

Q: I think that is the important thing. The trouble in Guyana and Trinidad is that ethnicity and race became linked with politics. That did not happen in St Vincent. After leaving England and completing a PhD in political science in New York, you began working in the Caribbean Secretariat in Georgetown, Guyana in 1975. Burnham was at the height of his power then. What was your impression of Guyana and Indo-Guyanese?

A: I suffered a bit of a culture shock when some Indo-Guyanese became concerned by my friendship with other black people. I guess at that time in Guyana, there was already a divide between Indians and Blacks. I had no problem crossing that divide, but my Guyanese friends were concerned by it. That was my first experience of living in a racialized situation. Growing up in a typical Indian village in St Vincent we never had that kind of antagonism. I got the impression that Guyanese felt that if I was not with them then I was against them, but it never bothered me.

Q: After 1964, Guyanese had become strongly politicized. Your reactions in Guyana clearly illustrate differences between Indo-Guyanese and Indo-Vincentians.

A: My father was quite politically aware. He had travelled to Trinidad and other Caribbean islands, and seen the differences between Indians and Blacks there. But I cannot remember him reminding us about these differences. He saw himself as a Vincentian, not as an Indo-Vincentian. Perhaps it was because we were a minority in a larger community, but he never suggested that we should not mix because we were different, but marriage was a different matter.

Q: What opinion did you form of Burnham during your time in Guyana in the 1970s?

A: I am convinced he was a demagogue and racist, and I believe most educated Guyanese thought so, too. But he had the support of the man in the street, and many Indians supported him, either because their bread and butter depended on him, or out of fear of recrimination.

Q: After about three decades since Independence, Indian politicians now lead the governments in Guyana and Trinidad and Tobago. How significant is that?

A: I think it is very significant that Indian political leaders have mass support. The electorate in Guyana had grown tired of PNC corruption. I would not like to think that Dr Jagan was elected because he is Indian. He is a man of principle and has support among non-Indians.

Q: You do not see him as representing Indo-Caribbean culture?

A: I believe there is an Indo-Guyanese culture and an Indo-Trinidadian one. The term "Indo-Caribbean" is a response to the Afro-West Indian thrust of the 1970s and 80s. There is a lot that is shared between Indians from various Caribbean territories, for example, their plantation experience and relations with Afro-Caribbeans.

Q: "Indo-Caribbean" comes out of an attempt to find the right label for a cultural group that was created by empire builders and abandoned when empire broke up. It is a new postcolonial phenomenon, and it will take time before the right label is found.

A: I define Indo-Caribbean culture in terms of race, ethnicity, national origin and regionalism. Indo-Caribbeans are easily identifiable by race. Their ethnicity is a little more complicated because of their mixed cultural experience in the Caribbean. Their national origin is obviously Indian, and their regional identity is just as obviously Caribbean. It is only when people emphasize one of these factors more than the others that they run into trouble. What we must never forget is that the Caribbean is a fusion of cultures, but within the mix, each group has its own cultural traditions.

Part Four

The Second Migration

Indian Migration

Large numbers of Africans and Asians were transferred to distant parts of the globe during the post-Renaissance period of modern history when Europe achieved military superiority worldwide and mastered technology for her ships to undertake transoceanic voyages with relative ease. Former land-based empires like those of the Romans and the Arabs did not engage in large scale transfer of populations over similar distances. But modern European nations, Britain in particular, not only established imperial outposts in almost every continent: they felt free to shift populations between them. These outposts were regarded simply as provinces revolving around European centres such as London in England. This is why a British character in Churaumanie Bissundyal's play *From Ganges to Demerary* can say: "Remember the British Empire is everywhere. There is no difference between Cawnpore and Demerary." On such a foundation of unquestioning self-assurance and [im]pure racial arrogance was the whole superstructure of Indian indenture built.

In India by the second half of the eighteenth century, Britain had acquired control of a land with immense resources of population, culture and wealth. At this time too, Britain was already deep in the sordid business of shipping human cargo from one outpost of her empire, Africa, to other outposts in America and the Caribbean. After the loss of her American colonies, and subsequent changes in the world economy, Britain stopped this trade in slaves in 1807 and abolished slavery itself in 1834. This created a need for fresh supplies of labourers in the British Caribbean; and what better reservoir to tap than India's populous millions!

For some years after 1834 there was much debate in Britain over the principle of Indian immigration. The first Indians with fixed labour contracts immigrated in 1834 to Mauritius, but those in Britain who had championed African emancipation, suspected that Indian immigration was simply a new form of slavery, and opposed it, causing immigration to be suspended until a report on the subject appeared in 1840. The report came down against immigration which was then prohibited to all British colonies except Mauritius. But further debate led to resumption of immigration to Trinidad, Jamaica and Guyana, which, together with Guadeloupe and Surinam, received the most Indians of all Caribbean territories until 1917 when immigration stopped altogether.

In time, most Indians who lived in the Caribbean, certainly those who were born there, came to regard the region as home. Cut off from direct contact with the languages, customs, and religions of India, and depending for survival upon their capacity to adopt Western/creole manners, it was inevitable that Indo-Caribbean people should begin to see India somewhat like third and fourth generation Irish Americans see Ireland: with pride, affection, solidarity, but with awareness of significant differences from the orthodox customs and traditions of the parent culture. Throughout the colonial period in the Caribbean, a trend towards indigenization or creolization encouraged belief in a common history of slavery/indenture that had endowed Afro- and Indo-Caribbean people with a single legacy of colonial victimization that was shared, binding. Ironically, this belief came to be questioned after Independence in the 1960s when the West Indies gained freedom from centuries of colonial rule.

No doubt, this is why VS Naipaul takes such a sour view of Independence, freedom and all that. For it is the threat of political disorder and physical insecurity following Independence that convinced thousands of Indo-Caribbean people to ignore their roots established during one hundred and fifty years residence in the Caribbean, and choose instead the dubious relief of further exile in Britain and North America. If the experience of Indians in East Africa and Fiji is anything to go by, Indian-derived people face a common pattern of events in former British colonies: one of shared victimization during colonial rule, and of disorder and insecurity after Independence, prompting flight to what Naipaul calls "the greater disorder" of the cities of Britain and North America.

In his novel *The Mimic Men*, Naipaul's hero Ralph Singh is surrounded by chaos, disorder and shipwreck on his fictional Caribbean island. The ships which brought Ralph's forebears from India arrived safely in the Caribbean, but safety was outwardly physical and temporary: spiritually, metaphorically, inwardly, Ralph feels insecure and shipwrecked. Ralph speaks for all Indo-Caribbean people and probably for others when he claims to be a victim of:

> the restlessness, the deep disorder, which [was produced by] the
> great explorations, the overthrow in three continents of estab-

lished social organizations, the unnatural bringing together of peoples who could achieve fulfilment only within the security of their own societies and the landscapes hymned by their ancestors.

This is where Indo-Caribbean experience began—with great post-Renaissance European explorations, the establishment of colonies, and massive trans-shipment of Africans and Asians from one colony to the other. Naipaul's perception is that this process of displacement, immigration and fragmentation did not stop in 1917, or with the coming of Independence. On the contrary, the process accelerated after Independence, no longer with ships taking people across vast oceans on voyages lasting many months, but with giant aircraft whisking their human cargo away, in a matter of hours, to equally alien destinations in the cities of Europe and North America. The consequence of such flights today is not different from the consequence of voyages made from India one hundred and fifty years ago: a sense of displacement, loss, and an incurable feeling of alienation, of not belonging.

David Dabydeen
The Intended
London: Secker & Warburg, 1991.

One of David Dabydeen's earliest essays dealt with racist assumptions in the artistic theories of the eighteenth-century English painter William Hogarth. This rather specialized subject was part of Dabydeen's PhD thesis at the University of London, and the thesis generated two books, *Hogarth's Blacks* (1985), and *Hogarth, Walpole and Commercial Britain* (1987) which give chapter and verse for racist ideas that were considered respectable and even scientific in Hogarth's time. Dabydeen's reputation as an author was later enhanced by two books of poetry, *Slave Song* (1984), which won the Commonwealth Poetry Prize, and *Coolie Odyssey* (1988).

The Intended is an autobiographical novel that follows the career of the unnamed narrator from his childhood in rural Guyana through adolescence in London in the 1970s to academic success at Oxford. It presents a pattern familiar in the Caribbean: of one parent emigrating for economic reasons to London, Toronto, or New York, then "sending for" the rest of the family. The pattern is not strictly followed in this novel since the narrator is not reunited with his family in London. Instead, he is sent to a Home for boys which he describes as follows:

> The Home was in fact a prison for youth, and the innocent who were taken there were soon converted to criminal ways. Boys abandoned by their parents through no fault of their own quickly grew into little gangsters. (pp. 79–80)

We are not told about the circumstances, for example, of the narrator's relationship with his father, which lead up to his being placed in the Home. Suffice to say that he is not converted to criminal ways and leaves soon enough, having made friends with one of the Home boys called Joseph, a black West Indian with acute perceptions and intuitions, though little formal education. This friendship and others with the Muslim Shaz and the Hindu Patel are maintained after the narrator moves from the Home to a room in a house owned by Mr Ali, a Pakistani. Recollections of these friendships form the substance of the narrator's experience in London.

Dabydeen's portrait of 1970s London is vigorous and bracing. With perceptions and observations slanted from an Indo-Caribbean view point, he is able to catch something of the variety and complexity of relationships in a contemporary multicultural, urban society. A journey by the London Underground is no simple matter:

> The white English remained utterly silent for the whole journey, "while" Asians were invariably curious about each other, and furtive glances would be exchanged . . . We could not talk to each other openly in the way people in Asia or the Caribbean offered greetings or waved hands, even to utter strangers (p. 16).

In Balham, in South East London, where the narrator lives, a distinctly acrid flavour emanates from the heady mixture of multicultural tensions and poverty. While there is no open racial conflict, one detects an undercurrent of hostility amidst the to-ing and fro-ing of the various groups, immigrant and native, all vying for survival in a milieu highlighted by porno shops, Asian corner stores, and prostitutes on the Bedford Road. Yet the most brutal incident in the novel is one that involves white combatants, two of whom kick a third into unconsciousness or death before they themselves are set upon by others and gouged by a broken beer bottle.

All this is witnessed by the teenage narrator, who is evidently not so immersed in his studies that he does not also have time for other things, including rites of sexual initiation. His first effort with his English girlfriend Janet fails, but he succeeds with Shaz's girlfriend Monica who is a prostitute. After he has penetrated Monica, he is seized by panic and has to reassure himself that he has not slipped out before resuming to "finish before anything went wrong so that I could feel that I had done it with a woman, broken my duck and scored an opening single as Shaz would have put it" (p. 220). The self-mocking, playful tone illustrates the unpuritanical zestfulness that pervades the entire novel. Some of this zest derives from the narrative itself which is fast paced, expertly switching back and forth between Guyana and London, without letting the reader feel any break in the sequence of events. This is because the London events are given in strict chronological sequence although interspersed with flashbacks to earlier periods in Guyana. As a whole, this Guyana experience is one of brutality, drunkenness, obscenity, cunning and greed amidst abject poverty.

The Intended is replete with literary references that are an essential part of the story. Chaucer and Milton are mentioned, but the chief reference is to Conrad's *Heart of Darkness*, which provides the title of the novel. We recall how at the end of Conrad's novella Marlow cannot bring himself to tell Kurtz's unnamed fiancée—the intended—the exact truth of Kurtz's monstrous degeneration into bestiality; instead he simply tells her what she wants to hear. Despite its racist assumptions, Conrad's novella is an illuminating exposé of colonial exploitation and human degeneration. These are the main themes of Dabydeen's novel, and they are directly linked to Conrad, not only by the title of the novel, but also by the narrator's constant efforts to analyze *Heart of Darkness* and explain his analysis to his friends. Joseph is so impressed that he wants to make a film of the story. But the novel's central Conradian insight has to do with Janet who is finally preparing to leave with her parents for Australia. During their last meeting the narrator tells Janet: " but you are fragrant, you are everything I intended" (p. 243). In the narrator's mind Janet is linked to a creamy white doll that was in his house in Guyana and which he was caught looking at during his first experience of masturbation. Is this one of the guilty secrets of colonial degeneration that he takes from the colonial outpost to the imperial metropolis but which he cannot bring himself to reveal to his intended? It is one of many; and it illustrates the Conradian resonances that ring with heavy suggestiveness throughout this novel.

Tilokie Depoo and Prem Misir, Eds.
The East Indian Diaspora
New York: Asian/American Center, 1993.

The East Indian Diaspora, subtitled "150 Years of Survival, Contributions and Achievements" contains twelve articles that were originally presented at the First International Academic Conference on Indians in the Diaspora, held in New York City during July 10–15, 1988. The Conference was organized by the East Indian Diaspora Committee, Inc. which describes its role as follows: "to promote a scientific understanding and diffusion of the culture and sociocultural achievement of Indians in the Diaspora" (p.3). The volume also contains an Introduction which provides excellent background information including a description of the East Indian Diaspora Committee, and an overview of each article which introduces the indenture system that spawned the original diaspora—Indians who left their homes to live and work overseas from the 1830s to 1917. In format and scope the articles are interdisciplinary: they cover a variety of topics from politics, economics and religion to literature, culture and the arts.

The opening article is a keynote address by Dr Cheddi Jagan, President of Guyana. (At the time of the Conference Dr Jagan was leader of the Opposition in Guyana). As one might expect, Dr Jagan gives an authoritative account of Caribbean political development packed with statistics, and animated by a virile passion for democracy based on working class solidarity. Despite the obstruction of reactionary forces, he argues, working class solidarity has been able, in several instances, to overcome racial divisions in Guyana. This leads him to assert that "Class is more fundamental than race" (p.29) and conclude that whereas reactionary forces consisting of the "Black bureaucratic capitalist and/or the Indian materialistic-minded comprador bourgeoisie" might obstruct progress, the future of the Caribbean lies in a truly integrated national culture based on: "the working class, the radical intelligentsia and the patriotic capitalist" (p.31).

Dr Jagan's address is followed by "Trade Unionism, Politics and

Indo-Caribbean Leadership" by Basdeo Panday, President of Trinidad and Tobago. [Mr Panday was at the time of the conference leader of the Opposition United National Front.] Mr Panday's article carries roughly the same kind of authority as Dr Jagan's, and is based on similar ideological principles of racial unity, working class solidarity and true democracy. Good editorial judgement ensures that Mr Panday's article, written mainly from a Trinidadian perspective, is placed where it nicely complements Dr Jagan's address, given largely from a Guyanese standpoint. Basdeo Mangru's "Severing the Bond: Migration of Indian Indentured Labour Overseas" throws fresh light on the circumstances and motives of diaspora Indians when they first left India. Firstly, Dr Mangru claims that immigrants were drawn from a larger variety of areas and groups than formerly believed. While in the 1850s and 1860s, for instance, most of the immigrants may have come from Bihar and Bengal, by 1881 a majority were drawn from the Northwestern provinces and Oudh. Secondly, Dr Mangru suggests that, at least in the early decades of migration, many recruits were so called "hill coolies" or dhangars who were black in complexion and negroid in appearance. As for the motives of potential immigrants, Dr Mangru states that some were discouraged from migration by innate conservatism, caste inhibitions, ignorance and distrust, while others were encouraged to migrate by the pervasiveness of rural indebtedness, crop failures, and lack of steady employment. Although the prevailing view is that most recruits were drawn from the lower castes, Dr Mangru claims that circumstances encouraging migration were widespread enough to draw many from higher castes as well. According to Dr Mangru, these "push" factors—dissatisfactions with living conditions in India— rather than "pull" factors consisting of the real or imaginary attractions offered by overseas territories were what finally induced most Indians to emigrate.

Almost half the articles in *The East Indian Diaspora*, including the three already discussed, focus on Caribbean territories with the largest settlement of Indians—Guyana, Trinidad and Tobago, and Surinam. Prem Misir's "The Significance of Public Policy in Limiting the Social Status of the Indian and African Working Class" deals with contradictions between the theory and practice of the Peoples National Congress administration in Guyana from 1964 to 1992, and Edward Dew's "Surinam: Transcending Ethnic Politics the Hard Way" provides a dispassionate survey of the turbulent interaction between race and politics in

Surinam in recent decades. But one of the chief merits of *The East Indian Diaspora* is that it also offers studies of what might be called a diaspora within a diaspora, in the sense that Indian immigrants who settled in the Caribbean themselves produced descendants who, mainly during the 1970s and 1980s, made a second migration, this time from their native Caribbean, principally to Britain and North America. Three articles deal with these Indo-Caribbean immigrants in the US and one—"Squatter Consolidation in Latin America, the Case of Guyanese East Indians in a Venezuelan Barro" (by Dhanpaul Narine)—presents an unusual case that confirms the disintegrative power of the diasporic impulse among Indo-Caribbeans.

In "Organizing for Social Action: Challenges Facing the Indo-Caribbean Community in New York," Tara Singh attributes some of the difficulties of Indo-Caribbean Americans to conservative preferences deriving out of a particular Indo-Caribbean brand of religious upbringing and social formation. Singh suggests: "Traditional values and conservative ideology have combined to lull Indo-Caribbeans into a false sense of security" (p.125) that makes them insensitive to their real circumstances in New York and, one may add, in Toronto, London and other places. Singh also hints at mental health problems which are considered more fully by Lear Matthews in "Mental Health Problems Among Caribbean Immigrants in New York: Implications for Intervention with East Indians." Like Singh and Matthews, Frankie Ramadar in "First Generation Caribbean East Indian Americans and Voluntary Community Participation" considers problems faced by Indo-Caribbean Americans. He warns that their failure to participate in voluntary, civic organizations places them: "at a disadvantage in competing for power, privilege and prestige" (p.142).

A few articles consider Indian diasporic experience in more general or global fashion, for example, "East Indians in the Diaspora: History at a Glimpse" which supplies a brief but useful historical survey of Indian indenture to the Caribbean. Arnold Itwaru also, in "Self as Other in the Diaspora" poetically evokes the pain of Indo-Caribbean alienation, while the concluding article by Ramjass Boodhram "My Experiences" reflects on the author's role as a juror in the notorious Howard Beach case involving an Afro-Trinidadian American who, in December 1986, was beaten and chased by white youths on to a parkway in New York City where he was struck down and killed by a car. Boodhram's reflections on the American criminal justice system form a suitable conclusion to *The East Indian Diaspora*, since they reveal broadly human dimensions of problems facing all immigrants, and drive home the urgent need for racial and ethnic harmony.

So catholic is the selection of articles in *The East Indian Diaspora* and so skilful their arrangement and editing, that they provide a thoroughly informed and wide ranging appraisal of their subject. While they acknowledge the injustice of Indo-Caribbean victimization, they suggest that Indo-Caribbean habits of neglecting social or civic obligations, for example, may result in their continued marginalization and victimization. Similarly, they argue that Indo-Caribbean indulgence in largely materialistic pursuits (personal success) can arouse envy and provoke other problems. Contributors to *The East Indian Diaspora* agree that solutions to these problems must be found if Indians in the diaspora are not to continue being dogged by their historic experience of victimization, marginalization and alienation.

Cyril Dabydeen
Jogging in Havana
Oakville, Ontario: Mosaic Press, 1992

Cyril Dabydeen is the most productive Indo-Caribbean writer now living in Canada. The author of eight volumes of poetry and two novels, he was born in Guyana and migrated to Canada in 1970. *Jogging in Havana* is his third collection of stories, and he has edited two anthologies of ethnic Canadian writing as well. *Jogging in Havana* contains some of Dabydeen's best fiction so far, despite the fact that stories in the volume employ many themes, situations and linguistic strategies found in his previous work. The dominant theme remains Canadianization or the process of cultural adaptation and mixing that ethnic immigrants to Canada must undergo before achieving nationality in a more complex cultural rather than political sense. One of the more successful stories "The Rink" is about a black West Indian immigrant, George, who makes strenuous efforts learning to ice skate, while his wife Ida and his friends constantly mock him and suggest, sneeringly, that he might do better to stick to the popular West Indian sport of cricket. As Ida puts it: "But George, you can't blasted well be able to skate! You, a black man trying to do a white thing. It isn't the sport fo' you" (p. 123). In inimitably succinct and pungent creole idiom, Ida neatly sums up the dilemma of cultural adaptation faced by all immigrants to Canada and especially by those who are ethnic or non-white. But at the end of the story, when George's daughter is "Skating pirouetting, as if she was born with skates on" (p. 125), it is clear that George's Canadianization has taken an inevitable step—his integration into Canadian culture through his children who are effortlessly Canadian in a way that he can never be.

Themes of displacement and exile, and racial and cultural integration are found in most stories in this volume whether they apply specifically to Canada or not. "Relations" and "God Save the Queen" are set in Guyana and deal with rural scenes of great tropical beauty that are disfigured by poverty, deprivation and family violence. In other stories, immigrant narrators who live in Canada reflect on the fate of their relations or friends in the Caribbean or elsewhere. In "Ain't Got No Cash" the Guyanese narrator who has immigrated to Canada visits a fellow Guyanese in New York where they discuss interethnic, cross-cultural relations that evolve out of colonialism, migration and exile.

In perhaps the best story in the volume, "A Plan is a Plan," black Caribbean immigrants discuss life for immigrants in Canada, especially sexual relations between blacks and whites. But the story's distinction relies less on Fanonesque revelations about interracial sexual relations than on the vigour of its creole language. On the whole, the stories in *Jogging in Havana* tend to support the view that Dabydeen's writing could benefit from more frequent and more enthusiastic use of creole speech and narrative.

Dabydeen is adept at condensed characterization, pithy description and palatable dialogue, standard skills of a short-story writer. Often he injects elements of humour or mystery chiefly with an aim to entertain rather than expose or criticize. In the title story, for instance, we get excellent sketches of people, places and issues, as foreign academics travel to Cuba and sample Castro's socialism at first hand. Yet there is little passion in the story, which is content to reproduce, without judging, the mixed reactions and varied, often contradictory impressions that come out of academic discussions and tourism in a milieu universally known for its socialist rhetoric.

Such objectivity insinuates a distinct documentary flavour to Dabydeen's writing, one in which the external features of situations are faithfully reproduced without any real desire to investigate too deeply. In its treatment of displacement, cultural mixing, and the integration of immigrants into Canada, Dabydeen's writing itself appears to undergo a process of integration by moving gradually away from its lively variegated Caribbean sources in terms of characters, settings and language, towards mainly Canadian situations that are less lively, more subdued, and noncommittal in tone. Because of this movement, *Jogging in Havana* and Dabydeen's writing as a whole appear to undergo a process of Canadianization or assmilation that is either a necessary peril or an inevitable outcome of immigration.

Indo-Caribbean Canadians

Indo-Caribbean Canadians, that is to say Indians who migrated to Canada from the Caribbean, came mainly from Guyana and Trinidad and Tobago. Some came from other Caribbean territories like Jamaica, Guyana or Trinidad and Tobago, which are also anglophone; and a few others may have come from the Dutch-speaking Caribbean territory of Surinam. Why the ancestors of these immigrants first left India for the Caribbean in 1838, or why, after more than one and a half centuries of residence in the Caribbean, so many of them should move to Canada is not the concern of this essay. Suffice to say that economic factors were strong in bringing Indians to the Caribbean in the first place, and again, one hundred and fifty years later, in inducing them to leave. Also by the 1960s and 70s, Indo-Guyanese and Indo-Trinidadians felt alienated not only by economic factors and social marginalization in a predominantly creole environment, but by mounting political tensions between themselves and their Afro-Caribbean countrymen. At any rate, whatever their real motives, this essay begins with the fact that Indo-Caribbean immigrants arrived in Canada in a huge exodus during the 1970s and 80s.

It is not possible to give the exact number of Indo-Caribbeans currently living in Canada because the relatively recent classification of "Indo-Caribbean" has not yet been adopted by Statistics Canada which still identifies Caribbean immigrants solely by their country of origin. But using these general statistics provided by Statistics Canada for Caribbean territories, it is possible to arrive at a rough estimate of the number of Indo-Caribbean immigrants who entered Canada since 1962. Assuming that 80% of immigrants from Guyana and 60% from Trinidad and Tobago are Indians, we arrive at a total of 91,649 Indo-

Caribbeans who came to Canada between 1962 and 1992. If another 10,000 are added to account for natural increase and illegal immigrants, the current Indo-Caribbean population of Canada can be estimated at 101,649 or about 100,000 in round figures. Although small numbers of these immigrants may be found in such provinces as Nova Scotia, Manitoba, Alberta, and Saskatchewan, most settled in Ontario, and predominantly in the greater Toronto area where they are noticeable in more suburban areas such as Scarborough and Mississauga.

Classifying Caribbean immigrants only by their territory of origin not only creates a problem in determining the exact number of Indo-Caribbean immigrants in Canada: it exacerbates a psychological dilemma for these immigrants. In the first place, when Indo-Guyanese or Indo-Trinidadians are classified simply as Guyanese or Trinidadians, they are perceived in Canada as Afro-Caribbean, for the simple reason that most Caribbean people are African in origin, and terms such as "Caribbean" or "West Indian" are almost universally regarded as signifying black or African descent. In the second place, Indo-Caribbeans are now considered as "South Asian" in Canada, a term that in its unique Canadian usage refers to people from India, Pakistan, Bangladesh, Nepal, as well as from the Caribbean, East Africa and Fiji. In both cases, whether Indo-Caribbeans are called West Indians or South Asians, they face an equal dilemma; for, on one hand, they are not wholly Caribbean (West Indian) in the sense that they do not originate from Africa; neither are they wholly South Asian since they do not generally speak South Asian languages, although they may retain other features of South Asian culture. Indo-Caribbeans therefore face a predicament in private or public social gatherings, for example, when they may be addressed in a South Asian language, or be expected to show familiarity with aspects of South Asian culture of which they are ignorant. This predicament is worse because there is no physical dissimilarity between Indo-Caribbeans and South Asians: both groups share an identical racial origin. But race alone does not make Indo-Caribbean Canadians South Asian, any more than their ethnicity—shared Caribbean speech habits and Caribbean culture—make them African.

If Indo-Caribbean Canadian authors are to be believed, this issue of identity is one of the most important factors that influence Indo-Caribbeans living in Canada. Indo-Caribbean immigrants have made probably their most distinctive impact in Canada through their contribution to literature. Neil Bissoondath, the major Indo-Caribbean writer in

Canada today, first arrived in 1973 as a student at York University in Toronto. After graduation, he went on to write stories and novels set both in Canada and his native Trinidad. His story "Insecurity" which appears in his first published volume *Digging up the Mountains and other Stories,*[1] describes frightening conditions on a fictional Caribbean island. This is especially true for Indian shop-keepers like Alistair Ramgoolam who has taken the precaution of sending one of his sons to live in Toronto, and is preparing to send up another son as a student. As a businessman, Ramgoolam is successful, but his thoughts betray disillusionment and fear:

> The island of his birth, on which he has grown up and made his fortune, was transformed by a process of mind into a kind of temporary home . . . He could hope for death here but his grandchildren, maybe even his children, would continue the emigration which his grandfather had started in India, and during which the island had proved, in the end, to be nothing more than a stopover. (p.72)

Whether or not Ramgoolam's feelings are typical of Indo-Caribbeans who migrated to Canada, his family reflect typical motives of Indo-Caribbean migration: firstly, educational and economic opportunity, and by the 1970s and 80s, disillusionment, anxiety, fear, and an increasingly desperate need for safe refuge.

In a later volume *On the Eve of Uncertain Tomorrows*[2] Bissoondath also has a story "Security," that forms a sequel to "Insecurity." In "Security" Alistair Ramgoolam is living with his family in Toronto, having escaped the harassment and panic of life in Trinidad. He no longer gets threatening telephone calls late at night, nor does he hear of the mysterious death of his close business associates and consequent police inaction over their cases. But although the sources of his Trinidadian insecurity are removed, Ramgoolam is far from secure in Toronto. His struggles to find employment are one thing; boredom of apartment living is another. What is worse is his dismay over the secular mores of an urban, industrial metropolis which appear frankly as barbaric to a devout (vegetarian) Hindu like himself. He regards his sons as: "Barbarians, everyone of them. Stuffin' themselves in restaurants with steak and hotdogs and hamburgers."

Ramgoolam's disquiet coincides with the feelings of older Indo-Caribbean immigrants, especially those who come from a rural background and are more traditional; but his greatest worry is his sense of alienation:

> It was from this loneliness, this sense of abandonment, that emerged Mr. Ramgoolam's deepest worry: would his sons do for him after his death all that he had done for his parents after theirs? Would they—and, beyond this, could they, in this country—fulfill their cremation duties, feed his hungry and wandering soul, have themselves ritually shaved beside a river, dispatch his soul to wherever with the final farewell ceremony? He feared they would not, feared they had grown too far from him and from the past that was his. (p.108)

The irony of the story's title is evident in the acute spiritual torment that afflicts Ramgoolam. The irony for Indo-Caribbean Canadians is that while they have escaped from the psychological insecurity caused by political instability, marginalization, lack of opportunity and inter-ethnic tension at home, coming to Canada has brought its own insecurity caused by urban-industrial alienation, race and colour prejudice, impersonal, secular mores, and the hectic pace and pressure of modern city living.

Bissoondath's report on Indo-Caribbean Canadian experience is corroborated by the work of another Indo-Caribbean Canadian writer—Cyril Dabydeen. Dabydeen has written fiction, poetry and criticism, and has edited anthologies of immigrant writing. His titles include *Goatsong*, 1977 (poems), *Elephants Make Good Stepladders*, 1982 (poems); *To Monkey Jungle*, 1988 (stories); *Dark Swirl*, 1989 (novel); and *A Shapely Fire*, 1987 (anthology). Like Bissoondath, Dabydeen portrays feelings of displacement, marginalization, anonymity and alienation that affect most Indo-Caribbean Canadians. In particular, Dabydeen provides a frank appraisal of racism encountered by "coloured" or non-white immigrants in Canada. His poem "Citizenship" records the experience of a non-white immigrant who is about to receive Canadian citizenship:

Walking along
heading for the Citizenship Court
Kent Street/Ottawa

I have been here seven years
Yet the same question
Where do you come from?
I'm identifiable
I'm different[3]

These lines would strike a chord of recognition in most immigrants who belong to so-called visible minorities in Canada; for skin colour is an inescapable badge of foreignness which stimulates stereotypical reactions from a largely white, host community. Still, it is notable how little anger or resentment there is in the poem. The degree of racism is mild and it invokes a response that is equally mild.

This mild response to Canadian racism, at least as it is reported by Indo-Caribbean Canadian writers, contrasts sharply with similar accounts of racism by Afro-Caribbean writers. Stories by Austin Clarke, for example, Canada's most distinguished black writer include much physical violence, outspoken language, and feelings of deep hurt and grave injustice. Dionne Brand's writing also registers bitter feelings about racism in Canada. Nor is there any doubt about the accuracy of these Afro-Caribbean accounts: for there have been many studies of discrimination against Blacks in the workplace, and news stories about the shooting of Blacks by police in Toronto as well as in other Canadian cities. Whether this means that racism towards Blacks is more acute than against South Asians does not necessarily follow. According to Dabydeen, while South Asians (including Indo-Caribbeans) have suffered from racial discrimination and outbreaks of so called "Paki-bashing," in which South Asians have been beaten and killed by gangs of Whites, a study of Canadian racism states:

> their [South Asian] reaction has generally been mild and subdued. Following a series of racially motivated attacks within Toronto subways directed principally at South Asians, the Metropolitan Toronto Police and the Toronto Transit Commissions jointly established a system designed to intercept attackers and prevent further incidents.[4]

The most recent victims of these racial attacks in Toronto have been Sri Lankans, but expressions of racist violence against South Asians are mercifully rare or sporadic, and do not appear prominently in Indo-

Caribbean Canadian writing. This implies that the Indo-Caribbean experience of racism in Canada, so far, at any rate, tends to be subtle and psychological rather than explicit or physical.

The work of other Indo-Caribbean Canadian writers such as Arnold Itwaru, Ramabai Espinet, Madeline Coopsammy, Sasenarine Persaud and Ishmael Baksh tends to confirm the view of Indo-Caribbean Canadian experience as largely one of increased material well-being coupled with inward unease that is the result of many factors including racism. Itwaru was born in Guyana in 1943 and has written fiction, poetry and criticism. His books include *Entombed Survivals*, 1987 (poems); and *Shanti*, 1990 (novel). As a woman writer, Espinet who was born in Trinidad in 1948 projects a fresh, feminist outlook that asserts the toughness and resilience of Indo-Caribbean women as home-makers and suggests that the disabilities which women suffered from patriarchal structures in the Caribbean might be reduced in Canada. News reports support this view in so far as they discuss issues of wife abuse, child care and employment equity in a more explicit way than in the Caribbean. In this respect, at least, immigration to Canada has brought some benefit to Indo-Caribbean women.

One of Espinet's poems "For Patricia Deanna" also throws light on an important aspect of immigrant experience in Canada—the issue of illegal immigrants and refugees. In Espinet's poem, Patricia Deanna is a young Caribbean woman, an illegal immigrant who in trying to escape from immigration officers, falls to her death from the balcony of her apartment. Espinet's description of Patricia as "pregnant, illegal and utterly alone" is poignant, and she successfully captures the young woman's fear, terror, powerlessness and desperation as she seeks, in vain, to evade the immigration "Hunter-man." Again, precise numbers are not available of Indo-Caribbean people who are either applying for refugee status or who live illegally in Canada. But the numbers are probably quite high, considering press reports and public meetings in Toronto, not so long ago, with Indo-Trinidadians claiming recognition as economic refugees. Many Indo-Guyanese are also known to have claimed refugee status on the basis of racial discrimination by the ruling, African-dominated People's National Congress in Guyana. A study in 1983 showed that most "apprehended aliens" in Toronto were Jamaicans (28%) and Guyanese (16%).

The work of Bissoondath, Dabydeen, Itwaru, Espinet and other Indo-Caribbean Canadians writers will undoubtedly help Indo-Caribbean Canadians to understand their fate in Canada. It may even help them to survive culturally. As we have seen in Bissoondath's story "Insecurity," physical survival is not a problem for people who are as thrifty, energetic and industrious as Indo-Caribbeans. In Toronto, for instance, they excel in law and medicine which, for peculiar historical reasons, had become traditional professions for them in the Caribbean. They also show a particular aptitude for retail business that is evident in the many Indo-Caribbean groceries, restaurants and roti shops that can now be found all over Toronto. While most of these establishments are patronized chiefly by Indo-Caribbean customers, the roti shop with its menu of spicy, "exotic" dishes and its familiar set up as another fast food outlet, has made the strongest impact on the widest number of Canadians. Indo-Caribbean real estate agencies are another successful business enterprise. Evidence of Indo-Caribbean success in business and the professions may be found in numerous advertisements in Indo-Caribbean newspapers such as *Indo-Caribbean World*, *Guyana Times*, *Equality* and *Caribbean Contact*. But cultural survival will not be assured until feelings of displacement, exile and alienation are transcended, and Indo-Caribbean identity is properly appreciated for both its similarity and difference from Afro-Caribbean and South Asian culture.

It would be ironic and perhaps tragic if, having emigrated from the Caribbean in order to evade marginalization, alienation and insecurity, Indo-Caribbean immigrants, now run a risk of further marginalization in Canada by being classified as "South Asian." To be grouped with South Asians whose numbers are much greater, and whose cultures are significantly different, may indeed threaten the survival of Indo-Caribbean Canadians by swallowing their culture into a larger group identity that erases its special features and renders them invisible. Another threat to survival is raised by Bissoondath's story "Security" which depicts a second generation of Indo-Caribbean Canadians who have become culturally differentiated from their parents because of their rapid absorption into the Canadian mainstream. If this absorption were to continue, Indo-Caribbean Canadian culture could be in jeopardy. In her essay "The Next Indo-Caribbean Generation in Canada," Kamala Jean Gopie confesses that Indo-Caribbean cultural survival is in doubt in Canada, and is possible only if Indo-Caribbean Canadians are able to overcome feelings of displacement, alienation and marginalization that have taken root in them during two migrations over the past century and a half. Whether most younger Indo-Caribbean Canadians become assimilated or not, it is difficult to predict the fate of the Indo-Caribbean diaspora in Canada. What is evident is that Indo-Caribbean Canadians have prospered in a materialistic sense; but this prosperity is accompanied by feelings of psychic disorientation which might justify a general description of the community as a condition of "insecure security."

Immigration in the Fiction of V S Naipaul

Many critics have commented on V S Naipaul's treatment of exile and alienation, and discerned what is perhaps the most important revelation in Naipaul's fiction: that we are all uprooted and lost, separated from our origins and exiled by birth itself, the primal act of separation that can never be reversed. This claim is supported by numerous references and images in Naipaul's fiction which illustrate our tenuous hold upon the earth. In Naipaul's early novels and stories, themes associated with this image—disorder, waste, and futility—emerge out of colonial circumstances of entrapment and social, economic, mental and spiritual limitation. But in *The Mimic Men* (London: André Deutsch, 1967), Ralph Singh discovers that however limited or disordered his native Trinidad may have been, London, "the centre of the world," is no better. London, for Ralph, represents a "greater disorder:" a feeling of rootlessness that cannot be blamed on anything manmade, artificial or historical such as colonialism. Ralph's alienation originates in a source that is shared by people in remote, insignificant colonies as well as in powerful metropolitan centres. In *In a Free State* (London: André Deutsch, 1971), which follows *The Mimic Men*, Naipaul examines the origin of alienation in immigrant characters in two stories, "One Out of Many" and "Tell Me Who to Kill."

"One Out of Many" is about Santosh, an Indian domestic who is transported from his impoverished life in Bombay to more materialistic comforts in Washington, DC, "the capital of the world." On the plane coming over from India, Santosh is so confused by the newfangled technology and routine of air travel that he vomits on all of his baggage. His disorientation as an immigrant in Washington is equally upsetting. His bedroom is a cupboard in the apartment of his employer, an official of the government of India. But, accustomed to sleeping under the open sky in the streets of Bombay, Santosh spends his first night outside his employer's apartment. In effect, he faces a process (acculturation) that ropes in all immigrants in one fashion or another. He is bewildered and pained by American speech, television, and manners in general. This painful reaction is exacerbated by his arrival in Washington in the mid-1960s, when protest over the Vietnam war and Black revolutionary ferment, including urban riots, looting and burning, were at their height. Eventually, despite his pain and bewilderment, and his mixed feelings about American Blacks, Santosh marries a Black woman in order to change his illegal immigrant status and become a citizen of what is reputedly the freest state in the world.

Santosh's marriage is the culmination of a process by which he becomes Americanized. Yet his acquisition of American citizenship and its democratic, individualistic, materialistic values provide no solution to his problem of feeling unsettled and disorientated. His concluding thoughts are these:

> Once, when there were rumours of new burnings, someone scrawled in white paint on the pavement outside my house: 'Soul Brother.' I understand the words; but I feel, brother to what or whom? I was once a part of the flow, never thinking of myself as a presence [in India]. Then I looked in the mirror and decided to be free [in the US]. All that my freedom has brought me is the knowledge that I have a face and a body, that I must feed this body and clothe this body for a certain number of years. Then it will be over. (p.61)

It is ironic that his immigration to the US should lead Santosh to miss the poverty-stricken, communal lifestyle of a virtual slave that he had in India. What he misses is the meaning, order and security that hierarchical Indian values of religion, caste and class provided for him in Bombay. By becoming free in America, he has lost this sense of security and its accompanying feeling of freedom, however false or illusory it was in Bombay. towards the end of the story, Santosh appears to realize that true freedom is impossible, that he was no more free in Bombay than he is now in Washington. But he prefers the illusion of freedom which he had in India.

The second story, "Tell Me Who to Kill." is about two Indo-Trinidadian brothers who immigrate to England. One brother is to work and provide money for the other, Dayo, to educate himself and probably get a profession. When they arrive in London, the unnamed working brother, who also narrates the story, is attracted by the anonymity of the big city, and the relief it offers from the intruding pettiness and interfering provincialism which are so constricting in Trinidad. He likes the order and routine of his factory job and, for a time, he and Dayo are happy. He makes enough money to pay for his brother's studies and start up a small restaurant business. But the displacement of immigration soon takes its toll, and feelings of hatred and frustration which he had in Trinidad begin to return. Only now, these feelings are directed against the English host society which, he claims, has spoilt his life. His business fails because, in his own words, he runs "into prejudice and regulations," (p.93) and because English youths either eat and don't pay, or break his plates and glasses, and bend his cutlery. Such random vandalism or gratuitous victimization intensify his feelings of alienation and resentment: "a lot of them against me alone. That is their bravery and education. And nobody is on my side." (p.94) These thoughts produce frustration, hatred, self-pity, and poison the career of the narrator and his relationship with his brother.

The narrator's greatest frustration stems from the collapse of their original plans, for Dayo fails as a student, and eventually marries an English girl. The narrator realizes that by immigrating to England, where he has no family or friends, he has entered a trap from which he cannot escape because he has nowhere else to go. His thoughts resemble those of Santosh:

"The life is over. I am like a man who is giving up. I come with nothing, I have nothing, I will leave with nothing."(p.101)

His sense of failure, loss, impotence, futility, and desolation is crippling. In the end, he describes his brother's wedding through images of death and decay that reinforce his own sense of a "spoilt life:"

"I love them [English people]. They take my money, they spoil my life, they separate us. But you can't kill them. O God, show me the enemy. Once you find out who the enemy is, you can kill him. But these people here they confuse me. Who hurt me? Who spoilt my life? Tell me who to beat back. I work four years to save my money, I work like a donkey night and day. My brother was to be the educated one, the nice one. And this is how it is ending, in this room, eating with these people. Tell me who to kill." (p.107)

The narrator blames English people for his failure, just as Santosh blames America for his disorientation. But although immigration contributes to the sense of alienation in both characters, it is not the cause.

The fact is that both Santosh and the narrator of "Tell Me Who to Kill" felt restricted or alienated in their own countries, India and Trinidad, respectively, before they emigrated. In India Santosh was bound to his religion, caste and employer, and he had a wife and children in the hills. He was imprisoned by obligations and rites of an old, custom-ridden, communal society. It is not that he is less free in Washington, or more free, for that matter; it is simply that the factors that limit his freedom have changed. Instead of restrictions imposed on him by hierarchical values of an old, Asian society, he now feels imprisoned by the physical processes of his body and its dependence on the materialistic comforts of American or Western civilization. It is true that the narrator of "Tell Me Who to Kill" does not enjoy the dubious benefit of similar hierarchical values, religious rites and social obligations in Trinidad. His main concern before emigration is a crudely competitive need to rise in the world. This need soured his life in Trinidad and filled him with hatred against his uncle's family and resentment of the world in general. Since both characters encounter circumstances of restriction and entrapment in their native countries, immigration cannot be regarded as the cause of their problems in Washington and London respectively. All that immigration does is to intensify their circumstances of limitation and promote a more convincing portrayal of their shared condition as "unanchored souls" with only a tenuous hold upon the earth.

While Santosh and Dayo's brother suffer many of the same intensifying ill effects of immigration, there is an important difference in their careers. Santosh felt "settled' in Bombay and enjoyed "respect and security" because of the social prestige of his employer in Bombay. This means that Santosh's dissatisfaction in Bombay is not nearly as severe as that of Dayo's brother in Trinidad. By moving from respect and security in Bombay to dissatisfaction in Washington, Santosh reveals contrasting values in two civilizations, both of which are shown to be inadequate in so far as they deny real human freedom. This contrast illuminates Naipaul's study of universal homelessness more clearly than the parallel move of Dayo's brother from frustration in Trinidad to greater frustration in England.

The events in "Tell Me Who to Kill" are more shrouded in mystery than those in "One Out of Many." After opening with the narrator's preparation to attend his brother's wedding, "Tell Me Who to Kill" switches to recollections of his family in Trinidad, before returning to events leading up to the wedding in England. The narrator also employs dreams and reminiscences, especially those related to his uncertain memory of Hollywood films in which failure, violence and death are common themes. No doubt the mysterious atmosphere and episodic structure of "Tell Me Who to Kill" are dictated, to some extent, by the narrator's uncertain and incoherent point of view. After all, the narrator's main problem is that he does not know who to kill. In other words, he does not know the cause of his problem and therefore cannot solve it. Santosh cannot solve his problem either, but he understands it better. He is helped by the saving illusions of an old society which enable him to accept his predicament in Washington with calm resignation. Without similarly binding obligations and customs in a young, rootless society like Trinidad, the narrator of "Tell Me Who to Kill" is left seething with anger and resentment.

The greater incoherence of the Trinidad story derives from issues that are less understood than those in "One Out of Many," in which basic issues of universal homelessness are clearly illustrated through a sharp, and articulate contrast between Indian and American culture. Since it provides less illumination of its subject it is tempting to regard "Tell Me Who to Kill" as a less successful story than "One Out of Many." This would be a mistake for the subject itself of "Tell Me Who to Kill" is the narrator's inability to understand his experience as someone who has twice suffered displacement and migration, firstly through his ancestors from India, and secondly from Trinidad. The double displacement explains why his feelings are more turbulent and confused than those of Santosh, and why his most considered reaction is one of uncomprehending puzzlement. His puzzlement is consistent with the view of alienation which "Tell Me Who to Kill" is meant to convey. It is a different, less explicit view than the one given in "One Out of Many," and within the structure of the whole volume, *In a Free State*, is intended to complement more articulate attitudes expressed by Santosh. Together, both stories project Naipaul's vision of alienation as a fundamental aspect of human experience, one that exists from our very birth, although it may later be exacerbated by the effects of colonialism, immigration, and so on.

Other sections of *In a Free State* also illustrate this vision of alienation, for instance, the "Epilogue," a brief, autobiographical account of the author's visit to Egypt where he reflects on the passing of empires, the transience of worldly glory, and the mortality of humankind. In the course of these reflections Naipaul contemplates an ancient stone carving which tempts him to believe: "Perhaps that had been the only pure time, at the beginning, when the ancient artist, knowing no other land had learned to look at his own and had seen it as complete." (p.255) But travelling back to Cairo through dusty towns and agitated, everyday crowds of Egyptians quickly brings him down to earth, and he concludes:

> Perhaps that vision of the land, in which the Nile was only water, a blue-green chevron, had always been a fabrication, a cause for yearning, something for the tomb. (pp. 255–256)

Reluctantly, Naipaul resists an all too natural temptation to believe in Edenic innocence. Like Santosh and Dayo's brother, he stiffly admits that Eden itself may be a fabrication, a comforting illusion invented to assuage the pain of human mortality. It is neither true that birth disconnects us from God, nor that death offers us hope of reconnection. Whether God was ever in the picture is uncertain. All we can be certain of is the inescapable reality of birth and death and, if we are lucky, the space of a number of years in between. This is the sober truth facing not only immigrants, Africans, Indo-Caribbeans or other victims of colonization, but everyone, whether they are post-imperial colonizers living in more or less stable, powerful metropolitan centres, or hapless, modern-day, postcolonial immigrants shifting aimlessly about from one distant stopover to the next.

NOTES

Introduction

1. Patrick Leigh Fermor, *The Traveller's Tree* (Harmondsworth: Penguin, 1984), p.9.

2. The first batch of indentured Indian immigrants arrived in Guyana in 1838. A similar batch of Portuguese first arrived in 1835, and Chinese in 1853.

3. Jamaica and Trinidad and Tobago became independent in 1962, and Guyana and Barbados in 1966. Although Trinidad and Tobago are separate islands, they form one state—Trinidad and Tobago. For the sake of brevity "Trinidad" is sometimes used for "Trinidad and Tobago" in this book. Guyana was formerly known as "British Guiana." The usage "Guyana" is used in all essays and reviews here.

4. Linden Forbes Sampson Burnham (1923–85) began his political career as a member of the PPP led by Dr Cheddi Jagan. In 1955, he formed his own party, the PNC, and in 1964 he won national elections and became prime minister. Although Burnham died in 1985, his party won elections under a new leader, Desmond Hoyte, and continued in office until 1992.

5. Dr Eric Williams (1911–82) was the founding leader of the PNM in 1955. His party won national elections in 1956 and he remained as prime minister until his death. He was an historian and author of several works including *Capitalism and Slavery*, (1964) and *History of Trinidad and Tobago* (1964).

6. Dr Jagan was born in 1918. As leader of the PPP he won elections in 1953, 1957, and 1961, and again in 1992. See the introduction to Dr Jagan's interview in Part Three for fuller details.

7. Pre-Columbian indigenes of the Caribbean and the Americas were also called "Amerindians". The terms "aboriginal" or "indigenous" are preferred in this book.

8. Cf the epigraph from V S Naipaul, *The Overcrowded Barracoon* (London: André Deutsch, 1972) p. 32.

9. C L R James, Appendix to *The Black Jacobins* (New York: Alfred A Knopf, 1938). Cyril Lionel Robert James (1901–89), affectionately known as "CLR," was the first West Indian man of letters to gain international recognition. He was a novelist, historian, scholar, critic, and political commentator. James was born in Trinidad, but in 1932 he left for England where he lived most of his life and eventually died. *The Black Jacobins* is a history of the successful revolution by African slaves in San Domingo (today's Haiti) at the end of the eighteenth

century.

10. V S Naipaul, *In a Free State* (London: André Deutsch, 1971), p. 61.

11. Dennison Moore, *Origins and Development of Racial Ideology in Trinidad: The Black View of the East Indian* (Turnapuna, Trinidad: Chakra Publishing House, 1995).

12. V S Naipaul, *A House for Mr Biswas* (London, André Deutsch, 1960).

13. Walter Rodney, *A History of the Guyanese Working People, 1881–1905* (Baltimore: The John Hopkins University Press, 1981).

14. Albert Gomes, *Caught in a Maze of Colour;* see review in Part One.

Part One: The Caribbean

Review of: *Caught in a Maze of Colour: Memoirs of a Colonial Politician*

1. After the abolition of slavery in the British territories in 1838, Britain brought indentured Portuguese labourers from Madeira to do the work that the freed African slaves used to do in the Caribbean plantations.

2. In 1962, two neighbouring islands—Trinidad and Tobago—were incorporated into the independent nation of Trinidad and Tobago. This explains frequent references to Trinidad as a separate British colony before 1962.

3. V S Naipaul, *The Middle Passage* (London: André Deutsch, 1962), 79.

4. For L F S Burnham, see Note 4, Introduction.

5. C L R James, *The Life of Captain Cipriani* (Lancashire: Nelson, 1932). See Note 9, Introduction.

6. Dr Eric williams (1911–1982) was prime minister of Trinidad and Tobago from 1956 to 1982. He also wrote several historical works, including *Capitalism and Slavery* (1964), and *History of the People of Trinidad and Tobago* (1964). V S Naipaul and his brother Shiva (deceased) are Trinidad-born writers. V S Naipaul's *The Middle Passage* (1962) achieved notoriety for its negative comments on Trinidad. Arthur Calder Marshall is an English author and journalist. His *Glory Dead* (1939) offers a nonfiction account of Trinidad. Samuel Selvon, author of such novels as *A Brighter Sun* (1952) and *The Lonely Londoners* (1956), was one of the best-known Trinidadian writers, famous for his expert use of local speech and language in his fiction. He died in 1994. Merle Hodge is a lecturer and author of *Crick Crack Monkey* (1979), a novel set in Trinidad.

Part Three: Indo-Caribbeans

CHHABLALL RAMCHARAN

1. Plantation Albion is one of the larger sugar estates in Guyana. It is in the country of Berbice.

2. A "bit" was a small silver coin worth eight cents at the time in Guyana.

3. The term "arkhati" signifies "recruiter" in Bhojpuri, the dialect of the region in India from which most indentured immigrants came. "Arkhatis" had a reputation for unscrupulous trickery and wiles in enticing or entrapping prospective immigrants.

4. New Amsterdam is the chief town in the county of Berbice.

5. Beginning in 1858, James Crosby (1811–1885) gave distinguished service as Immigration Agent General in Guyana for twenty-two years. His vigorous advocacy of the rights and privileges of Indian immigrants had such an effect on the immigrants that long after his death in 1885 they referred to the Immigration Agent General's office as "Crosby."

6. In the primary or elementary school system, after graduating from the top class, Sixth Standard, with a Primary School leaving Certificate, one could be appointed as a teacher or "pupil teacher" in primary schools. Then one could gain higher qualifications by taking the Pupil Teachers Examinations at different levels, eg. First Year, Second Year, etc.

7. The "matia" was the local Hindu temple.

8. Georgetown is the capital city of Guyana.

9. Guyana is divided into three counties—Demerara, Berbice and Essequibo. Georgetown is in Demerara, the smallest county.

10. Immigrants were bound by their terms of indentureship to work for a period, usually five years, before returning to India. If immigrants did not return at the end of their period of indentureship, they could receive a grant of land in lieu of return or they could renew their contract. Since the immigrants in 1955 had not received land, the return to India portion of their indenture agreement was unused and they were redeeming it many years later.

11. "Baboo" was a derogatory Anglo-Indian term for native Indian clerks or any Indian in an official capacity. Since "Crosby" had become synonymous with Immigration (see Note 5, above) the "Crosby Baboo" was the local Indian immigration official, that is, Chhablall Ramcharan.

12. In the exchange rates of the day, one British pound was the equivalent of four hundred and eighty Guyana dollars.

13. The "Arya Samaj" is a reform Hindu movement initiated in India by swami Dayanand Sarasivati in 1875. The aim of the movement was to purify Hindu practices by returning to Vedic teachings. The movement was established in Guyana in 1910. The Samajists advocated abnotheism and rejected idol worship. They had educational aims as well. They advocated upgrading the status of women and they criticized Brahmin authority. There was prolonged rivalry between the Samajists and the more traditional Sanatanists.

14. For Dr Jagan see introduction to Dr Jagan's interview.

15. Ayube Edun was originally a goldsmith. He began to champion the rights of sugar workers in journals such as the *Tribune* and *Labour Advocate* in the 1920s. He founded the Manpower Citizens' Association (MPCA) in 1937 with the aim of representing sugar workers in their struggle for better eco-

nomic, social and political conditions.

16. For Burnham see Note 3, Introduction.

17. "Bajan" is a West Indian colloquialism for "Barbadian," and since most Barbadians are Africans, the "Bajan Quarter" was African.

18. Balram Singh Rai served as Minister of Community Development and Education in the PPP government of 1957, and as Minister of Home Affairs in the PPP government of 1961. He now lives in England.

19. The British Guiana East Indian Association was formed in 1919 as an advocacy group for Indians. The first president was a J A Luckhoo.

20. As an ally of Ayube Edun, C R Jacob was influential in representing the interests of sugar workers in the 1930s and 40s.

21. Dr Jund Bahadur Singh began as a sick nurse and dispenser and later qualified as a doctor. He was appointed to both Legislative and Executive Councils and was awarded the DBE. He and his wife Rajkumarie promoted cultural and charitable causes among Indians.

22. See introduction to Dr Jagan's interview.

23. This interview was taped before the election in 1992 when the PNC lost power finally after 28 years of continous rule. The election was won by a coalition of Dr Jagan's PPP and Civic, a loose association of concerned citizens rather than a political party.

RAHMAN GAJRAJ

1. When Indian immigrants completed their period of indenture, they were given a certificate of exemption which meant that they were no longer bound by contract.

2. See Note 3, C Ramcharan's interview.

3. Enmore is a sugar plantation on the East (Altantic) coast of Demarara. It is about 12 miles from Georgetown.

4. Albuoystown was a less affluent district in Georgetown.

5. A "logie" or range was the typical barrack-room dwelling built originally for housing African slaves and later used to house indentured immigrants. It was a long narrow building with single partitions separating the families housed in it.

6. Water Street is the main area of commercial activity in Georgetown.

7. Stabroek market is the largest covered market in Georgetown. It occupies a central position on Water Street close to the ferry terminus.

8. "Bookers," the short name for Bookers Bros. McConnell Ltd, was an English firm that held the largest commercial interests in Guyana during colonial times. Apart from numerous business activities in Georgetown, Bookers owned most of the sugar plantations in the country.

9. Portuguese were regarded as separate from whites or Europeans because they came originally as indentured immigrants to Guyana and consequently had a social status lower than that of the ruling whites. The fact that they were

mostly peasants, and from Madeira rather than Portugal, was also a factor.

10. Francis Kawall and Mahadeo Panday were Indian businessmen who played pioneering roles in working for the social welfare of Indo-Guyanese.

11. J A Veerasammy was both the first Indian to become a magistrate and the first to represent Guyana in inter-colonial cricket.

12. Kunwar Maharaj Singh was a member of the Indian Civil Service who was sent by the Indian government to see what progress had been made in the condition of Indians in Guyana since a report, a few years earlier, by Messrs D B Pillai and V N Tivary who had also been sent out by the Indian government to assess the conditions of Indians in Guyana.

13. See Note 9, C Ramcharan's interview.

14. The Georgetown Cricket Club (GCC) was regarded as the headquarters of cricket in Guyana. Their ground—Bourda—is still the only venue of Test matches played in Guyana.

15. See Note 19, C Ramcharan's interview.

16. See Note 21, C Ramcharan's interview.

17. A E Seeram was a lawyer who played a leading role in the affairs of the British Guiana East Indian Association. He was elected president in 1934 but decided to live in Trinidad in 1935. Francis Kawall was a businessman. He succeeded Seeram as president of the British Guiana East Indian Association.

18. The Ruimveldt riot was the result of labour unrest that had been building up before culminating on 3 April 1924. The police killed thirteen and wounded eighteen people.

19. The Man Power Citizens' Association was a labour union formed to represent the sugar plantation workers. It was registered on 5 November 1937, thirteen years after the Ruimveldt riots. Cf Note 15, C Ramcharan's interview.

20. The League of Coloured People represented the interests of Guyanese of African descent.

21. Queen's College wa an elite secondary school for boys run by the government. It was founded in 1844.

22. The population of Georgetown then consisted mainly of Blacks, Browns, Whites, and Portuguese.

23. The coloured or brown group were those of mixed blood—principally African and European.

24. See Introduction to Dr Jagan's interview.

25. After the suspension, the British governor appointed an interim legislature consisting of individuals who were not connected with the People's Progressive Party of Dr Jagan.

26. In the 1964 election, the PPP won 24 seats and the PNC 22, but the PNC, led by Burnham, entered a coalition with the United Force (7 seats) led by Peter D'Aguiar in order to form a government.

27. Fires were set and riots broke out in February 1962 over the ruling PPP's budget with new taxation proposals. Later on 18 April 1963, a general strike

was called in protest against the PPP's Labour Relations Bill. It was supported by the Trades Union Council and the Civil War Service Association and included workers from commerce, industry and the government. The strike lasted 80 days, with mob violence, fires, and looting.

MARGARET JAGESAR

1. By "Naparima Theological College," Jagesar means St Andrew's Theological College, which was established by Canadian Presbyterian missionaries in the vicinity of Naparima High School in 1892. The College trained local ministers.

2. The *Ramayana,* one of the sacred texts of Hinduism, tells the story of Lord Rama whose life and actions provide a model for Hindus in much the same way that the life of Jesus provides a model for Christians.

3. A home for Indian girls was first opened by Canadian missionaries at Tunapuna in 1890. In 1905 it moved to Princess Town. With Christian instruction, the girls received training in "primary school work and domestic duties."

4. In 1917 a separate high school for girls was established by Canadian missionaries at La Pique, San Fernando. It was to be patterned on the Naparima High School for boys which already existed.

5. Bhadase Sagan Maraj (1919–71) rose to prominence as an Indian political leader in Trinidad in the 1950s. He was a millionaire and a sugar union leader who founded the Peoples' Democratic Party (PDP) in 1953. This became the Democratic Labour Party (DLP) in 1957. Maraj's support came mainly from Hindus, and he was unable to unite all Indians. His greatest success was in the 1958 federal elections when the DLP won 6 out of 10 seats allotted Trinidad. See Note 6, Dr Ibbit Mosaheb's interview.

LILIAN BANKAY

1. In Guyana, where many houses are built on stilts because the land is below sea level, the open space between the house door and the ground is called a "bottom house."

2. Dr J P Lachmansingh was first a trade union leader and later a member of Dr Jagan's PPP. Yet later, he defected to Forbes Burnham to form the PNC.

3. The "Balak Sahaita Mandalee" was a society to help needy children. It consisted mainly of women members.

4. See Note 22, Gajraj's interview.

5. See Note 21, Ramcharan's interview.

ROBERT JANKI

1. Helena is a plantation near to Mahaica, a village on the East Coast of the county of Demerara in Guyana. Janki later moved to Georgetown, where he went to school.

2. Dr James Barnett Cropper, one of the most influential Canadian Presbyte-

rian missionaries who served in Guyana, was appointed as superintendent of former plantation lands which were bought by the government and issued as allotments for settlement by indentured Indians in lieu of their return passage to India.

3. Bishop's High School was the elite government school for girls in Georgetown.

4. See Note 21, R Gajraj's interview.

5. See Note 9, Ramcharan's interview.

6. Secondary school exams were administered by Examination Boards in the UK. The Cambridge Senior School Certificate examination was taken nationwide.

7. The *Daily Argosy* was one of the national daily newspapers.

8. See Note 9, R Gajraj's interview.

9. The Luckhoos are probably the most famous family of lawyers in Guyana. The patriarch J A Luckhoo was president of the British Guiana East Indian Association. He later became a King's Counsel and was the first Indian appointed as Puisne Judge in the Supreme Court of Guyana.

10. See Note 21, C Ramcharan's interview.

11. The "Sanatan Dharma Sabha," to give the Maha Sabha its full name, is a religious movement formed in India to defend orthodox Hinduism against the doctrines of the reform movement, the Arya Samaj. The British Guiana Sanatan Dharma Sabha was founded in the 1920s to carry out social and educational work as well as propagating the principles of orthodox or Brahmanic Hinduism.

12. Cf Note 3, Bankay's interview.

13. Berbice High School played a role in Guyana similar to Naparima High School in Trinidad—as the main institution of secondary education for Indians.

14. See Note 19, C Ramcharan's interview.

15. Because of unrest in several West Indian colonies, including Guyana, a Royal Commission led by Lord Moyne was sent in 1938 to investigat social and economic conditions.

16. See Note preceding Dr Jagan's interview.

17. For Forbes Burnham, see Note 4, Introduction.

18. Reid was Minister of Health in Burnham's party, the PNC.

19. On Peter D'Aguiar, see Note 26, interview with R Gajraj.

SIMON RAMESAR

1. Since this interview (1992), Professor Ramesar has retired. Since that time too, the United National Congress (UNC) led by Basdeo Panday, an Indo-Trinidadian, has been elected to form the government of Trinidad and Tobago.

2. Cf Note 11, R Janki's interview. The Trinidadian Sanatan Dharma Maha Sabha was a much more powerful organization than its Guyanese counterpart. Its educational programme in building schools owed much to the leadership of

Bhadese Maraj (See Note 5, Jagesar's interview). The phase "refactory minority" is a misquotation. Williams's actual phase was a "recalcitrant and hostile minority" as quoted by Selwyn Ryan in *Race and Nationalism in Trinidad and Tobago* (University of the West Indies), p. 192.

IBBIT MOSAHEB

1. Rev John Morton was originally minister of a Presbyterian church in Bridgewater, Nova Scotia, Canada. He first went to the West Indies in 1864, and in 1867 was appointed as a missionary to Indians in Trinidad. He is credited with establishing the work of the Canadian Mission in the Caribbean.

2. In 1926, the Canadian government commissioned five passenger and freight ships to act as carriers of people, trade and mail between Canada and the West Indies. The service was named after famous English sailors, thus, "Lady Nelson," "Lady Drake," and "Lady Hawkins." Hence the term "Lady boats."

3. For Eric Williams, see Note 5, Introduction.

4. Eric Williams, *Capitalism and Slavery* (London: André Deutsch, 1964).

5. See Note 9, Introduction.

6. See Note 6, Margaret Jagesar's interview.

7. In 1940, during the Second World War, the US gave Britain fifty old destroyers, in return for which Britain ceded a number of bases, including some in the Caribbean Commission.

8. For Albert Gomes, see the review of his autobiography in Part One.

9. Sir Learie Constantine (1901–71) was born in Trinidad and first went to England in 1923 through his skill as a cricketer. He lived mostly in England and died there. His career spread beyond cricket into politics, diplomacy, writing, law and broadcasting. He was knighted in 1962 and given a life peerage in 1969, when he took the title of Baron Costantine of Maraval in Trinidad and of Nelson in the county of Palatine of Lancaster. He was also posthumously awarded the highest honour of Trinidad and Tobago—the Trinity Cross.

10. Norman Washington Manley (1893–1969) is regarded as the "father" of the nationalist movement in Jamaica. He founded the People's National Party (PNP), one of the two main Jamaican political parties, the other being the Jamaica Labour Party (JLP), led during his lifetime by his rival Sir Alexander Bustamante. Manley became chief minister of Jamaica in 1955, but he lost a referendum held in September, 1961 on the issue of whether Jamaica should join the Federation of the West Indies. He was succeeded by his son Michael as leader of the PNP.

11. Sir Grantley Adams (1898–1971), was first elected to the Barbados House of Assembly in 1934. He was perhaps the most distinguished Barbadian politician in the colonial period, and his career was crowned when he became prime minister of the West Indian Federation in 1958.

12. See introduction to Dr Cheddi Jagan's interview.

13. "Busta" or Sir Alexander Bustamante (1884–1977) began as a trade union leader when he formed the Bustamante Industrial Trade Union in 1939. He later founded the JLP and served as chief minister of Jamaica from 1944 to 1954. He was elected as the first prime minister of independent Jamaica in 1962.

14. Dr Rudranath Capildeo (1920–1970) was winner of the Trinidad scholarship. In addition to his university post, he qualified as a barrister. As leader of the DLP he became leader of the Opposition in 1962.

15. Adrian Cola Rienzi (1905–72) was born Krishna Deonarine and was active as a trade union leader.

16. Basdeo Panday is a lawyer and the President-General of the All Trinidad Sugar Estate and General Workers' Union. His party the United National Congress (UNC) now forms the government of Trinidad and Tobago.

ISMITH KHAN

1. Ismith Khan has lived in the US since 1948. He is the author of three novels: *The Jumbie Bird* (London: Hutchinson, 1961); *The Obeah Man* (London: Hutchinson, 1964; Toronto: TSAR, 1994); *The Crucifixion* (Leeds: Peepal Tree Press, 1987). He has also written many short stories.

2. "The Indian Mutiny" is the name given (by the British) to a revolt against British rule that included much of the Bengal army in India in 1857. The action began as a mutiny but became widespread enough for Indian historians to regard it as the first Indian war of independence.

3. Indians who were recruited in this way came mostly from the United Provinces in North East India.

4. In October 1884, in San Fernando, Trinidad, the celebration of Hosay, a Muslim festival, led to riots in which the police killed thirteen Indians and wounded many more. See review of *Eight Indians* in Part Two.

5. Queens Royal College, commonly known as QRC, was a prestigious secondary school for boys run by the British colonial government. Cf Queen's College in Guyana.

6. *The Trinidad Guardian* is the leading daily newspaper in Trinidad and Tobago. Samuel Selvon (1923–1994), Ismith Khan's friend, was a distinguished West Indian novelist and author.

7. Subhas Chandra Bose (1897–1945) was an Indian nationalist who opposed Gandhi's policy of non-violent resistance toward British rule in India. For a short while, Bose led a provisional government of India under Japanese sponsorship.

8. Norman Mailer, the American author.

9. See Note 7 for Sam Selvon. Like Selvon, George Lamming and Sir V S Naipaul both emigrated from the West Indies and established successful literary careers in London in the 1950s.

10. Neil Bissoondath was born in Trinidad but lives in Canada where he is a

leading novelist and short-story writer.

11. Caryl Phillips, who was born in St Kitts, grew up in England where he still lives. He is a novelist, playwright and author and teaches in the US.

JANICE SHINEBOURNE

1. Along with the indigenous "Amerindians," the Guyanese population consists of descendants of African slaves and descendants of immigrants from India, Europe, China and Madeira. Indians, Chinese and Portuguese were brought, under a system of indenture or contract, to work on British-owned sugar plantations. Most of these immigrants remained in Guyana after the terms of the contract were fulfilled.

2. The "middle passage" is the second or middle part of a three part voyage in which, up to the nineteenth century, ships first went from Europe to Africa; then from Africa with a cargo of slaves to the Caribbean; and finally from the Caribbean back to Europe. The "middle passage" achieved notoriety because the cargo on this part of the voyage was human.

3. Berbice High School was a secondary school run by Canadian Presbyterian missionaries. It was located in New Amsterdam, the largest town in Berbice. See Note 13, Janki's interview.

4. Edward Brathwaite and Derek Walcott are the two best known Caribbean poets writing in English. In the 1960s the perception of Brathwaite's poetry as Afro-centric and Walcott's as Euro-centric provoked a controversy that aroused some hostility towards Walcott, who was thought to lack patriotism and nationalism.

5. Queen's College was a government boys's secondary school and St Stanislaus a Catholic boys' secondary school in Georgetown, the capital city of Guyana. These were the most prestigious boys' schools in the country. See Note 21, Gajraj's interview.

6. *Expression* was a literary journal that ran briefly in Guyana in the 1960s.

7. Martin Carter is the best known poet in Guyana. His collections of poetry include *Poems of Resistance* (1954) and *Poems of Affinity* (1980).

8. A J Seymour (1914–1989) is the most distinguished man of letters produced by Guyana. He was a poet, editor and author and was very influential among younger Guyanese authors. Apart from his own collections of poems, and other writings, Seymour founded and edited the literary journal *Kyk-over-al*.

9. Edgar Mittelholzer, *Corentyne Thunder* (London: Secker and Warburg, 1941).

10. V S Naipaul, *Miguel Street* (London: André Deutsch, 1959); *A House for Mr Biswas* (London: André Deutsch, 1961).

11. Dr Cheddi Jagan, President of Guyana when he died in 1997. His political career began in the 1940s. See the introduction to Dr Jagan's interview.

12. In 1964, Dr Jagan was defeated in elections held under a new system of

proportional representation, and Forbes Burnham (1923–1985), leader of the People's National Congress (PNC), became prime minister (and later president). Burnham's party remained in power until 1992, during which time Dr Jagan was leader of the Opposition.

13. Ricky Singh is a well known Guyanese journalist who now lives in Barbados. He is one of several Guyanese professionals who had to emigrate during Burnham's regime because their writings or views were not politically acceptable. The *Guyana Graphic* was a leading daily newspaper in Guyana.

14. When she was interviewed, Janice Shinebourne was on a visit to Toronto to take part in a literary festival held in the Toronto complex called Harbourfront, where she read her story, "The Maid in Bel Air." The story is about two black middle-class families, the Semples and Vincents. Mrs Vincent dies, and the story contrasts the reactions to this death by the Semples and by their maid, Vera, who comes from the rural district of Plaisance.

15. Bookers is the name of a British firm which had the largest commercial interests in Guyana in the 1950s and 60s. For example, Bookers owned major sugar estates in Guyana.

16. Bishops High School was the government girls' high school in Georgetown with similar social prestige as Queen's College and St Stanislaus College. See Note 3, Janki's interview.

17. Wilson Harris is the most critically acclaimed author produced by Guyana. Harris has lived in England since the 1950s and has produced more than a dozen novels which have a reputation for obscurity and profundity. His first novel was *Palace of the Peacock* (London: Faber, 1959).

18. Wilson Harris, *The Secret Ladder* (London: Faber, 1963).

19. Edgar Mittleholzer's novels were published as follows by Secker and Warburg in London: *The Children of Kaywana*, 1952; *Kaywana Stock*, 1954; *My Bones and My Flute*, 1955; *Kaywana Blood*, 1958.

20. Peter Kempadoo is a Guyanese author who now lives in Africa. He is the author of two novels: *Guiana Boy* (London: Hutchinson, 1964) and *Old Thom's Harvest* (London: Hutchinson, 1965).

21. Kenneth Ramchand is a critic and professor of English at the University of the West Indies in Port of Spain, Trinidad.

22. *The Trinidad and Tobago Review* is an interdisciplinary journal that appears monthly in Trinidad and Tobago.

23. *Race and Class* is a journal published in London by the Institute of Race Relations.

RAMABAI ESPINET

1. Ramabai Espinet is the author of a volume of poems *Nuclear Seasons* (1991). She has also edited *Creation Fire* (1990), an anthology of Caribbean women's poetry.

2. See Note 1, Mosaheb's interview.

3. J J Thomas (1840–1889) was a Trinidadian intellectual with strong literary interests. He was secretary to *The Trinidad Monthly*, the first literary journal in Trinidad, and in 1872 he organized the Trinidad Athenaeum, a literary society. He is best remembered for his book *Froudacity* (1889) in which he exposes misconceptions and errors in *The English in the West Indies* (1888), a book written by the English historian J A Froude, giving his impressions of a visit to the West Indies.

For C L R James, see Note 9, Introduction.

ALVIN KALLICHARAN

1. Rohan Kanhai was one of the finest of all West Indian batsmen. He was born in 1935, in Port Mourant, Guyana, and made his debut in Test cricket in 1957. He served as a model and inspiration to the younger Kallicharan.

2. The Shell Shield is a cricket tournament in which teams from each West Indian territory participate. The tournament gives exposure to promising cricketers who may later be picked to reprsent West Indies.

3. Joe Solomon was born in 1930 also in Port Mourant. He was a less distinguished batsman than Kanhai but deserves to be celebrated for his fighting qualities and for being only the third Indo-Caribbean to reach Test cricket level.

4. Basil Butcher, who is African, makes up the third member of a triumvirate of Guyanese players from Port Mourant—Kanhai, Solomon, Butcher—who made a spectacular appearance in the West Indian team in the 1960s.

5. In his very first Test innings against New Zealand at Bourda, Guyana, in 1972, Kallicharan scored 100 not out. In his next Test in Trinidad he made scores of 101 and 18.

6. Kerry Packer is an Australian entrepreneur who opposed the cricket establishment in the 1980s by setting up a World Series of cricket matches and luring the best international players to take part by paying them handsomely. The result was a temporary disruption of Test cricket because of the absence of some of the main players in Packer's World Series.

7. Clive Lloyd, also from Guyana, was an aggressive batsman who became the most successful captain of the West Indies. Lloyd is African, and later in this interview Kallicharan makes veiled comments about his appointment as captain, thus confirming that racial considerations also affected cricket.

8. Kallicharan was also a member of the English county cricket team, Warwickshire.

9. Kallicharan is less than explicit, but he is linking political and racial attitudes with economics and sport.

10. Throughout the 1970s and 80s, South Africa was banned from playing Test cricket because of its policy of racial segregation, or apartheid. During this period, the South Africans offered huge salaries to famous international cricketers to play in South Africa. However, international Test cricketers who played in South Africa were banned from Test cricket, as Kallicharan was.

CLEM SEECHARAN

1. New Amsterdam is the chief town in the county of Berbice in Guyana.

2. See Note 9, Janki's interview for Luckhoo. J A Luckhoo was the patriarch of the family. Dr Wharton was the son of cane cutters. He began his studies in medicine at the University of Edinburgh in 1893.

3. Marcus Garvey (1887–1940) was a Jamaican who founded the Universal Negro Improvement Association (UNIA). The aim was to unite "all the Negro peoples of the world into one great body to establish a country and a government exclusively their own." Although he failed in the end, Garvey built an enormous mass movement, which spread his ideas of black self-improvement and liberation in many countries, including those in the Caribbean.

4. In 1936, following a dispute, Italy successfully invaded Ethopia, then known as Abyssinia. The Ethiopian emperor Haile Selassie took his case to the League of Nations. His failure to win support was seen as yet another example of white colonialism over black people, and an ensuing sense of outrage became widespread, reaching British colonies in the Caribbean. Ethopia was liberated by British forces in 1941 during the Second World War.

5. See Note 13, Introduction.

6. In 1898, as a result of a prolonged economic depression in the West Indies, Sir Henry Norman was appointed to lead a Royal Commission to investigate the sugar industry in the region. His secretary was Sydney Olivier, who (as Lord Olivier) was later to become governor of Jamaica. The principal recommendation of the Norman Commission was greater recognition for the role of the peasantry in the future of the West Indies.

7. Cf Note 2, Jagesar's interview.

8. See Note 13, Ramcharan's interview.

Part Four: The Second Migration

INDO-CARRIBEAN CANADIANS

1. Neil Bissoondath, *Digging up the Mountains* (Toronto: Macmillan, 1985).

2. Neil Bissoondath, *On the Eve of Uncertain Tomorrows* (Toronto: Penguin, 1990).

3. Cyril Dabydeen, *Goatsong* (Ottawa: Mosaic Press, 1977), p.33.

4. Daiva K Stasiulis, "Racism and the Canadian State," in *Explorations in Ethnic Studies* VIII (Jan. 1985), p.20.

INDEX

Index